DISCARD

# THE URGE TO SPLURGE

Laura Byrne Paquet

# THE URGE TO SPLURGE

A Social History of Shopping

ECW PRESS

Published by ECW PRESS
2120 Queen Street East, Suite 200, Toronto, Ontario, Canada M4E 1E2

NATIONAL LIBRARY OF CANADA CATALOGUING IN PUBLICATION DATA

Paquet, Laura Byrne, 1965–
The urge to splurge: a social history of shopping / Laura Byrne Paquet
ISBN 1-55022-583-9
1. Shopping—History. 2. Shopping—Social aspects. I. Title.

HC79.C6P36    306.3    C2003-902204-8

Design and typesetting: Yolande Martel
Production: Emma McKay
Printing: Quebecor
Cover design: Paul Hodgson
Endpapers painting: courtesy cliché Bibliothèque nationale de France

Diligent efforts have been made to contact copyright holders; please excuse any inadvertent errors or omissions, but if anyone has been unintentionally omitted, the publisher would be pleased to receive notification and make acknowledgments in future printings.

This book is set in Minion and Franklin Gothic

The publication of *The Urge to Splurge* has been generously supported by the Canada Council, by the Government of Ontario through the Ontario Media Development Corporation's Ontario Book Initiative, by the Ontario Arts Council, and by the Government of Canada through the Book Publishing Industry Development Program. **Canadä**

DISTRIBUTION

CANADA: Jaguar Book Group, 100 Armstrong Avenue, Georgetown, Ontario L7G 5S4

UNITED STATES: Independent Publishers Group, 814 North Franklin Street, Chicago, Illinois 60610

EUROPE: Turnaround Publisher Services, Unit 3, Olympia Trading Estate, Coburg Road, Wood Green, London N22 6T2

AUSTRALIA AND NEW ZEALAND: Wakefield Press, 1 The Parade West (Box 2266), Kent Town, South Australia 5071

PRINTED AND BOUND IN CANADA

ECW PRESS
ecwpress.com

*For Paul:*
*I couldn't have done it without you.*

# Table of Contents

Introduction    11

1    Around the World in Search of Merchandise    23

2    A Fair Is a Veritable Smorgasbord    29

3    To Market, To Market    39

4    Eat, Drink, and Be Shoppers    53

5    From Mesopotamia to Minneapolis: It's a Mall World    85

6    On the Road Again: From Peddlers to Avon Ladies    101

7    Please Mr. Postman: Catalogs, TV Shopping,
and the Internet    121

8    Department Stores: The Original One-Stop Shops    139

9    Fashion Victims    161

10    Born to Shop: From Bridal Showers
to Christmas Stockings    179

11    Don't Miss Our Gift Shop on the Way Out    197

12    Extreme Retail Therapy: Shopaholics
and Kleptomaniacs    221

13    The Politics of Shopping    229

14    Our Conflicted Attitudes to Shopping    237

Sources    255

Bibliography    267

# Introduction

*And you may find yourself behind the wheel of a large automobile*
*And you may find yourself in a beautiful house with a beautiful wife*
*And you may ask yourself—Well . . . How did I get here? . . .*
*Same as it ever was, same as it ever was, same as it ever was, same*
    *as it ever was.*
                    —Talking Heads, "Once in a Lifetime," 1980

The idea for this book hit me more than a decade ago, and it sprang from a picture.

While doing some research on urban planning, I stumbled on a reproduction of an 1815 watercolor of the Palais Royal, an early shopping arcade in the heart of Paris. The picture, by German artist Georg Emanuel Opiz, shows a large and varied crowd under a vaulted roof illuminated by dangling lamps. Painted signs on the archways announce the names and wares of adjacent shops and businesses: *Café américain, Ombres chinoises, Change de toutes sortes de monnaies.*

A Café américain more than a hundred years before Rick Blaine opened his fictitious watering hole in Casablanca? A currency exchange? I was intrigued.

Detailed study of the picture only intrigued me more. The gentlemen are well dressed. Many are in military uniform, complete with bicorn hats, since the picture was painted toward the end of the Napoleonic Wars. Most of the women are wearing the skimpy, classically inspired gowns in vogue at the time, made with flimsy fabrics. A woman in the foreground caresses a soldier's cheek. Behind him, another soldier chucks the chin of a woman leaning against the window of the currency exchange. Amid the hubbub of people staring into shop windows, leading small children by the hand, and chatting with friends, it's clear that something else is going on: the place is a hotbed for courtesans.

Something about the liveliness of that picture just wouldn't leave me. I also couldn't shake the revolutionary idea—revolutionary to me, anyway—that people were strutting, preening, dreaming, and spending in enclosed shopping areas long before the Mall of America and Bloomingdale's opened their doors. I had always imagined that, until fairly recently in human history, "shopping" had consisted only of utilitarian trips to an unadorned country store or plain market stall. Further, I thought that materialism was a modern condition, forced on us by out-of-control advertising.

I couldn't have been more wrong.

## Me seller, you buyer

It turns out that we've wanted stuff for about as long as there was stuff to want. Back in the Stone Age, when Gog figured out a way to make a better flint ax, no doubt everybody suddenly felt a desperate need to "keep up with the Gogs" and acquire the latest in chipped stone technology. Granted, our Neolithic ancestors couldn't trek to Stone Mart, the way they might if they actually lived like the Flintstones. But they could trade, and this sort of prehistoric "shopping" led to the division of labor and, hence, to the entire history of human civilization.

Remember that the next time somebody sniffs at you for spending Saturday at the mall.

But it isn't simply the acquisition of stuff that appeals to us. Most of us don't want to sit, like Citizen Kane, in an empty Xanadu stuffed to the rafters with unloved treasures. The joy isn't in the having. It's in the getting. It's the thrill of the hunt. Human beings have always liked to engage in the public playfulness of trade—when they've had the money, the time, and the leisure to do so. The only factors that have changed are the scale, the affordability, and the speed of the process.

In this, shopping has a lot in common with architecture, transportation, communication, and just about every other institution that shapes our modern world. The monster home, the supersonic jet, the cell phone, and the bacon double cheeseburger are just more finely honed and ostentatious versions of the workman's cottage, the donkey cart, the postal letter, and the bowl of porridge. And the regional mall is just a brighter, shinier, bigger version of the Middle Eastern marketplace where an early Christian may have bartered with an austere tentmaker named Saul. The stage today is bigger and better lit, but the process modern marketers call "the retail drama" has been going on for centuries.

People started exchanging goods as soon as they were able to make more goods than they could use. If I'm good at sewing coats made of mammoth fur, and you're good at making weapons from saber-tooth tiger teeth, maybe we can trade so that I have a nice weapon and you have a warm coat. That'll show those uppity Gogs.

Eventually, trading became so complicated that people began using small, portable objects that everybody wanted as a medium of exchange. We usually think of this medium as being gold or silver coins, but it could be anything—beans, shells, cigarettes, whatever you had handy.

## Passive-aggressive gift-giving and Biblical curses

Of course, not all societies came up with the marketplace as a response to these needs. In some parts of the world, gift exchange was the preferred way to circulate goods so that all people got what they needed. In these societies, such as in the Haida culture of what is now British Columbia, people gained prestige by giving the biggest gifts, not by earning the most money. Receiving a gift imposed a burden on the recipient, who was obliged to give a future gift.

In other places, such as ancient Persia, citizens simply paid taxes (euphemistically called tributes) to the local authorities. These taxes might be paid in money, but they were often paid in goods, such as grain or wine. The rulers then redistributed this largesse as they saw fit for the good of all. If recent communist experiments are any indication, this system was not foolproof, as rulers sometimes have a different idea of what constitutes the common good than the actual commoners do.

Despite these alternative models, marketplaces did evolve in a number of ancient societies, including Mesopotamia, Egypt, Greece, and the Roman Empire. By about 590 B.C., the Greek city of Tyre, in what is now southern Lebanon, was famous for its markets. The Old Testament book of Isaiah refers to Tyre, whose "merchants are princes, whose traffickers are the honorable of the earth." Ezekiel goes into much more detail, describing the wealth of goods these merchants received in trade: silver from the Iberian peninsula, bronze from Greece, ivory and ebony from coastal lands, emeralds and rubies from Syria, olive oil from Israel, wine and spices from Damascus. However, Ezekiel also prophesied that Tyre, for all its wealth and power, would come to a bad end:

> When thy wares went forth out of the seas, thou filledst many people; thou didst enrich the kings of the earth with the multitude of thy riches and of thy merchandise.
> In the time when thou shalt be broken by the seas in the depths of the waters thy merchandise and all thy company in the midst of thee shall fall.
> All the inhabitants of the isles shall be astonished at thee, and their kings shall be sore afraid, they shall be troubled in their countenance.
> The merchants among the people shall hiss at thee; thou shalt be a terror, and never shalt be any more.

Clearly, we've always been a bit conflicted about the value of the marketplace. We still are. Modern-day Ezekiels decry shopping as proof that society is shallow, destructive, and empty; boosters argue that without shopping the economy would come to a halt. Just recently, the latter view was floated in a memorable way.

**If we don't buy shoes, the terrorists have won**

In the terrible days after September 11, 2001, President George W. Bush exhorted his compatriots to shop for their country. "I ask your continued participation and confidence in the American economy," he said in an address before a joint session of Congress on September 20. About six weeks later, in a speech in Atlanta, he noted with approval that despite the terrorist threat, "People are going about their daily lives, working and shopping and playing, worshiping at churches and synagogues and mosques, going to movies and to baseball games." Put this way, shopping was as noble a pursuit as praying, as much a part of American life as baseball. Shopping, it appeared, would save the U.S.A.

The sentiment was widely derided at the time, and it did seem a rather facile response to a cataclysmic attack. But in a way—and it pains me to admit this—Dubya was right. Love it or hate it, shopping makes the modern western economy go round.

Here's a sobering fact: in the United States, "personal consumption expenditures"—the economist's phrase for the money that individuals, not companies, spend on goods and services—is equal to roughly two thirds of the gross domestic product. If we stopped shopping, the economy as we know it really would collapse.

However, most of us probably aren't thinking about improving the country's bottom line when we head to the mall. At the most basic level, we shop because we need things: bread, a warm blanket, shingles to fix the hole in the roof.

But once we've bought the minimum number of clothes we need to protect us from the elements, and enough food to sustain us through another day in the salt mines, what keeps us going back to the cash register? When we have sensible loafers, why do we want Manolo Blahnik stilettos? Don't we realize that if we just stopped shopping, we'd have more money, more free time, less stress, and less debt?

Well, sure. But there are many reasons we shop, and very few of them have much to do with either supporting the economy or keeping ourselves fed and warm.

Daniel Miller, an anthropology professor at University College London, believes that we—particularly women—shop as a way of showing love to others, particularly our families. According to *Shopping, Place and Identity,* a book he co-authored, "shopping is an investment in social relationships, often within a relatively narrowly defined household or domestic context, as much as it is an economic activity devoted to the acquisition of particular commodities."

For instance, a woman concerned about her husband's cholesterol level might buy low-fat cheese, to show she loves him (even if he'd rather eat something more decadent). A child might insist on an expensive toy as a birthday gift for a playmate, hoping that the friend will like him better as a result.

But what about the executive who buys an expensive tailored suit for herself? Even purchases like that are based largely on concerns about relationships, Miller and other theorists argue. By investing in high-end clothes, the shopper is hoping to attain or maintain status among other people—in other words, to foster relationships.

### Market segmentation now, market segmentation tomorrow, market segmentation forever

Many marketers have a related explanation, one they've supported by funneling millions of dollars into data analyses and focus groups: we shop because we want to affiliate ourselves with our peers, or the people we want to be our peers. Sarah buys organic salsa because she sees herself as a funky, downtown woman who likes ethnic cuisine and cares about the environment. Jack buys a cowboy hat because he goes to country bars and sees himself as a rugged individualist, even though he works in a suburban bank. Some of us pattern ourselves after movie stars or TV characters; others aspire to imitate the neighbors or the boss or the cool kids at school. (It's no accident that the people who show us the possibilities of fashion are called *models*.)

Corporations are doing their darnedest to pin down these peer groups and to predict what they're going to buy. One of the most popular systems for doing this is called PRIZM (Potential Rating Index for ZIP Markets), developed by Claritas Inc. It segments every neighborhood in the U.S. into one of 62 clusters, based on census data, demographic surveys, and other public information. Every ZIP code in the country has been analyzed and the top clusters in each ZIP code listed.

PRIZM is more fun to play with than a newspaper horoscope, particularly since each cluster has a cool, evocative name. Because I live in Canada and don't have a ZIP code, I went to Claritas's "You Are Where You Live" Web page and plugged in a ZIP code for a neighborhood I know fairly well: 10022, the east side of midtown Manhattan. I've always thought that if I won two lotteries (financial and green card), it would be a fun place to live.

The Web search revealed that four PRIZM clusters dominate in 10022: Urban Gold Coast, Young Literati, Bohemian Mix, and Gray Power. Were any of them me?

Urban Gold Coast folks are aged 45 to 64 with a median household income of $73,500. (Throughout this book, all dollar figures are in U.S. dollars unless stated otherwise.) They're most likely to go to the theater, bank on-line, use olive oil, watch *Mystery*, and read *Self*. Hmm, close, but too old and rich for me.

How about the Young Literati? They are aged 25 to 44 and have household incomes of $63,400. They're most likely to plan for large purchases, use a discount broker, take vitamins, watch Bravo, and read *GQ*. OK, now we're in the age ballpark, but not spot on yet.

The Bohemian Mix cluster falls into the same age group, but the household income is much lower: $38,500. They're most likely to have call answering, shop at the Gap, read *Elle*, watch *Face the Nation*, and have a rollover IRA. We're getting closer to my carefully nurtured self-image. Even though *Face the Nation* puts me to sleep, I'm the proud owner of multiple Gap turtlenecks.

What about Gray Power? Not surprisingly, they're aged 55 and up. Household income is $41,800. They're most likely to belong to a country club, take a cruise, own a safe deposit box, watch the Travel Channel, and read *Modern Maturity*. This is scary. I have a safety deposit box, I've taken two cruises, and I've been known to watch the Travel Channel when I'm in the States.

Good heavens. I'm a retiree stuck in a Gen-X body.

All kidding aside, the peer-group idea does have merit. Look around the next time you're at a party with a group of close friends. Chances are, most of the people in the room will be wearing similar clothes, will have similar foods in their kitchen cupboards, and will do similar things in their leisure time (which, of course, will require them to buy similar accessories, from downhill skis to video games).

Two researchers—Cele Otnes of the University of Illinois and Mary Ann McGrath of Loyola University—have countered the "shopping as affiliation" theories with one of their own, based on their study of male shopping habits. They contend that, among men at least, shopping is all about making the best decision and getting the best deal. "[M]en who profess to enjoy shopping still typically do so in order to fulfill one entrenched tenet of the masculine code—achievement," they wrote in the *Journal of Retailing*. "We argue that in contrast to Daniel Miller's theory that women shop to express love to their families and social networks, men shop to win."

Still other explanations abound for our love affair with the mall. Medical researchers, for instance, are trying to figure out whether the physical act of plunking down a credit card and carting off a new pair of shoes gives some of us an addictive rush, similar to the high that hooks gamblers and alcoholics.

There are countless other theories, and I'll explore many of them in this book. But the theory that appeals to me most is perhaps naively simplistic: we shop because, in most cultures, shopping has always been part of the way we experience the world. From the patrician haggling for pottery in the marketplaces of ancient Rome to the teenager shopping for CDs on the Internet, we have always liked to acquire things.

### High-definition shopping

Before I start looking into the history of shopping, I want to issue a small caveat: the book you are about to read focuses on a largely Anglo-American approach to buying and selling. The history of shopping is simply too long and too sprawling to incorporate extensive details from around the world, much as I was sorely tempted. So I chose chronological sprawl over geographical sprawl.

With that in mind, let's take a look through the dictionary to learn a bit about the way our relationship to shopping has evolved in the English-speaking world. The word *store* is one of the first buying-related words to show up, sometime around 1225. It comes from the Latin *instaurare*, meaning to set up or renew, and originally referred to a warehouse rather than to a retail outlet. The noun *shop* enters Middle English later that century, derived from an Old English word meaning *stall*. In its first incarnation, *shop* meant a workshop. The fact that you could also buy the craftsman's wares there was almost incidental.

But, slowly, shops became more elaborate. *Shop window* first appears between 1400 and 1450. People had realized that a display of goods could prompt passersby to buy something they might not have contemplated otherwise. However, the seller was still the person who made the product, in most cases. It wasn't until around 1520 that English devised the word *shopkeeper*—someone whose primary job is selling rather than manufacturing. And the act of buying and selling the ordinary goods of life in a central place acquired a name in the middle of the sixteenth century: *marketing*.

All that merchandise, at least a little of it displayed in inviting windows, led to new temptations. In the 1670s, when Restoration London was in full, decadent swing, the *shoplifter* gained a name for his light-fingered trade.

Clearly, a culture of buying and selling had evolved. But the idea of perusing the latest wares as a form of amusement didn't have a name until around 1760. As King George III took to the throne, his subjects were *shopping* for the first time. (It would be another hundred years, though, before they would refer to themselves as *shoppers*.)

Stores became more elaborate, the better to display the increasingly wide selection of manufactured goods pouring from the factories of the Industrial Revolution. Temptations for yearning shoppers multiplied, to the point where the urge to help oneself to the merchandise was so overwhelming that mere *shoplifting* didn't seem to describe it. *Kleptomania* entered the lexicon around 1820.

As brand names grew in popularity toward the end of the 1800s, people began speaking—either proudly or disdainfully, depending on their social class—of *store-bought* goods. By the 1920s, when automobiles made it possible to transport home large quantities of purchases, customers needed *shopping carts* and *shopping bags*. By 1940, they were taking their cars to the *shopping center*; two decades later, they headed to the *shopping mall* and the *shopping plaza*. And by 1965, the range of goods available was so vast that they needed a *shopping list* to keep track of them all.

### Conquering with dollars instead of gunpowder

While the urge to splurge has been with us for thousands of years, shopping wouldn't become the pastime of the masses until the mid-nineteenth century, when a combination of rising wages, industrial development, urban growth, and efficient transportation would make lots of goods available to a large number of people who could afford them. Shopping went from rich man's hobby to middle-class mania.

By the end of the 1800s, few people seemed to be completely immune to the lure of shopping. Even the famous nineteenth-century clergyman Henry Ward Beecher couldn't resist buying far too much of a type of Ceylon coffee he particularly liked. After tasting it for the first time, he promptly ordered five 100-pound sacks of it. His wife insisted that it would take them 50 years to drink that much coffee, and promptly sent four of the bags back. In an interesting footnote, Beecher was also one of the first people to knowingly provide a celebrity endorsement, lending his august name to ads for Pears' Soap.

As the twentieth century dawned, shopping would lead to a new round of exploration and colonization. At this point, however, the people leading the charge weren't sailors and kings; they were industrialists. Once it was Christopher Columbus and Vasco da Gama setting forth to foreign lands with dreams of profit. As the Victorian age gave way to the modern era, the wayfarers were Nestlé and Cadbury, Kellogg and H.J. Heinz, all of which opened manufacturing plants in far-flung Australia in the early years of the twentieth century.

Where manufacturers led, retailers followed. This new colonization of the planet continues to this day. Drive around any major metropolis in the developed world—and, increasingly, the wealthy enclaves of not-so-developed nations—and you'll see their flags flying high: Ikea and Safeway, the Body Shop and Gucci, Laura Ashley and Roots and the Gap.

The urge to splurge hasn't just colonized the world; brand-name stores, and the branded goods in them, have literally changed the way we see that world. If we meet someone wearing a Rolex, we make different assumptions about their power and status than we apply to someone sporting a Timex. People who shop for sweatshirts at Wal-Mart and those who buy furs at Bloomingdale's often inhabit completely different universes—a fact that both retailers and the shoppers themselves go to great lengths to maintain. Not for nothing did Naomi Klein call her book lamenting the rise of global corporate culture *No Logo*.

The siren song of branding seduces us early in life. James McNeal, a marketing professor at Texas A&M University, has determined that 10 percent of the nouns an average 18-month-old child knows are brand names. Even more disturbing, a recent British study estimated that one out of every four babies speaks a brand name as their first word.

"Pampers" doesn't have quite the same ring as "Mama," does it? Out of the mouths of babes comes one of the more vivid examples of the power of shopping.

### "Same as it ever was, same as it ever was"

Shopping has such power over us because it's the point where so many elemental things in our lives coalesce. In the shop is where we find out the concrete value of those hours spent laboring at a computer, in an assembly line, or in front of a schoolroom full of fractious kids. Is the blood and sweat we've poured out over days and weeks enough to buy a tin of gourmet peanuts, a cashmere sweater, a big-screen TV? Is our hard work enough to make sure our kids get enough protein? Are all those mornings of hauling ourselves to work on the 7:14 train going to translate into summer afternoons on a golf course, where our colleagues will enviously admire our titanium clubs?

It's no surprise that an activity that has had such a lasting effect on our cities, our economies, and our very concept of ourselves continues to fascinate scholars, moralists, and the rest of us. It always has. If something about our modern patterns of buying and selling amuses or bothers you, it's almost certain that you're not the first to feel that way.

Sixteenth-century Londoners fretted that their churches were turning into malls, and nineteenth-century New Yorkers wailed that Christmas had become too commercialized. Medieval clerics chided their flocks for being obsessed with fashion. King James I worried that kids were wasting too much time hanging around the seventeenth-century equivalent of a mall. From Sunday shopping to counterfeit money, and from souvenir-crazed tourists to shopaholics, just about every shopping issue that confronts us today has attracted the attention of someone else, sometime in history. Shakespeare probably grumbled to Anne Hathaway about surly ink merchants, and I wouldn't be surprised if Calpurnia nagged Julius Caesar to do something about the high price of eggs.

We're not the first people to wonder just how we got to this stage of fascination with buying and selling. When it comes to shopping, the situation really is the same as it ever was. It's all just a question of degree.

# 1 Around the World in Search of Merchandise

*Veni, vidi, VISA: I came, I saw, I shopped.*
—Bumper sticker, late twentieth century

Before I dig into the meat of this book—shopping—I'd just like to digress briefly into the wonderful world of global exploration, conquest, and warfare. After all, the demands of the marketplace have fueled empires and revolutions for thousands of years.

Just consider the Romans.

The Roman Empire was about many things: power and heroism, land and slavery. It was also, in many ways, about trade. As well as conquering villages, building aqueducts, and generally throwing their weight around, Roman soldiers brought back souvenirs for the folks back home. As it happens, a browser on a shopping binge with a thousand friends in steel dresses can get really good deals on Phoenician dyes. Early conquered people who found themselves debating prices with a guy in a mean-looking helmet likely concluded, more often than not, that the customer brandishing a big sword is always right.

The Romans preferred to get some goods in particular places. Just as French burgundies and Swiss watches have acquired a place-specific sheen in our time, oysters from Londinium were a Roman delicacy, and historians suspect that they were some of the earliest things bought and sold on the banks of the Thames. There wasn't much on the site of Londinium before the Romans showed up. The conquerors' fondness for local products was part of the reason they stuck around, laying the foundations of the city that would become London.

But the Romans, just like us, were a little guilty about their loot, even if it had been, well, looted. Playwright-philosopher Lucius Annaeus Seneca warned, "Poverty wants some, luxury many, and avarice all things." Of course, one of Seneca's pupils was Emperor Nero, who didn't exactly leave his mark on history as a pleasure-denying ascetic. A few decades after Seneca mused on greed, the historian Pliny the Younger began to notice that hard Roman currency was draining east in exchange for exotic goods.

### That's a spicy meatball!

Romans just couldn't seem to live without the spices that flowed over the Silk Road from the Far East. The spices were passed along mountains and deserts, and each intermediary charged huge markups along the way. Many of those intermediaries were Arabs, who found themselves strategically positioned between Europe and Asia. They did their best to keep their European customers in the dark as to where the precious cargo came from. For instance, they convinced Greek historian Herodotus that cinnamon was found only on a mountain range somewhere in Arabia, where vicious birds protected it from nosy interlopers and had to be distracted by bloody flanks of donkey meat. Not the kind of place nice Greek writers wanted to go at all.

By the first century, the Romans had pretty much figured out where their spices came from, but that didn't really matter. Their suppliers had them over a barrel. The Romans had to have spices, which both preserve meat and, if the preserving doesn't quite work, conceal the rancid taste. Pepper was so prized that the Visigoths demanded it, alongside gold and silver, before they would call off their siege of Rome in A.D. 408.

In the Middle Ages, most of Europe's spice trade was funneled through Venice. A family of Venetian merchants, the Polos, even managed to make it as far as China in the late 1200s. One of them, Marco, took to telling stories of his adventures while imprisoned in Genoa. A Pisan named Rustichello wrote the stories down, embellishing them here and there to make the final package a better read. The enthusiastic stories of the spices available in Java, India, China, and other exotic places whetted the appetites of generations of dreamers. But it would be another 150 years before world events spurred many Europeans to follow in Marco Polo's footsteps.

In 1453, the Arabs took Constantinople, the one back door the Europeans had been able to use to avoid dealing with the Arabs. Now that their rivals controlled the entire overland spice trade (trekking over the barren wastes of Siberia apparently not being an option), Europeans took out their maps and started thinking outside the box they were trapped in.

The Portuguese, on Europe's westernmost edge, suddenly noticed that, while they were far from India as the crow flies, they were actually as close to it as anybody if you had to sail there. So the Portuguese figured out how to sail around Africa. As the story goes, when Vasco da Gama finally landed in Calicut, India, in 1498, his men shouted, "For God and spices!"

Soon, the Portuguese, Dutch, and English were colonizing India and the archipelago between modern Malaysia and Australia, not to mention various bits of Africa they found along the way. Of particular interest were the Moluccas, now a part of Indonesia, which the Europeans called the Spice Islands, since they were stuffed to the rafters with nutmeg, mace, and cloves. The first empires fought bitterly over these specks of land, which finally went to the Dutch.

## Binge imperialism

After bravely sailing around the treacherous waters of the Cape of Good Hope, after securing a pilot from Indian merchants at the African port of Malindi, after finally making it to Calicut, Vasco da Gama would learn a painful lesson about the folly of going too far out of your way looking for bargains. His ten-month voyage turned out to be largely for naught, because the ruler of Calicut wasn't particularly impressed by the cheap baubles da Gama had brought with him to trade. Partly because of his inferior goods, and partly because local merchants didn't want any new competition, the Calicut ruler refused to sign a trade treaty with da Gama, who ended up having to fight his way out of the harbor.

He did get a modern shopping center in Lisbon named after him, though.

Six years before da Gama stepped foot on India's Malabar coast, a crazy Genoan sailing for Spain had decided that the best way to go east was to sail west. Because of Christopher Columbus's dismal geography, he was convinced that China and the Indies were roughly where North and South America turned out to be. Columbus would make several trips back and forth across the ocean, including a few after he was dead, as his remains were shipped back and forth so often that now nobody is sure where they are.

Spain managed to find lots of gold and silver in the territories it occupied, but the other colonial powers in the Western Hemisphere weren't so lucky. The English and French had come to North America looking for valuable goods; what they got was a lot of fish, furs, and trees, which were useful but not particularly flashy. In the Seven Years' War, France would lose the vast swath of land that would become Canada. Britain offered to give it back in exchange for the islands of Martinique and Guadeloupe, which were small but rich in sugar. France rejected the offer and kept the islands. What good were "a few acres of snow," as Voltaire so memorably described my home and native land?

### Don't mess with the tea bootleggers

Planting colonies around the world fit into a deliberate European strategy that involved, basically, controlled shopping. In mercantilism, European economies tried to have exports exceed imports. So, for the British, their cousins in Virginia and Nova Scotia and Jamaica weren't just a source of raw goods; they were also, quite literally, captive markets.

In the late 1600s, the English Parliament passed a series of *Navigation Acts*, which required that English ships carry all goods going into and out of the colonies. If somebody in New York wanted, say, a Dutch pewter mug, the mug had to be shipped through England, where it would have duties and merchant commissions slapped on it. Manufacturing your own pewter mugs, or anything else, was strongly discouraged. The strategy worked. In 1759, New England exported £38,000 worth of finished products to the Mother Country—and bought £600,000 worth of manufactured goods from England.

Unsurprisingly, the colonists were a little miffed about this arrangement. The erstwhile captive markets began getting restless. They were paying through the nose to keep the economy humming back in the Mother Country. And what had Britain ever done for them? Well, OK, Britain had ejected the French from New France and saved the Thirteen Colonies from being overrun by Gallic hordes. But that was in 1763. By the 1770s, the American were already looking to Britain and asking, "What have you done for me *lately*?"

Ironically enough, the tinderbox that set off the American Revolution wasn't an attempt to raise prices, but a plan to lower them. The 1773 *Tea Act* eliminated the customs duty on tea sold by the East India Company, and allowed the company to export directly to the Americas.

Were tea-loving American shoppers dancing in the streets? Heck, no! By the time the *Tea Act* was passed, enterprising Americans had started smuggling Dutch tea into the colonies and reselling it at prices below that of official British tea. But when the *Tea Act* lifted the duty, English tea threatened to be competitive again.

Naturally, something had to be done about all this cheap, legal tea. In a display that would have made today's more violent anti-globalization types proud, a band of rabid Bostonians dressed up as Indians and headed for the docks. Three hundred and forty-two chests of tea went into Boston Harbor, and the colonists went on to invent Starbucks. To this day, many Americans view tea with slight suspicion.

On the other side of the world, another country of tea drinkers learned that resistance is futile when it comes to buying and selling. In 1639, the Tokugawa Shogunate had decided to isolate Japan from the rest of the world. Under this policy of *sakoku*, no one could leave or enter the country. That annoyed a good number of people, including sailors from other countries who wanted to use the place as a coal refueling station and traders who saw a big, untapped market just ripe for exploitation.

On July 8, 1853, U.S. Commodore Matthew Perry came steaming into the entrance of Edo (later Tokyo) Bay with four heavily armed ships. Using diplomacy rather than firepower, Perry convinced the Japanese to open two ports to U.S. ships and trade. Without Perry, we'd all be walking around humming to ourselves instead of tuning out the world with our Sony Walkmans.

So there it is, in a nutshell: a pocket history of world exploration and colonization, all filtered through the prism of finding stuff to buy and sell. Onward to the marketplace.

# 2   A Fair Is a Veritable Smorgasbord

*A fair is a veritable smorgasbord-orgasbord-orgasbord*
*After the crowds have ceased*
*Each night when the lights go down there can be found*
*All around*
*On the ground*
*Oh what a rat-ly feast!*

          —Templeton the Rat, in the animated version
          of *Charlotte's Web*, 1973

The summer I turned nine, my parents bought a pool at a fair.

It was 1974, and we were at the Canadian National Exhibition in Toronto. The Ex sprawled over a 190-acre site just west of downtown, and it was the highlight of the summer for kids from miles around. First of all, it was much more exciting than the boring old Royal Agricultural Winter Fair, held on the same site later in the year, where the chief excitements were watching cows chew their cud and finding out whether apple cider could make you drunk. Second, there was a midway, with roller coasters, and a Tilt-a-Whirl, and carnies haranguing teenage boys to win stuffed animals for their girlfriends. And third, there was the Food Building, where you could get five-cent hot dogs and cheap cups of Coke.

But none of us went to the International Building if we could help it. That's where grownups went to look at lawn mowers and Corningware. On the boring scale, it ranked right up there with the cud-chewing cows.

But I was nine, and I couldn't exactly wander off by myself. Besides, the International Building was air-conditioned, so at least I could catch my breath for a few minutes before begging my dad to take me on the Wild Mouse.

Then we saw the pool. I'm sure my parents had been considering this major purchase before we went to the Ex, but I hadn't heard a word about it. When they stopped to talk to the sales clerk, I couldn't believe it. Now *this* made our stop at the International Building worthwhile.

I still remember seeing that aboveground pool marooned on the concrete of the exhibition hall floor in all its turquoise, fiberglass-fenced glory. This was the kind of thing you couldn't buy at the local mall. In my mind, something as fantastic as a pool could only come from a fair.

### Fair play at the fair

Throughout history, fairs have always had a whiff of the exotic about them. In the past, they usually coincided with a change in seasons, a religious festival, or a sporting event, which added to their ceremonial air.

In ancient Greece, events such as the Olympic games attracted lots of people who had little interest in sport. Delphi was known for its spring fair, while the fall fairs of Thermopylae were popular places to buy and sell medicinal plants.

Historically, fairs often sprang up whenever a large number of people gathered together—the prospect of a captive audience is simply irresistible to folks with a cartload of merchandise to sell. Special conditions that sometimes reigned during major events also made fairs easier to stage. The often-warring Greek city-states, for example, suspended all hostilities during political assemblies and sports events, so it was easier for buyers and sellers from different regions to travel safely during those times. Nonetheless, during periods of tension, soldiers guarded fairs to dissuade enemy soldiers from giving in to the sizable temptation to plunder the place. If looters showed up, the guards rang a bell to warn people to scatter.

Fairs were the simplest way to distribute large quantities of goods quickly, which was particularly important at harvest time. They were an intermediate step between the producer and local marketplaces—a merchant could buy enough cloth or pottery at a fair to supply his market stall for the rest of the year. To attract the greatest number of visitors and the widest range of goods, fairs often evolved at the crossroads of major trade or pilgrimage routes. Many grew up near waterways, since the goods had to get to the fair somehow and roads were often few and far between.

(By an interesting coincidence, crossroads also have supernatural connotations. Blues musician Robert Johnson is said to have gone "down to the crossroads" to sell his soul to the devil. It figures that the devil would do a brisk business in soul-buying on the very spot where a major fair might have been.)

The Romans carried the custom of fairs throughout Europe, but the system fell apart—like just about everything else—when the western empire collapsed in the fifth century. Fairs continued to flourish in other places, such as Kinsai, China, but it would be almost two centuries before a significant fair rose from the ashes of the Western Roman Empire: the fair at Saint-Denis, outside Paris.

The European fairs of the Middle Ages varied in size and focus. Some were devoted to particular products, such as cloth or horses; others sold a little of everything. Most of them were largely wholesale events, but they attracted crowds of locals, who came to buy, sell, and enjoy themselves. As a tavern keeper in Lyons put it, "for one merchant who comes to the fairs on horseback and has plenty of money to spend and find good lodgings, there are ten others on foot, who are only too happy to find some modest *cabaret* to lay their heads." Those who couldn't afford any accommodations at all might get up before dawn to walk to the fair, spend the day enjoying themselves, and then trudge home late that night.

Regular textile fairs were established in Bruges and other Flemish towns in the late tenth century. Baldwin, Earl of Flanders, fostered their growth by waiving duties on anything bought or sold. Like modern air travelers scooping up cheap perfume, cigarettes, and liquor at a duty-free store, people flocked to these gatherings. There's nothing like the prospect of saving taxes to attract shoppers.

The middle of the twelfth century saw the rise of great fairs in the Champagne and Brie regions of northeast France. At these fairs, money-changers stayed busy exchanging coins from all over Europe. The "troy ounce" measure for gold can be traced back to one of these fairs, at

Troyes, where traders weighed coins to determine their value because the coins were often so damaged that it was hard to tell what they were worth.

The French fairs, which lasted for a month or more, attracted vendors from all over Europe. Buyers could examine cloth from Burgundy, linen from southern Germany, silk from Florence, furs from Russia, and leather from Catalonia. They could also hear the latest political news and see demonstrations of new craft processes.

The Champagne fairs had declined in importance by the middle of the fourteenth century, and subsequent fairs across Europe would wax and wane in popularity. By the end of the sixteenth century, the fairs at Antwerp had become *the* place for traders from northern and southern Europe to meet and mingle. Again, local authorities had ensured the success of the events by refusing to levy customs charges on the merchandise bought and sold.

I suspect the free trade advocates of the late twentieth century had these fairs in mind when they promoted the open movement of goods. Of course, in Renaissance Europe, people weren't really concerned that the local textile mill would move to Mexico to take advantage of looser labor and environmental laws.

### Why only history buffs still go to Renaissance fairs

Fairs weren't without their problems. They were vulnerable to events outside their control. In 1622, an exclusive fair at Piancenza, where international banking took place, closed when the supply of silver from the New World petered out. Three years later, Charles I banned all English fairs for several years, until an incidence of plague subsided. While medical understanding of infection was still rudimentary at the time, people instinctively knew it wasn't a great idea to gather crowds in one place when epidemics were afoot in the land.

By the beginning of the 1700s, competing trade venues such as the exchanges of Amsterdam were making fairs increasingly irrelevant. As the century went on, critics began to grumble that the fairs' duty-free status hurt the competitiveness of settled merchants. And once the Industrial Revolution took hold, mechanized factories began spewing out more goods than the medieval-scale fairs could handle.

One of the first industries to mechanize was the cloth industry, and its effect on the textiles fair at Chester in northeast England was remarkable. Between 1778 and 1815, dealers and speculators built three major trading halls there, but they couldn't keep up with the output of mills in Belfast, Manchester, Yorkshire, and elsewhere. By 1808, people were already beginning to notice that the crowds at the Chester fair had diminished; factory owners were finding more efficient ways to sell their goods, such as through marketing agents in major cities.

The tide was turning, but fairs didn't disappear without a fight. Take the case of England's long-lived Sturbridge Fair (also spelled Stourbridge, depending whom you ask).

This fair, held just outside Cambridge, had existed since at least 1211, when it received a charter from King John. By the 1300s, it was an international event that gave English merchants and individuals the chance to buy goods from around the known world: Venetian glass, French wine, Asian spices and porcelain, Spanish iron, Norwegian tar, and more. Considering the distance the goods had to travel, and the expense and danger of bringing them to this wheat field in southeast England, the variety was even more amazing.

From its early days, the late-summer event had the potential for rowdiness; in 1395, Richard II ordered the local sheriff to detain anyone breaking the peace during the fair. Shoppers who behaved badly seemed to have been a constant concern; in 1548, a crier opened the fair with a long, convoluted proclamation, which began by urging attendees to "keepe the Kings peace" and to "leave theire weapons at theire Innes."

But merchants weren't blameless, either. Customers worried—and with good reason—that the vendors were out to cheat them, and the people who ran the fair tried hard to allay shoppers' fears. After all, a suspicious shopper buys less. The 1548 proclamation goes on to describe, at length, the legal weights, strengths, and prices for various goods. Vintners, for example, were ordered to sell their goods "no dearer than they doe at London." There were also a lot of rules designed to prevent the sale of adulterated food. On and on the proclamation goes, for some 2,000 words. For the sake of the criers, I hope that the merchants of Sturbridge Fair sold a remedy for sore throats.

There was more to Sturbridge Fair than buying and selling. Like the theme parks, hockey rinks, and submarines that draw shoppers to modern mega-malls, a variety of amusements entertained the visitors to Sturbridge Fair. Customers could watch bull baiting and bear baiting, laugh at a staged comedy, or play "nine-holes."

In fact, by 1604, the range of entertainment had become so vast that King James I ordered the University of Cambridge to ban all such amusements entirely within five miles of Cambridge, so that they wouldn't interfere with students' concentration on their studies. The sober king was concerned that, if these distractions continued, "the younger sort are or may be drawn or provoked to vain experience loss of time or corruption of manners." I suspect that King James would not be impressed by the scene in the food court of the average modern mall, either.

Fair-goers attracted the attention of other folks concerned about their spiritual well-being, too. From the mid-1600s until the early 1700s, at least, a preacher gave sermons on Sundays during the fair. The open-air pulpit stood in the middle of a large square called the Duddery, surrounded by booths selling clothes and fabrics. In earlier centuries, it had been home to a maypole. Writer Ned Ward described the site in 1700 as "an old weather-beaten pulpit, where on Sunday a sermon is delivered for the edification of the strolling sinners."

Sinful or not, the fair went on, becoming more and more of a spectacle. By the beginning of the 1700s, the opening procession had evolved into an early version of the Macy's Thanksgiving Day parade. It actually served much the same function: to alert the locals that a special time for buying and selling had arrived. The crier still led the way, followed by a motley crew of constables, musicians, politicians, members of Parliament, judges, and local merchants. In their wake came a herd of boys on horseback, who raced each other around the grounds when the official ceremonies were over.

### Marooned by savings:
### Robinson Crusoe goes shopping

With the growth of newspapers, the fair became even more famous. When an announcement of the fair appeared in the London papers in 1705, describing what the opening ceremonies would be like, the fair recorded its best attendance in a decade. One visitor came and spent two weeks at the fair, enjoying the sights and sounds, drinking tea every afternoon and consorting with "some very agreeable ladies of Cambridge town and education."

Daniel Defoe, best known for writing *Robinson Crusoe*, paid a visit to the fair in 1723. He hailed it breathlessly as "not only the greatest in the whole Nation, but in the World." From his description of the fair, it's easy to see why he would come to this conclusion.

The fair stretched for a square half mile over a wheat field overlooking the River Cam. The small river, which connected to larger waterways, made it relatively easy to ship heavy goods from London and other parts of England.

The stalls stretched out in rows like streets. Shoppers buying retail patronized the booths in a row called Cheapside, named after a famous shopping street in London. "[S]carce any trades are omitted, Goldsmiths, Toy-shops, Braziers, Turners, Milliners, Haberdashers, Hatters, Mercers, Drapers, Pewterers, China-Ware-houses, Taverns, Brandy-Shops, and Eating-houses, innumerable, and all in Tents, and Booths," Defoe noted approvingly.

Customers buying wholesale frequented another row, which led to the Duddery. That square was large enough that merchants could pull up large wagons to stock their booths, which by this date was essential. The massive textiles stalls in the Duddery, Defoe related, looked like "vast Ware-Houses pil'd up with Goods to the Top."

Not surprisingly, this enormous event attracted hordes of novelty-seekers from London, 54 miles away. So many people came that London entrepreneurs followed them. Shoppers who didn't want to walk could avail themselves of the services of some 50 hackney coaches, brought up from the capital to shuttle people back and forth between Cambridge and the fair site, a few miles out of town. Others hopped rides in little rowboats called wherries—again, imported from London—that plied the River Cam. Every inn for miles around was full, and people who weren't so particular about their accommodations slept in stables.

The vendors themselves slept in their booths. If they wanted to cook for themselves, they had no shortage of fresh food, since local farmers and grocers went from tent to tent every morning selling fresh meat, bread, butter, eggs, and cheese. But many merchants ate and drank instead at the fair's taverns and coffeehouses.

The fair had a definite rhythm. Wholesaling and trading among the lower classes took up the bulk of the fair; after that was largely finished, the local gentry showed up. "[A]nd tho' they come for their diversion; yet 'tis not a little Money, they lay out," Defoe noted—the lament of the window-shopper everywhere. Finally, at the end of the two-week festival, there was a horse fair and horse races.

"In a Word, the Fair is like a well Fortify'd City, and there is the least Disorder and Confusion (I believe) that can be seen anywhere, with so great a Concourse of People," Defoe concluded.

### This fair is a circus!

Defoe had the good fortune of seeing the fair just before it began to seriously fall apart. By the mid-1700s, Sturbridge Fair was in decline, and it wasn't the only one.

Across England, the entertainments that had always been part of the fairs started to take over the events completely, with showmen, drinking booths, and stalls selling cheap gifts filling the void left behind by the vanishing wholesalers. The change happened first in the cities. Bartholomew Fair in London was already a largely frivolous event by the early 1700s, and Sturbridge Fair was increasingly given over to pantomimes, student pranks, and dancing as the century went on. Summer and fall fairs in Liverpool were largely entertainment events by the end of the eighteenth century, as was the Great Fair at Coventry by 1850.

Practical fairs held on longer in the countryside than in the city. In 1810, for instance, visitors to a small fair in Essex could buy cloth, clothing, shoes, gifts, and food from about 30 traders. Forty years later, however, the fair attracted only 17 traders, and the usual showmen and snack vendors predominated.

Middle-class Victorians, not surprisingly, were appalled at the rowdiness of these working-class fairs. Complaints began and new restrictions were put in place to control drinking and noise, although town councils were reluctant to completely give up the revenues the fairs brought in. Sometimes the councils moved them to sites farther from town as a compromise.

The 1855 proclamation of the Sturbridge Fair shows the administrators' increasing concern with public order. The proclamations had often warned people to keep the peace, but the warning was beginning to sound primmer and, well, Victorian. Prince Albert, in the name of his wife Queen Victoria, commanded

> [t]hat all unhonest women, all vagrant and unruly persons avoid and withdraw themselves from this Fair and the precincts thereof immediately after this proclamation, that Her Majesty's Subjects may be quieter, and good rule the better maintained . . .

As it happened, despite being both Victorian and English, fair-goers weren't really that interested in quiet, orderly entertainment. The Sturbridge Fair died a slow death. In 1882, it had dwindled to a three-day event, but it didn't close for good until 1934. It was the end of an era, but few events in human history can claim to have lasted for over 700 years.

### Fairly modern

Sturbridge Fair and its kin may be gone, but fairs never disappeared completely. They just changed function. Instead of serving as wholesaling and retailing venues for everyday goods, they evolved into events where merchants and the public could see the latest, greatest manufactured products. The "Great Exhibition of the Works of Industry of All Nations," held in London in 1851, was just such a fair.

In fact, it was the first of the world's fairs, which would later include the Centennial Exhibition in Philadelphia in 1876, the 1939 New York World's Fair, and Expo '67 in Montreal. These later fairs would draw crowds that the merchants of Sturbridge couldn't imagine in their wildest dreams. The 1939 fair, held in a 1,200-acre drained swamp in Queens, logged more than 44 million visits; attendance at the Montreal fair topped 50 million.

Some of these fairs have become part of folklore. Shoppers first encountered Crackerjack and Aunt Jemima pancake mix at the 1893 Columbian Exposition in Chicago. The St. Louis Fair claims to have given the world ice cream cones, hamburgers, and hot dogs. The Montreal fair came to symbolize the pride of a nation celebrating its 100th birthday. And the New York fairgrounds were the setting for the climax of the movie *Men in Black*, in which it was revealed that the site also had an alien clientele.

Aside from the world's fairs, countless trade fairs take place all over the world—everything from the Cannes Film Festival and the Frankfurt Book Fair to less glamorous events for lighting manufacturers and hardware dealers.

Las Vegas has become to trade shows what places like Sturbridge were to fairs. For most of the last decade, the city has hosted 35 of the largest 200 U.S. trade shows; in 2002, five of the country's 10 largest trade shows took advantage of at least a small slice of the Vegas's 17 million feet of exhibit space.

With so many buyers and sellers congregated in one place, some weird evolutions happen. One of the best known Las Vegas trade shows, Comdex, attracts computer industry professionals who have a reputation for not gambling. The week of Comdex is, however, reputed to be the biggest week of the year in Las Vegas for hookers and strippers. When Comdex organizers banned exhibitors pushing pornographic software and other raunchy products, a parallel event emerged: AdultDex, billed as "the trade show where silicon meets silicone."

The consumer show is yet another descendant of the medieval fair. These annual events descend on convention centers just as predictably as the fairs at Troyes or Sturbridge ever did: the spring boat show and the fall home show, the Christmas craft sale and the winter antiques market.

And there are more of these trade and consumer shows than you might think; the Center for Exhibition Industry Research, in its latest census, has tracked more than 13,000 events in the U.S. and Canada, each of which occupies at least 3,000 net square feet. Annually, 16 cities host more than 200 shows each.

And, finally, there are the annual end-of-summer exhibitions, like the Canadian National Exhibition, where I saw that wonderful pool. The CNE, as it's called, has been running since 1879 and shows no sign of throwing in the towel just yet; it attracts about 1.4 million visitors annually and pumps about C$35 million into Toronto's economy.

It's been a long road from the ancient Olympics to the modern midway. And while we have many alternatives to the temporary trading event, from air-conditioned malls to Internet shopping, there's something about the bustle of the exotic that keeps us coming back to fairs.

# 3   To Market, To Market

*To market, to market, to buy a fat pig,*
*Home again, home again, dancing a jig;*
*To market, to market, to buy a fat hog;*
*Home again, home again, jiggety-jog;*
*To market, to market, to buy a plum bun,*
*Home again, home again, market is done.*

—Traditional nursery rhyme

Markets, as I mentioned in the introduction, have been around from the day somebody realized he could trade his excess grain for his neighbor's extra goat. And when people started to settle in cities, markets evolved into full-scale social events. Although visitors to these markets could usually buy a little bit of everything, from Brussels sprouts to boots, I'm going to focus on food shopping in this chapter. When I have a choice in life, I usually find it useful to hone in on food.

### Before "everyday low prices" there were "every eighth-day low prices"

In ancient Rome, markets were held regularly, often every eighth day. The fact that the market took place on specific days was important. Because a farmer had to devote most of his time to caring for his crops and livestock, he couldn't be hauling himself into the city every day to sell his produce. If the market took place just once or twice a week, he could spend as little time as possible away from his farm, while being certain that as many people as possible would be gathered in one place to buy his products.

These markets were more than opportunities to buy and sell; they also gave shoppers the chance to exchange news, to hold political meetings, to hear the latest proclamation from whoever was in power that month, and to be entertained. As the Roman Empire was Christianized, markets were often held in conjunction with saints' days. This strategy ensured that the greatest number of people would be attracted to the city or town on the same day—or, as historian Cornelius Walford once put it, "in order that trade might attract those whom religion could not influence."

The custom of holding frequent, scheduled markets spread throughout the Roman Empire, although the interval between each market varied widely from place to place. The Roman administrators also exported the Greco-Roman idea of market courts, which settled disputes between buyers and sellers. The Romans appear to have introduced the concept of markets to England—in fact, the English word *market* comes from that Latin *mercatus*. Traces of Roman market areas have been found near Cornwall, Cambridge, Newcastle, and other sites.

With the fall of the western empire, these rather sophisticated markets faded into memory for much of Europe. The invading barbarians had ravaged the landscape, and most people barely eked out a living from it. Any excess production went to the local lord as taxes. But when the agricultural economy began to recover, surpluses began to appear once more. At the end of the fifth century in what is now Italy, marketplaces re-evolved to help people trade what they couldn't use.

These small, informal markets appeared wherever people needed to buy things. Some emerged in conjunction with the courts held weekly in many towns. Others sprang up in churchyards on Sundays, where crowds of parishioners presented an irresistible opportunity to traders. At first, markets were held in the open; as time went on, many vendors sold from covered stalls.

But a vendor couldn't, in most cases, just wander into a churchyard or market street and set up shop whenever and wherever he pleased, for free. He had to pay a fee called *stallage* to the owner of the market, who might be the town council, a bishop or abbot, a group of citizens, or the local lord. In exchange for this fee, the seller was allowed to enter the town and to set up a stand in a particular spot. Most market owners also provided a range of services for vendors and buyers, which usually included methods for allocating space and resolving disputes.

Early on, authorities realized that it made sense to keep all the buyers or sellers in one place. Towns that had a defined market district—or better yet, a market building—found it easier to regulate commerce than towns that simply allowed vendors to set up on the streets and then tried to collect fees and tolls from them as they worked. Unsurprisingly, the incentive for vendors to sell quickly and bolt without paying their taxes was high.

Like Roman markets, these medieval markets took place on set days, again to ensure the highest concentration of farmers and locals. The set market day also helped the traveling tradesman, who would move from town to town selling his wares at different markets. Many towns carefully chose their market days so that they wouldn't conflict with those in nearby burgs.

### Tax cuts for the rich

Markets were major economic engines, and kings eventually decided they wanted a piece of the action, much as today's Mafia dons want a taste of neighborhood mercantile success in exchange for "protection." In England, some time before the eighth century, rulers started sending royal agents out to coastal towns to exact tolls on goods-laden ships entering port. By the beginning of the thirteenth century, kings had come up with another way to pluck the merchant goose: they required all fairs and markets to be licensed. English monarchs, like most of their counterparts across western Europe, were in desperate need of revenues to pay for the Crusades, which had been going on for a century by this point. Apparently, an expensive adventure to meddle in the Middle East can really do a number on your balance sheet. Who knew?

All this taxation didn't sit well with the folks who were already earning a nice living through stallage fees—in many cases, the local lords. The barons who presented King John with a draft of the Magna Carta demanded "that merchants shall have safety to go and come, buy and sell, without any evil tolls, but by antient and honest customs." By "evil tolls," they meant any fees, duties, or other charges that were so high that they ate up the merchants' profit.

In other words, the founding document of English democracy was a tax cut for the rich.

Of course, businesspeople are going to demand more than they think they can get, so that the other party can negotiate. In the finished Magna Carta of 1215, King John agreed that merchants could travel through England safely, and that they could "buy and sell, without any *unjust exactions*"—the king, of course, being left to decide what was just and what was unjust.

As it turned out, John reneged on the deal as soon as he could, and for years the Magna Carta was part of an elaborate version of political "capture the flag" played out by the king, the nobles, and the Catholic Church. Eventually, John had the good grace to die and the Magna Carta was back in business. Shopping was safe once again.

### Medieval zoning and other regulations

Other laws and limits soon came to bear on the medieval marketplace. Also in the thirteenth century, a lawyer proclaimed that English markets had to be at least six miles apart, so that they wouldn't steal each other's customers. The specified distance ensured that sellers could get to town, sell their goods, and get home within daylight hours, before highway robbers were about.

(Nighttime bandits aren't as much of a concern as they once were, but we still regulate the distances between commercial enterprises. If you buy a franchise of Bob's Donut and Live Bait Shop, for example, Bob will promise not to sell another franchise within a certain distance of your establishment. Similarly, city planning boards carefully consider applications for new shopping malls, trying to determine whether there are enough people within easy driving distance to sustain the operation.)

The medieval controls on markets strongly emphasized fairness. Each market had a set opening hour, so that everyone who wanted to buy had an equal chance at the goods. If someone shopped before the opening bell rang, he—and the vendor he bought from—would face severe penalties.

Vendors faced further penalties if they sold nonstandard products. At regular meetings called the assizes, market authorities specified the standard size of a loaf of bread and the standard strength of a gallon of ale, these being the mainstays of the English diet at the time. Interestingly, they didn't set prices, because many transactions involved bartering rather than the use of scarce coins.

As in markets and fairs throughout history, the question of weights and measures was contentious. In the late 13th century, Edward I decreed "that one weight shall be kept in every fair and town; that the weigher shall show the buyer and seller that the beam and scales are fair, and that there shall be only one weight and measure in our dominions, and that they be stamped with our standard mark." These were fine words, but temptations to cheat were rife, especially when times were hard.

Each market had a court of vendors, usually presided over by the mayor or a local justice, to settle disputes between buyers and sellers about weights, measures, quality, and pricing. These courts were called, memorably, Courts of Piepowder. The name has been traced through the Old French *pied puldreaux*, which goes back to the Latin *curia pedis pulverzati*. Both terms referred to people with dusty feet, which has been taken to mean peddlers.

These courts particularly frowned on efforts to "forestall" a particular product. Forestalling involved buying up a good chunk of the local stock of something such as poultry, eggs, or cheese, and then either sending it out of the area to be sold or selling it all yourself, thereby increasing local demand and ensuring that you could charge a higher price. This practice was unpopular because medieval Europeans strongly believed that it was immoral to make too much profit on your labor. More seriously, in an era when people couldn't just nip over to Safeway if the local Kash 'N Karry was out of bread, forestalling could also lead to dangerous food shortages.

### City slickers and country cousins

As Europe became more urbanized and city markets became increasingly voracious, the business of regulating marketplaces became more complicated and bitter. In particular, relations between city markets and their country cousins got a bit testy.

In 1487, the Common Council of London passed an ordinance designed to keep people from taking goods out of the city to sell at other markets and fairs. This edict immediately caused an uproar among the good citizens of Bristol, Coventry, Cambridge, and many other places, who didn't much like the idea of hauling themselves all the way to London to buy cloth, household goods, and other products. The outcry was so great that Parliament was forced to annul the London law.

London might have lost that battle, but as the centuries went on, it would certainly win the war. Let's jump forward in time by three centuries, and see how city and country markets were faring in the early days of the Industrial Revolution.

By the late 1700s, many English market towns were struggling to stay afloat. Farmers and other producers were increasingly bypassing the local stalls to sell their goods to city-based factors—the steady, guaranteed income was attractive, and it saved the farmer the bother of selling the products himself in the market. To add insult to injury, when food was scarce, peddlers from cities descended on country markets and bought up as much food as they could, leaving the locals with nothing. Some towns tried to combat the problem by outlawing wholesale selling until an hour after the market opened, so the locals could slip in and buy enough for their needs, but the problem remained a serious one.

The crux of the issue was that London's needs were simply overwhelming. In 1800, with a population of roughly one million, London was the world's largest city. Not since the days of the Roman Empire—when the population of Rome, according to some estimates, topped two million souls—had the Western world faced the problem of feeding so many people in one place. The fact that roads were bad, canals slow, and other methods of transportation largely nonexistent made bringing food to market a labor-intensive proposition.

In the early 1800s, for example, women from the market gardens ringing London carried strawberries and other fruit into the city in panniers. Foot transport was gentle enough not to bruise the fruit. In the early 1830s, some of these gardeners started using well-sprung carts to haul their goods along roads that had recently been "macadamized"—paved using a new process developed by Scottish engineer J.L. McAdam. A cart could carry 20 times more fruit than a woman on foot could, but the produce was inevitably jostled and bruised, and couldn't command as high a price.

Steamships and rail transportation would have a much greater impact on London's markets. The shopper of 1850 could choose from a much larger selection of fruit and meat than her grandmother would have found in the stalls 50 years earlier. Steamships made it cheaper and easier to import fruit from Europe, while railroads made it possible to ship "country-killed" meat from further afield in England. This variety eventually improved the availability of food in the countryside as well, as food sellers from villages and small towns traveled to London and major provincial cities by rail and bought stock from wholesale markets to resell at home.

### Where teenagers (and others) loitered before the mall

Just like fairs, mid-nineteenth-century markets could be magnets for rowdy behavior that market owners worked hard to control. Saturday nights were a particular problem. In the larger venues, hundreds of stalls lined the crowded marketplace. Shoppers viewed the wares by the dim light of candles, smoky grease lamps, or glaring gaslight. Clots of street sellers thronged the byways; it was their busiest night of the week, and the air was loud with their cries. A carnival air prevailed, since many factory workers were paid late Saturday night and had their only day of rest on Sundays.

The problem wasn't limited to London's enormous markets. In 1852, a group of aggrieved residents complained to the administrators of the market in Coventry about "great disorder and bad language used by Persons attending the Market on a Saturday Evening." As a result, the owners started closing the market on Saturday nights at 11:30 P.M., giving shoppers and vendors a one-hour warning by ringing a bell at 10:30 P.M.

However, not all Saturday night shoppers were bent on trouble. One oyster seller in London spoke fondly of her weekend customers:

My heartiest customers, that I serve with the most pleasure, are working people, on a Saturday night. One couple—I think the wife always goes to meet her husband on a Saturday night—has two, or three, or four penn'orth, as happens, and it's pleasant to hear them say, "Won't you have another John?" or, "Do have one or two more, Mary Ann." I've served them that way two or three years.

Similarly busy but decidedly quieter markets were often held on Sundays, when housewives would take what remained of their husbands' pay (after the excesses of the night before) to buy a nice Sunday dinner. The better-off street sellers avoided working Sundays, if they could, hoping to take their day of rest just as many other people did.

Food markets were large, lively, and well stocked, but even these vast marketplaces eventually couldn't accommodate all the demands of the booming city, whose population would soar to 4.5 million by 1901. Across the ocean, the growing cities of the New World were facing a similar problem.

### "Start spreading the news, I'm buying New York . . ."

European colonial powers brought the idea of public markets with them to North America. However, medieval ideas of marketplace ethics went through a series of major shifts on this side of the pond. New Amsterdam, the city that would become New York, is a case in point.

Dutch traders had set up rudimentary camps on Manhattan Island in the early 1600s. These were just temporary places to trade with native fur trappers and prepare animal hides for shipping. The permanent settlement of New Amsterdam can be dated to May or June 1626, when the director of the New Netherland colony, Peter Minuit, bought Manhattan for 60 guilders worth of trinkets (about $24). There is much chuckling about how Minuit swindled the natives out of property now worth about $60 billion, but the natives may have had the last laugh. Many scholars believe that Minuit actually negotiated with the wrong tribe. Ooops.

For the first 13 years of the city's existence, the Dutch West India Company controlled all commerce on the island. It gave up that monopoly in 1639, and Manhattan hasn't been the same since. Small stalls sprang up in New Amsterdam, and "Scotch traders" or "sojourners" (peddlers) began dropping in with exotic wares, but the town wasn't exactly a shoppers' paradise yet.

For one thing, there wasn't much money floating around, for a variety of reasons. First of all, the colonial powers were stingy about distributing hard currency to their far-flung colonies, but they weren't keen to have colonists minting and printing their own money either. Further to the north, the governor of New France got around the currency shortage by signing playing cards, so you could spend the king of diamonds and nine of clubs.

In the early 1600s, colonial authorities in New England and New Netherland came up with a similar solution. They noticed that Indians used wampum as currency and adopted that system. But that bright idea quickly led to problems. Genuine wampum beads were made only from clam and whelk shells native to Long Island Sound and Narragansett Bay; their rarity was part of the reason they were valuable. But once wampum was legal tender, demand for it soared among both natives and colonists. The market was soon flooded with counterfeit wampum, made from stone, wood, glass, and other cheap materials. Prices shot up and people got grumpy.

The colonists pleaded with the folks back home to send money, or let them mint their own. England caved first, allowing New Englanders to demonetize wampum and make their own money. As a result, New Netherland was flooded with New England wampum. Various administrators tried to control the value and use of wampum in New Netherland. Beaver pelts were used as alternative currency, but people would keep spending wampum on the banks of the Hudson until the early 1700s. And the places they were spending it grew increasingly sophisticated.

## Cleaning up the town

When Petrus Stuyvesant arrived in New Amsterdam in August 1647 as the new director-general of New Netherland, the ramshackle settlement had no grammar school, no paved streets, and a large population of farm animals roaming free. Stuyvesant was not impressed, and immediately decided to clean the place up and make it more like a pleasant, tidy Dutch town.

His ideas of orderliness extended further than physical cleanliness. He wanted New Amsterdam to be efficient and law abiding as well. One of the first things he did was set up a farmers' market on the shore of the East River. By 1656, the location had moved to the mouth of a canal that ran along the route of today's Broad Street. Farmers from Brooklyn and Bergen simply sailed boats up the canal and conducted business from the decks. Markets held on open areas near wharves were common in cities all along the Eastern Seaboard.

Unfortunately, even in the 1600s, New Yorkers took a dim view of anybody trying too hard to tame them. When the English sailed into New Netherland in 1664, Stuyvesant tried to rally the locals against New York's first wave of unwanted tourists. Sadly for him, the local Dutch apparently took one look at the English and decided they'd rather sell them wooden shoes than fight them off with muskets. Waves of entrepreneurial immigrants have been transforming the city ever since.

### Markets on the move

In the early 1700s, when populations were small, North American marketplaces were more like medieval European markets than the large daily markets that existed in London or Paris at this time. In the colonies, since producers needed to be on their farms at least part of the time, the markets were open only one or two days a week. Mondays were frowned on as market days, because that would mean sellers would have to prepare their goods and travel on the Sabbath. From the beginning, Americans were much more concerned about the intersection of religion and commerce than many Europeans were—not surprisingly, since many of the fledgling colonies were founded by religious groups.

Cities grew quickly, and markets changed along with them. Within a few decades, many American cities allowed certain perishable goods—milk, for instance—to be sold daily. The number of marketplaces grew; by the late 1720s, five municipal markets lined the banks of the East River in New York. And sellers and shoppers alike were beginning to see the value in covered marketplaces, where both goods and people would be sheltered from the elements.

Civic officials set up the first enclosed public markets in the middle of wide city streets, for the simple reason that since the street was public property, they didn't have to pay anyone for the land. These early market buildings were plain, functional and probably unloved. They were just crowded, smelly places to buy meat and bread, after all.

One of the earliest substantial public markets in the U.S. was Faneuil Hall in Boston, built in 1742 by merchant Peter Faneuil and expanded in 1805. With its brick facade and pretty cupola, it was a statement of civic pride. It would also become, like many markets, a community center of sorts. During one meeting early in the American Revolution, 1200 people reportedly crammed into the small civic hall on the second floor to discuss ways to harass the British. (This fact is even more amazing when you realize that the entire population of Boston was 16,000 and the hall—which currently has a legal capacity of 860 people—was half the size it is today.)

Other public markets throughout the U.S. Northeast housed additional civic functions, including fire halls, police stations or meeting rooms. City authorities figured that as long as they were paying for one public works project, they might as well throw in the works. Fire halls were a particularly prescient addition, since most markets—unlike Faneuil Hall—were made of wood and prone to combustion.

As commerce became more varied and important, it soon became impractical to have a market in the middle of a city street, snarling traffic in both directions. (This appears to be an ancient problem; the Latin word for *market* also meant *traffic*.) The fact that markets in the middle of the street had to be built as one long corridor also caused trouble. Since products were usually segregated in separate areas—profitable butchers near the entrances, other foodstuffs further inside the building—shoppers had to walk great distances to pick up all the goods they needed. In the days before shopping carts, this was particularly unpleasant. (But at least they didn't have to contend with Muzak.)

In the mid-nineteenth century, many markets were moved into street-side locations, where they still often took up at least a city block. But the change of location, coupled with advances in building technology, meant that they no longer had to be constructed as one long corridor. Iron and steel frames made it possible to build square buildings with vast interior spaces uninterrupted by columns or walls.

**Marketing the market**

Around the same time, city officials and merchants realized that a pleasant environment encouraged shoppers to spend more. Where aesthetic considerations had failed to move builders, commercial considerations succeeded: market buildings became more substantial and elegant. Merchants also began investing a bit more thought and money into making food shopping an event. Christmas Eve of 1851, for instance, saw a market hall in Cincinnati tarted up with chandeliers and gilt-framed portraits of worthy personages such as Washington. Altogether, the festive display set the merchants back $1,000. But it must have worked, if the elaborate Christmas decorations in today's malls are any indication.

In New York's markets, shoppers would have likely appreciated any attempt at beautification. In the 1870s, the city was home to nine major markets. The days when markets only opened one or two days a week were long gone; these buildings saw heavy, constant use. Most of the buildings were old and the exteriors were decrepit. The comings and goings of crowds of customers and suppliers left the surrounding streets messy and foul smelling, particularly in summer. But shoppers who could overlook all this had a treat awaiting them inside.

"The ricketty [sic] old buildings are crammed to repletion with everything edible the season affords," wrote journalist James D. McCabe, Jr., in 1872, going on to list the variety of fruits, vegetables, meat, fish, and poultry available from all over the country. "Indeed, one who has the means can purchase here almost everything the heart can desire."

The choicest morsels went early. When the markets opened between 4 A.M. and 5 A.M., the first customers were restaurateurs, hotel caterers, servants in wealthy mansions, owners of upscale boarding houses, and shopkeepers buying supplies for their stores. Prices and quality at this hour were the highest of the day.

Once these well-funded and picky shoppers had left, the next wave descended. These folks included the owners of less-fashionable boarding houses, "who are too smart to come when the prices are high and the articles good and fresh," and miserly millionaires, who "will haggle to the last penny," according to McCabe. By 10 A.M., not much was left for the poorest classes to pick through.

Late sleepers weren't completely out of luck, though. Small food stores scattered throughout New York and other cities, both in America and abroad, were increasingly giving public markets a run for their money. By 1870, New Yorkers were making two-thirds of their food purchases in venues other than public markets.

## Why we still want food with dirt on it

Although cities such as Newark and Seattle continued to build market buildings well into the twentieth century, public marketplaces seemed to have hit their high point by 1900. Customers were moving out of crowded downtown tenements into low-density suburbs, where big central markets didn't make economic sense. Food manufacturers were churning out nifty processed foods that were much more interesting than piles of rutabagas and potatoes, and they were selling them at competitive prices in tidy new grocery stores. Advances in canning and refrigeration made it possible for housewives to shop once a week rather than once a day.

The death knell started to sound. Public markets were torn down all over North America and, to a lesser degree, in Europe. Bright, sterile, air-conditioned supermarkets were the way of the future, people said. Only your crazy neighbor who thought radio and automobiles were passing fads would shop at a public market.

There was only one problem with this theory. Some of the markets refused to die. Sure, they got a little seedy around the edges. And, granted, they weren't the primary shopping destinations they once were. They were hardly going to put the local Safeway out of business. But people loved them. The St. Lawrence Market in Toronto soldiered on, as did the Atwater Market in Montreal. The building that housed the 17th Street Farmers Market in Richmond, Virginia, was torn down in 1961, but a few vendors and customers insisted on sticking around. In the mid-1980s, a new, open-air market was rebuilt and the market came back to life.

The revival of the 17th Street Farmers Market isn't an isolated story. It seems that, for some people at least, the siren call of fresh, local produce persists. Between 1994 and 2002, the number of U.S. farmers' markets—which can be anything from a few seasonal stands set up in a parking lot to a year-round, indoor market—boomed by 79 percent. There are now more than 3,100 of these markets across the country.

It's the same story in many other places. In my home province of Ontario, the number of farmers' markets had dwindled to just 60 by the 1980s; by 2002, that number had doubled and the markets were racking up total annual sales of about C$500 million. Over in the U.K, meanwhile, 120 towns and cities held farmers' markets in 1999.

Some of this revival can be attributed to a concerted effort by governments and farmers' associations to resuscitate the markets, which can be a significant source of revenue for small-scale farmers. Some of the interest can be traced to the roaring success of "festival marketplaces" such as the Faneuil Hall Marketplace in Boston. Even though many of these latter developments aren't terribly food oriented, their sense of theater and fun has made downtown markets in general hip and trendy again. In fact, the State of Massachusetts has been thinking of building a $40-million public food market in Boston—a twenty-first-century version of the 1826 Quincy Market, whose buildings now house trendy fashion boutiques and gourmet stores.

And so, as with so much in the world of shopping, everything old is new again. People have liked buying their food right from the farmer for a few millennia now. Despite the ubiquity of huge supermarkets with their heaps of shiny produce, I wouldn't count the farmer's market out just yet. After all, the shine on those supermarket apples is usually produced by some combination of fungicide, chlorine, and detergent. The day will probably come, sooner rather than later, when many of us will prefer our apples dirty.

# 4    Eat, Drink, and Be Shoppers

*I never make a trip to the United States without visiting a supermarket. To me they are more fascinating than any fashion salon.*
—Wallis, Duchess of Windsor, April 8, 1964

In the checkout line, I look into my cart and gasp. How did all that *stuff* end up in there?

I shouldn't be surprised. After all, I came to the College Square Market Loblaws—a new supermarket in suburban Ottawa—specifically to experience the peculiar joys of shopping in a gigantic grocery store. And one of those joys is choice.

At 115,000 square feet, the College Square store sells much more than meat, milk, and mayonnaise. There's a cigar shop, a travel agency, an electronics store, a photo shop, and a full-size drugstore. A huge center aisle is filled with children's clothes and toys, while another is stocked with home office supplies. A third aisle and a separate meat counter are devoted to kosher foods. The far side of the store is replete with bath towels, throw pillows, cookware, and lawn furniture. Upstairs, there are offices, a community meeting room, a cooking demonstration room, and a Goodlife fitness center. Only an ascetic inured to the siren song of ingenious marketing could come in looking for a loaf of bread and leave with nothing more.

## Traipsing through the aisles

Like any new grocery store, College Square is an artful stage set designed to get your mouth watering. For decades, produce has been the first thing you encounter in most grocery stores. There's nothing like all those bright colors and appetizing aromas to make you hungry, and various studies have shown that hungry shoppers buy more. College Square keeps the produce section but adds lots of other appetizing goodies at the entrance to vie for your attention.

The doors open onto a fanciful marketplace, anchored in one corner by a giant fiberglass tree that looks as though it came from Disney's overstock. The first thing that catches my eye is a sushi stand, overseen by an Asian clerk. Sushi is trendy but not brand new; exotic but not threatening. It says to shoppers: this is a store where you can feel sophisticated but safe. Two or three or five years from now, some food trend currently known only to Manhattan and L.A. cognoscenti will have swept the sushi stand from its prestigious real estate.

If sushi isn't your thing, don't worry—the minds at Loblaws and other supermarkets have created other aromatic "home meal replacement" options to get those taste buds jumping. Home meal replacement is the big buzzword in grocery retailing right now, and the business has expanded dramatically beyond deli potato salads and rotisserie chickens. The elegant stands ringing the entry to College Square offer sandwiches, hot pizza, and Singapore noodles, among other goodies. I walk away with four samosas and a tub of Bombay chicken salad I had no intention of buying when I walked through the door. By the time I get to the nearby produce section, I'm pumped.

The lowly produce section, where our moms once picked up heads of iceberg lettuce and bags of onions, has gone through a renaissance of its own. Mounds of exotic fruits and vegetables glisten under special lamps that highlight their color while not overheating them. In some stores, the veggies are displayed against black backdrops, like performers on a stage; at College Square, they're heaped in faux wicker baskets as though they'd just fallen off a stall in a farmers' market. Whatever your fantasy—theater or nostalgia—if marketers have determined it will move radicchio and kiwifruit off the shelves, you'll see it played out.

Toward the back of this wide entry aisle are a variety of other products designed to get the imagination racing: a seafood counter piled high with salmon and shrimp on crushed ice (live lobsters pace around an enormous tank nearby); several cases full of cheese; a large deli counter; and another case full of fresh pasta, sauces, and upscale soups. Into my cart goes a jar of carrot and orange soup, too exotic to resist—it sounds just like an "I'll order that, I'd never make it at home" appetizer from a chichi restaurant.

The last section of the first aisle, the bakery, hits me with another wave of hunger-inducing aromas. Mmmmm, donuts.

I haven't even made it into the second aisle, and I'm ready to eat the metal cart.

### Supermarkets, by the numbers

I'm not the only one. The average American makes 2.2 grocery-buying trips every week, a figure that includes quick trips to the 7-Eleven to buy milk and bread. That number is down from 3.4 trips a decade ago.

However, the lines are probably just as long, because we have a penchant for all shopping at the same time. Looking for a quiet day to shop? Pick Tuesday—statistics show it's usually the slowest day of the grocery week. Stay away from the stores on Saturdays, when 22 percent of all grocery shopping is done. Other times to avoid include long weekends, Christmas Eve, the day after a major catastrophe (such as a blizzard, blackout, or hurricane), and any afternoon between 4 P.M. and 7 P.M.

Despite the fact that we're making fewer trips, we're spending more each time we go. If you always seem to be behind the woman with three dozen coupons and a massive quantity of dog food cans, this is probably why. In 2002, the average American grocery store was raking in $361,564 a week, almost double the average weekly sales a decade earlier.

So what exactly are we dropping in our carts? Let's say Joe and Jane Average American take $100 to their local supermarket. In 2001, according to the Food Marketing Institute, they will spend $50.41 of that money on perishables: meat, dairy, baked goods, produce, deli goods, and frozen foods. (If anyone has ever looked closely at the expiration dates of some of the food in my freezer, they'd realize I have a different definition of "perishable" than do Joe, Jane, and the Food Marketing Institute.) Our average shoppers will also spend $10.21 on nondairy beverages, $6.25 on snacks, $13.59 on other food items (largely things in boxes, bags, bottles, and cans), and $3.96 on health and beauty items. Various other catego-ries, including things like aluminum foil and birthday cards, make up the total.

Interestingly, the fewer people there are in your house, the more money you're likely to spend per person on groceries. People living alone spend $52 on their groceries per week; if there are five or more people in the household, that figure drops to $24 per person per week.

Part of this has to do with more people sharing the same staples, but I think there may be other forces at work. Small households may have more disposable income per person and fewer inhibitions about playing with it. There are two of us in my household. When I grocery shop with my husband, he has an enormous appetite for gourmet oils, spices, and sauces we almost never use. Often, we succumb to shared temptation. I have my own weaknesses for overpriced goodies, of course, but if you want to hear about them, my husband may well have to write his own book.

But, speaking of my impulsive shopping habits . . . how, precisely, did grocery stores become so adept at making me want to buy?

### Fewer mouths to feed

A lot of it has to do with increased competition. These days, supermarkets can't count on getting your grocery dollar anymore. One U.S. analyst has defined 15 different kinds of grocery formats, including wholesale clubs (such as Costco), convenience stores, supercenters (such as Super Target), and Internet food retailers. Seven of these 15 types didn't even exist in 1980. All of them are making a finely honed pitch for shoppers' money.

In addition, more food dollars are going to non-traditional sources. In 1930, Americans spent 21 percent of their food dollars on food made somewhere other than home, usually a restaurant. In 2001, "away from home" meals (including home meal replacement products) accounted for 46 percent of American food spending.

Finally, even though we're eating more, we Westerners just aren't reproducing like we used to. In Canada, Australia, and most of Europe (except the Czech Republic and Albania), the fertility rate is less than two births per woman, or below the level needed to maintain current populations without immigration. In many other countries, including the United States, the fertility rate is high enough to ensure stability without immigration, but not growth. As a study from the Washington, D.C.-based Food Marketing Institute put it, "With minimal growth in the number of people to feed, retailers can grow only by taking business away from competitors."

For all of these reasons, supermarkets are getting more inventive every day. Many of those inventions hinge on our modern preoccupations: lack of time, worries about our health, fascination with novelty and, paradoxically, nostalgia.

What, precisely, are we nostalgic for? If you asked most people under 60, they'd probably mention farmers' markets, whose comeback I described in chapter 3. But if you ask a senior, you might hear a wistful reminiscence about the stores of the 1930s and 1940s, where the grocer knew your name, the butcher cut chops to your specifications, and a nice young man delivered your order right to your door.

Were things really better in the old days? Perhaps. But before I get into discussing prewar grocery stores, I want to go back a bit further— to the 1300s, actually.

### A little bit of everything, all in one place

Back in Europe in the Middle Ages, guild restrictions usually controlled who could sell what. As a result, shoppers often had to do the rounds of a number of very specialized stores to buy everything they wanted or needed. But even though big cities such as London and Paris supported all sorts of specialty shops—hatters, haberdashers, cobblers, ironmongers, and so on—one type of merchant sold a wide range of groceries and dressmaking supplies. In Britain these retailers were called mercers, and in France they were known as *merciers*. Both words can be traced back to *merx*, the Latin word for "general merchandise."

Customers apparently liked these stores. By 1300, French *merciers* had acquired an evocative nickname: *paradis des femmes*, or ladies' paradise. Even back then, it seems, shopping was popular with us chicks. And, if you want to be sexist about it, the range of goods mercers sold was strongly weighted toward the housewifely arts. The records of an eighteenth-century mercer in a small town in northern England show that he sold, among other things, treacle, flour, beer, soap, beeswax, tobacco, vinegar, books, fabrics, needles, and more. Aside from the beer and tobacco, it's pretty much a cooking, sewing, and cleaning sort of inventory.

When the Europeans brought the mercer idea over the pond with them, the colonists turned it into the trading post and the general store. Originally, customers of these stores could choose from an even wider variety of products than their European cousins could find at a mercer. As city populations rose, though, urban general stores were able to specialize in food. By 1700, *grocer* was a trade distinct from a general storekeeper.

Grocers sold nonperishable goods that didn't come from local farms, such as coffee and olive oil. Originally, they set up shop near public markets, to capitalize on the markets' ability to attract large numbers of food shoppers. But as public markets became increasingly noisy and dirty, grocers moved into residential neighborhoods, where they could offer customers a cleaner alternative.

*Clean* is a relative term, though, since grocery stores didn't exactly have a pristine reputation. When cities were small, grocers had to hedge their bets by diversifying into other ventures. Memorably, a Boston grocer in the mid-1700s rented his second floor to a madam, a strategy that could certainly give modern superstores an edge over the competition. Just imagine the two-for-one sales!

Less imaginative grocers in New York, Boston, and elsewhere got liquor licenses and set up in-store saloons. It was a logical sideline, since whiskey made in the U.S. Midwest was cheaper than imported tea and coffee in the years after the American Revolution. Not surprisingly, business boomed. By 1819, there were 1,300 licensed grocery stores in New York City alone.

Out in the countryside, meanwhile, lots of general stores also sold hooch and served as saloons, although I haven't found a record of any of them stocking hookers. The upstairs apartments in country stores were often rented to other sorts of professionals, such as lawyers and doctors.

Country stores in North America faced an increasingly different environment from urban establishments. City stores had large, growing populations to draw from, so they could afford to specialize in food. As settlement pushed inexorably westward, the rural general store had to draw from a wider and wider geographic area. Often, the shopkeeper would be the only retailer for miles around. So just as urban general stores turned into grocers, rural ones became ever more diversified.

### Let us gather 'round the cracker barrel

Those of us who weren't around at the time tend to think of those old-time general stores as places like Ike Godsey's folksy establishment on *The Waltons*. Folks like Ike were fairly common back in the day. And they really did sell just about anything you might require—it just wasn't cheap. Just as shoppers in Canada's Arctic today pay C$2.49 for a pound of bananas and C$16 for a case of Coke, settlers of North America's wide-open spaces paid a premium for living in the back of beyond. You couldn't blame the storekeeper, at least not completely. Not only did he have to keep inventory for months or years before earning a cent on it; in the years before the coming of the railroad, he also had to physically transport all his stock himself.

Once or twice a year, Joe Storekeeper would head with his horse and wagon to the nearest major city—which might be hundreds of miles away—to pick up supplies. Often, he'd be armed with a list of goods his regulars had requested. His wagon would be laden with items his customers had made or grown, which they often used instead of cash to barter for manufactured goods.

In the city Joe would use those goods, along with whatever precious cash he'd managed to take in over the last few months, to buy new stock. For a week or so, he'd live the high life. Rural storekeepers were important customers for city wholesalers, and sales reps (called drummers) knew the importance of showing them a good time. Then, as now, a successful sales rep could wangle tickets to the latest play *and* hold his liquor.

Finally, after enjoying the big city and picking up enough supplies to sustain the store for the next half year or so, the storekeeper would pack up his wagon and creak back to his shop in what would later become Michigan or Missouri or Manitoba. That store was likely at a crossroads, to ensure that the greatest number of people could reach it quickly. It would draw customers from a maximum radius of about 20 miles—

that's the longest distance farmers could conveniently haul heavy goods to trade.

Until the mid-1800s, the building would look more like a house or a small farm than a store to the modern eye. Measuring about 20 feet by 30 feet in many cases, it was usually made of wood or logs. Windows were minuscule or nonexistent. Glass was hard to get, windows just let in the cold, and there wasn't much need to create an eye-catching display, since the customers didn't have a variety of other shopping options. If the storekeeper had a little money to spare, he might install a covered porch, to give shoppers a bit of shelter from the weather while they loaded up their wagons. There might be outbuildings to store excess stock and bartered items, as well as a chicken coop to provide fresh eggs.

Inside the store, barely controlled chaos reigned. There were barrels of coffee and tea, packets of tobacco and spices, jars of candy, bolts of cotton and woolen fabrics, bottles of whiskey and rum. Kettles and axes dangled from the ceiling (well secured, one hopes); dishes and books were stacked haphazardly on shelves. Gunpowder and patent medicines were squirreled away in unpredictable spots. The floor was dusty, since products such as sugar and flour had to be scooped out of barrels or large boxes and put into individual bags for each customer. And that dust likely bore the imprint of several pairs of paws. With all that food lying about in half-empty barrels and bags, the country store would be a haven for mice if the storekeeper didn't keep a cat or two in residence.

Many of the products would need final processing at home before you could use them. Ready-made clothing wasn't common until the second half of the nineteenth century. You bought fabric and thread and either made the clothes yourself or paid a seamstress or tailor to do it for you. Coffee was sold as beans, which you ground yourself and then roasted in a frying pan. Cookies, cakes, and bread came from your own oven, not a cellophane-wrapped package. The one baked product you might find at the general store was crackers—but you'd have to fight your way past the regulars gathered around the cracker barrel if you wanted some.

The wood or coal stove in the corner of the typical general store was a magnet for layabouts from miles around, who huddled close to the warmth and traded gossip. Contrary to popular legend, not all shop-keepers found these characters either lovable or amusing. Some regulars made a lot of noise, demanded free coffee and snacks, and made paying customers—particularly women—uncomfortable.

Over all of this, the all-knowing storekeeper presided. Only the storekeeper and his clerks had the faintest hope of finding what you wanted to buy. Since most things were stocked behind the counter, you had to ask for them. And once the clerk fetched the product, you'd often have to ask the price. In the days before the U.S. Civil War, when bartering was still common, rural storekeepers marked their products with a code rather than a price tag. The code, which each owner devised independently, recorded the wholesale price of the item and the various markups to be charged (the price varied depending on whether the buyer paid cash for the item, bought it on credit, or bartered for it). All in all, a transaction in such a store was a personal and time-consuming process. Heaven help you if you were timid.

### Technology comes to the cracker barrel

Small changes made their way into the general store over the decades. James Ritty, an Ohio saloonkeeper who called himself a "Dealer in Pure Whiskies, Fine Wines, and Cigars," had a problem with employees pocketing the cash his customers used to pay for their drinks. Inspired by a mechanism that counted how many times a ship's propeller went around, he and his brother invented the cash register, patenting the design in 1879 as "Ritty's Incorruptible Cashier."

Two other nineteenth-century technologies would ultimately have a more sweeping effect on rural stores: the telegraph and the railroad. After they were invented, drummers could travel directly to stores, dropping off catalogs. The storekeeper could order directly from the drummer, or send in orders months later by telegraph or mail, and the merchandise would be shipped by rail.

This new convenience freed storekeepers from the risk, drudgery, and expense of the twice-yearly buying trip, although quite a few of them probably missed the free drinks and ribald shows of the big city.

The railroad made an even bigger difference in the way goods were packaged and displayed, and this would affect both country general stores and the increasingly prosperous city grocers.

## Branding goods instead of cattle

When each storekeeper was stocking his own shop from his own wagon, there was no incentive or even need to package goods in small, uniform containers. But railroad cars were part of the machine age, and for maximum efficiency it made sense to put goods into small, solid containers that were easy to identify, stack, and separate.

The U.S. Civil War spurred demand for packaged food—mobile armies needed to be fed, as did folks on the ravaged home front. It wasn't the first time that armed conflict had led to culinary innovation. After all, we have Napoleon to thank for canning.

The little emperor was so eager to find a way to transport food on military maneuvers that he convinced the French government to offer a 12,000-franc prize to anyone who developed a solution. After 14 years of work, Paris confectioner Nicholas Appert came up with a reliable way to preserve food in glass jars, and won the prize in 1810. Around the same time, an Englishman developed the tin can.

Even so, the idea of canned food didn't really take off for several decades. Unless a war or some other disaster caused a food shortage, people didn't really see the advantage of expensive tinned products. And it didn't help that a practical can opener wasn't invented until 1865. More to the point, consumers didn't trust tins and packages at first. They were used to seeing, touching, and smelling their food before buying it. How could they know that the coffee packed into those fancy sealed tins was the genuine article?

Eventually, however, the convenience and lower costs of packaged food won the day. Brand names and logos played a key role in developing consumer trust, beginning with the first trademarked food (Underwood Deviled Ham) in 1843. A shopper who had bought Jell-O or Grape-Nuts previously and enjoyed them could come back the following week and buy another package of the same product, fairly confident that the quality would be similar.

By the end of the 1800s, Ivory soap, Chase and Sanborn coffee, Borden's condensed milk, Smith Brothers cough drops, and Quaker Oats were just a few of the brand names that consumers across North America would easily recognize. In Britain, Lever Brothers was marketing Sunlight Soap and Vim; Australians could buy Persil laundry detergent and MacRobertson's chocolates.

## A family reunion with Aunt Jemima and Uncle Ben

It didn't take long for manufacturers to realize the value of these labels and logos and to start seriously promoting them. Soon, grocery bags emblazoned with corporate graphics made their way into the most isolated rural store.

Interestingly, later theorists would argue that those graphics and logos played an important part in personalizing the shopping experience after the small neighborhood grocery store morphed into the sterile supermarket. A commentator quoted by British retailer W.G. McClelland argued that "[t]he package is an extremely important substitute for the personal relationship that people desire." If you can't be on a first-name basis with your grocer, I suppose you can have a lasting emotional connection to Mr. Clean and Betty Crocker.

Shoppers weren't the only people who welcomed the change in packaging. Suddenly, the storekeeper spent a lot less time weighing and wrapping bulk goods, and cleaning up the inevitable spills.

Packaged goods even changed the way the country store looked. Large items still dangled from the ceilings, and barrels were used well into the twentieth century to store some goods. But storekeepers now needed more shelves and tables to display tins and boxes. They started to assemble the packages into pyramids and other eye-catching displays. Since villages and towns had grown up around many country stores by the end of the nineteenth century. It was increasingly important to grab the attention of passersby. Those geometric product displays became the centerpieces in increasingly large and elaborate windows.

Competition had come to the country store, and later developments would increase pressure on rural grocers. But the fiercest battleground for food shoppers' loyalty would be the booming cities, where economies of scale led to a revolutionary development: the chain store.


## Stores in chains

The company that would change our centuries-old concept of the corner grocer and the country store didn't start out as a grocer at all. The Great American Tea Company began as a forestaller of sorts. Company employees met tea ships coming into New York harbor, bought entire cargoes, and sold the tea on the wharf. The company was founded on the notion of selling high volumes at low prices, a strategy it built on when it finally opened a permanent teashop in lower Manhattan in 1861.

That first little shop was a theatrical riot of color, from the red and gold facade illuminated by a giant, gas-lit capital T to the cashiers' wickets shaped like Chinese pagodas. A bright green parrot squawked from a central cage, and Saturday night shoppers enjoyed music from a live band. Loyal customers received little gifts like china and pictures. Soon, the shop was offering all kinds of other grocery products besides tea.

Like the newfangled department stores that were building their empires on the "high-volume, low-price" principle, the company grew quickly. By 1865, it owned five stores in Manhattan. Four years later, owners George Gilman and George Hartford decided they needed a more thrilling name for their enterprise. Seizing on the recent completion of the railroad across the United States, they renamed the firm the Great Atlantic & Pacific Tea Company. We know it today as A&P.

Instead of setting up enormous flagship stores, as the department stores had done, A&P prospered by building numerous small shops. It was still able to capitalize on the benefits of buying in bulk and sharing delivery wagons and other equipment. By 1900, the chain had 198 stores.

These outlets had little in common with a modern supermarket besides the fact that they sold food. Goods were stacked on shelves that ran around the perimeter of the store, behind imposing counters. Shoppers stood in a largely empty space in the middle of the store, scanning the shelves and waiting for a clerk to serve them. The clerks behind the counter scurried back and forth, scooping sugar into bags, slicing cheese, pouring liquid goods into containers, and weighing every bulk purchase. Down from the shelves came tins of pipe tobacco, cakes of soap, bottles of soda. In small stores, one clerk would serve you from start to finish, moving from shelf to shelf. In larger shops, each section had its own clerk, and you'd move from area to area. It wasn't the most efficient system ever devised.

Even so, these stores were popular, but they couldn't meet all of a shopper's food needs. Produce, meat, and other perishables were still largely the preserve of greengrocers, butcher shops, and public markets. Without widespread, affordable refrigeration, there was little choice but to sell perishable things day by day.

## The chains get more links

Things might have run along in this pattern indefinitely, with shoppers using a combination of public markets, grocery stores, greengrocers, and butcher shops, if American cities hadn't started to creep outward.

At first, the only way into and out of the city, aside from a horse and buggy, was the streetcar. A network of streetcar lines made it possible for well-off clients to commute back and forth to work, but shopping was a different story. Nobody well heeled enough to live outside the city wanted to bother hauling all that bulky food back on public transit, and many people balked at paying for long-distance delivery.

Low densities in the suburbs meant public markets were rarely cost effective, but these conditions were perfect for the small grocery store. From the beginning, the 'burbs were dominated by chain stores. Most downtown independent storekeepers had neither the capital nor the desire to set up second stores in far-flung neighborhoods. And anyone who thought about setting up his *first* store in a suburb was usually beaten to the punch by the well-financed chains—not only A&P, but newer chains such as Kroger.

In the early 1900s, these suburban grocery stores differed little from their downtown kin. Most were small, around 500 to 600 square feet, and served customers who generally traveled to the store on foot or via a short streetcar ride. Most offered credit and local home delivery.

In many countries, grocers increasingly saw themselves as professionals with a unique set of skills. Through the infant discipline of market research, for instance, they were learning ways to differentiate customers. In 1916, an Australian trade paper called *The Grocers' Assistant* published a series of articles advising readers how to deal with different customer types. These included the "easy-going customer," who seemed not to care what she bought or how much it cost; the "suspicious customer," whose main characteristic was her conviction that the storekeeper was cheating her; the "faddy and particular customer," who demanded lots of attention; and the "bargain hunter and cutter," who knew the price of every item and would haggle for the best deal.

Customer service wasn't the only thing that was changing. As chains grew bigger, they looked for ways to chop prices. After all, these stores depended on high volumes to make a profit, so they'd try just about anything to convince customers that their store offered the best value.

Beginning in 1912, A&P turned many of its 400 stores into "economy stores," dropping both home delivery and credit. Traditional grocers gasped at the heresy, but the strategy worked. And an even more heretical development was on the way.

### The Lord helps those who help themselves

The next key innovation came from another chain grocery store, the delightfully named Piggly Wiggly. In 1916, founder Clarence Saunders opened a self-service grocery store in Memphis, Tennessee. Gone were the clerks behind their glass-fronted counters. Instead, shoppers themselves moved through the store, selecting goods and putting them in baskets.

It seems hard to picture grocery shopping being conducted any other way, but in 1916 this concept was revolutionary. Even though some stores had experimented with self-service around the turn of the century, and at least two stores in California were using it by 1914, Saunders was one of the first to promote the idea on a large scale.

Grocery retailing is a deeply conservative business, so it's perhaps not surprising that grocers were slow to learn a lesson that their fellow retailers in the department store business had grasped half a century back: let customers wander around the store, examining the merchandise without pressure, and they'll buy more.

It's hard to overemphasize how much this one policy changed the nature of shopping, whether the customer was buying dress fabric or lettuce. Indeed, before browsing was widespread, we didn't really *shop*, in the sense of examining a wide range of merchandise, getting ideas, fantasizing, dismissing, and making impulse purchases. We simply *bought*. As Thomas Hobbes might have said, if he'd demonstrated any interest in retailing, a trip to the store before browsing was common was often solitary, poor, nasty, and brutish—although not necessarily short.

But even though they allowed browsing, the first self-service grocery stores weren't the temples of temptation that modern supermarkets are. One photograph of an early Piggly Wiggly shows a claustrophobic space that looks about the size of a small convenience store. The whole area between the entrance and the aisles was enclosed behind a forbidding-looking fence of wooden spindles and chain link, to prevent choice-addled shoppers from running off with the merchandise.

With only four short aisles and one checkout, it would seem congested if more than a dozen shoppers came at once. But since the store saved money by eliminating most clerks, it could offer lower prices. Many shoppers warmed to the idea immediately.

In the 1930s, when the self-service concept was still in the midst of catching on (remember, grocers are *very* cautious), a man named J. William Horsey took over Canada's Dominion Stores grocery chain. The company's 500-odd stores still offered counter service, and they were bleeding money. Out of frustration and curiosity, Horsey checked out a self-serve Loblaws store across the road from a Dominion outlet. As another grocery store king, Frank Sobey, recalled years later, "[The Loblaws store] was full of customers, and *the customers were doing all the work*. They were fetching their own goods and taking them to the cashiers. Bill Horsey decided right then that that was the way Dominion had to go."

But not all customers were comfortable just picking goods off the shelves at will. It must have felt a bit like going behind the counter of a jewelry store or backstage at a theater. Some people didn't have a clue where to start looking for particular products. To ease customers' nervousness and confusion, two brothers who ran a self-service grocery store in Pomona, California, tried stocking all the items in alphabetical order. They even changed the name of the store to Alpha Beta in 1917. Like many grocery store brainwaves that would come out of California in the next couple of decades, though, the idea didn't fly.

Difficulty finding things wasn't the only gripe people had about self-service grocery stores. Some customers, particularly the well-heeled ones, resented being forced to schlep their own goods around and missed the deferential clerks. Others railed that self-service grocery stores were just one more way that modern society was becoming less personal and more fragmented. By taking the social aspect of the grocer behind the counter out of the equation, they argued, retailers had made shopping just an exercise in empty consumption.

Counter-service stores didn't disappear overnight—in small-town North America, they lasted well into the 1940s, and they stuck around even longer in Britain and Australia—but the critics eventually lost this war.

In any case, the grocery chains soon had another headache on their hands that was far more pressing than a few people complaining about self-service. A new competitor showed up that almost put them out of business.

## Drive-in shopping

Grocery chains had gleefully dropped home delivery to cut costs, but they were slow to accommodate car-driving customers. Margins on grocery products were already small. The expense and hassle of setting up large parking lots near their stores wasn't worth the effort, the chain grocers sniffed. They had missed one of the bedrock truths of North American life in the twentieth century: we love our cars, and we'll go to just about any lengths to use them.

In the 1920s, a few retailers in car-crazed California and the U.S. Southwest tried innovative ways to accommodate their customers. In Los Angeles, companies built drive-in markets: U-shaped or L-shaped buildings that housed a variety of individual shops surrounding a large parking lot. They were moderately successful, but they were usually a collection of affiliated concessionaires rather than one large store.

It would take a couple of imaginative upstarts to realize that stores had to give customers a place to stash their Model Ts while shopping and had to increase sales volumes to a level high enough to pay for the parking lot.

The first man to put these ideas together was Michael Cullen, who managed a Kroger grocery store in Herrin, Illinois. He tried to interest his bosses in his idea for larger stores, but it didn't appeal to them. So he quit and opened his first large-format store in Jamaica, New York, in 1930. At over 5,000 square feet, it was ten times the size of a usual grocery store, so he gave it a suitably gigantic name: King Kullen. "World's Greatest Price Wrecker!" boasted Cullen's ads. He promoted the store's low prices to Depression-impoverished customers, and they made the place a hit. He didn't have a parking lot, but he reassured customers that there was lots of street parking. Within five years, Cullen had 15 stores.

For a guy who misspelled his own name on the store marquee, he was doing pretty well.

Meanwhile, in 1932, two businessmen opened an even bigger emporium in an empty auto plant in Elizabeth, New Jersey. Not content to be price wreckers, they touted the Big Bear store as "The Price Crusher." The store didn't look like much, but it offered a mind-boggling (at the time) 15,000 square feet of grocery space, along with another 35,000 square feet of concessionaire stands selling products such as auto accessories, candy, cosmetics, and paint. There was also a parking lot across the street, and a good thing, too—the widely advertised low prices drew customers from 50 miles around. All of a sudden, boring old grocery shopping had become an *event*.

"Depression-weary housewives enjoyed visiting the [super] markets, for the circusy, bizarre atmosphere that prevailed provided release for the suppressed emotions piled up within many women by the dreary monotony of Depression days," recalled a writer in *Progressive Grocer* magazine in 1952.

A new name had to be coined for these gigantic new stores. At first, the press dubbed them *cheapies*. Hollywood appears to have coined the word *supermarket*, although no one seems sure how or when. The first store to use the term was Albers Supermarket, which opened in Cincinnati in 1933.

### How to profit from losing money

At first, established grocers couldn't believe the success of these new stores. How could something that looked like a drafty warehouse attract shoppers? Chain stores had spent a lot of time and money making their stores both appealing and efficient. Gleaming white tiles assured shoppers that the store was clean. Big windows let in lots of light.

Chain stores had pioneered the idea of "loss leaders"—goods sold at or below cost as a way to lure customers into the store, where the retailer would make up the loss on the cheap products with higher markups on other goods. Supermarkets just took the idea to another, wider level.

Times were tough and people were avid to economize where they could. Fancier grocers may have looked down their noses, but supermarkets presented serious competition. Other entrepreneurs imitated Big Bear and King Kullen, sucking customers away from small corner groceries for miles around.

By 1937, one third of mighty A&P's stores nationwide were unprofitable. Granted, supermarkets weren't the only factor affecting grocery store sales—the Depression took its toll on retailers of all sorts—but giant supermarkets weren't helping matters.

A&P eventually saw the light, opening its first supermarket in 1935, in Paducah, Kentucky. Between 1929 and 1949, it closed and consolidated thousands of shops; the number of stores in the chain plummeted from 15,418 to 4,600. The extreme tactic worked wonders for the bottom line: annual sales tripled to $3 billion.

### Shopping carts, electric doors, and lady clerks, oh my!

The cheapies had thrown down the gauntlet. Once they appeared on the scene, the race was on among stores all along the grocery continuum to make their establishments stand out from the crowd.

In the 1930s, grocery shopping became more fun, more convenient, and more tempting. Every other month, stores installed some new device or fixture to make customers happier and stores more profitable. For example, instead of stacking products on tables scattered throughout the store, many stores installed the back-to-back cantilevered shelves known in the business as gondolas.

In 1937, an Oklahoma City grocer named Sylvan Goldman invented the shopping cart, after noticing that shoppers would stop shopping when their baskets were too full to carry easily. Customers didn't take to the concept at first. Goldman had to hire people to push full carts back and forth near the store entrance, so shoppers could get the hang of the idea.

Next, someone had to come up with an easy way for people to get those laden carts out of the store and into the parking lot. Publix Supermarkets, a Florida-based chain, installed magical "electric eye" doors that swooshed open when a customer approached.

Inside the store, shoppers were doing more work—or, looked at another way, gaining more control over the shopping process. In the late 1930s, A&P engineers invented a refrigerator case that allowed customers to select their own packaged meats, rather than waiting for a butcher behind a glass case to serve them. The meat section was one of the last areas of the grocery store to succumb to the self-serve craze.

However, World War II limited the innovations of both the supermarkets and the more traditional grocers. Labor was scarce, so shoppers in 1944 were more likely to see a woman stocking the shelves or operating the cash register than they would have been a decade earlier. Materials such as metals were restricted, so even innovations such as an open refrigerator case, introduced by the Penn Fruit Market chain in 1943, were slow to take off. Manufacturers couldn't get enough materials to make them in any quantity.

Japanese military victories in Asia cut off sources of tin for food cans, and food rationing depleted the stocks on store shelves, but supermarkets found other goods to fill the space, such as beauty products and cleaners. Customers appreciated the convenience, and these goods gained a permanent home on supermarket shelves.

The war threw up another obstacle—gas rationing—for supermarkets that depended on car-driving shoppers to buy large quantities of goods. Resolutely, store owners simply urged customers to car pool. In the same vein, they encouraged shoppers to bring their own bags, so that paper could be saved for the war effort. (Not coincidentally, this campaign also saved the store money—just as similar environmentally inspired efforts in the 1980s did.)

## Postwar glory days:
## There's a baby born every minute

Once the war ended, though, the brakes came off the evolution of grocery stores. The baby boom swept the supermarket into grocery dominance—first in the United States, then in other developed countries. Most of those one-and-a-half-story Cape Cod houses in most of those Levittowns had a car, a refrigerator, and a couple of hungry, growing children.

In 1946, supermarkets accounted for just 3 percent of American grocery stores but 28 percent of total grocery sales volume, according to grocery store historian James Mayo. Eight years later, with just 5.1 percent of all stores, they controlled almost half the total grocery volume. By 1956, the *average* supermarket was 18,000 square feet—larger than the Big Bear store that had made national news a generation earlier, and three and a half times the size of the first King Kullen. The era of the small store was waning, and that of the big store was waxing.

The chains had realized that the gig was up for little stores. Partly to circumvent anti-chain store taxes, but mostly to compete with the larger supermarkets, chains such as A&P closed most of their remaining small stores in the years after the war and replaced them with supermarkets.

For the postwar grocery shopper, bigger stores meant more choice. Manufacturers came up with a wider range of products to stock on all those miles of shelves, and one of the first areas of the store to change was the frozen food section.

Birdseye had been making frozen food since 1923 and had marketed precooked, frozen steak and chicken in 1939, but its inroads into grocery stores were minimal until better refrigerator cases could be mass-produced after the war. Grocery stores were hesitant to stock frozen products, thinking customers would find them too expensive. The main frozen foods sold during the Depression and war years were fruits and vegetables.

Customers' resistance to frozen food finally collapsed when Swanson introduced the first "TV dinner" in 1953, a 98-cent tray of roast turkey, corn bread stuffing, whipped sweet potatoes, gravy, and peas. For many people, the TV dinner represented everything wrong with postwar America. They were prepackaged. They were meant to be eaten while watching television rather than conversing. And, well, they were just plain new. But for families in the 1950s, TV dinners were fun and freed up time for other activities.

Today, frozen and other ready-to-eat meals are consuming ever-larger portions of the grocery bills of time-stressed consumers. Frozen foods accounted for just 2.16 percent of grocery revenues in the U.S. in 1991, according to the Food Marketing Institute; a decade later, that figure was up to 7.13 percent. Savvy marketers are even selling frozen dinners that require some sort of minimal preparation, so that we can fool ourselves into thinking we're "cooking."

Another relatively new product in the grocery store in the early post-war years was milk. Even though it's one of the staples of the supermarket now, milk accounted for negligible sales in U.S. grocery stores until World War II. Most people relied on a milkman, and the convenience of that system made them reluctant to get milk any other way. But when gas rationing during the war meant that delivery trucks couldn't make their rounds as often, people started buying milk at the grocery store. The habit stuck.

### Dazzle them with architecture

The new supermarkets were not only bigger and better stocked. They also looked different. More and more stores were now freestanding structures, surrounded by parking lots, so the facade had to look interesting from all sides. Devices such as a small tower in the front were popular in the 1940s and 1950s. By the early 1960s, modernism took over in force, with sweeping arches and funky colors that had more in common with George Jetson's apartment building than with King Kullen's converted garages or the plain, functional boxes of the early postwar boom.

Inside these stores, the endless surfaces of white tile gradually disappeared. In a small store, they'd connoted cleanliness, but they made an 18,000-square-foot store look like a giant operating room. Instead, shoppers were treated to pastel colors, often used to distinguish different departments of the store. Air-conditioning and piped-in music arrived.

Managers who wanted to cater to stressed-out young mothers bought grocery carts with child seats (patented in 1947) and installed "kiddie corrals," where families could leave their children while shopping. Freestanding "islands" were added to produce departments to make them look bigger and more inviting. Some stores even started playing around with the basic rectangular grid of aisles—Grand Union once experimented with a "wagon wheel" layout, where aisles were arranged as spokes around a central area. That last innovation went nowhere, but the others remained.

As the 1960s progressed, chains learned that upscale customers weren't all that excited about futuristic architecture. Particularly when a supermarket was being dropped into one of their ritzy neighborhoods, these high-income, profitable customers wanted a store that was both beautiful and similar to its surroundings. George Jetson's supermarket looked alien in an environment of clapboard houses and wide lawns.

No problem, said the cheery chain-store managers. They responded with Spanish colonial haciendas, red brick buildings with clock towers, and supermarkets modeled on New Orleans townhouses. Inside, there were murals and mosaics, surfaces of natural stone and wood. Customers ate this up—for a while.

As the decade wore on, the North American economy tanked. Almost overnight, perks were passé and value was vital. Shoppers realized that all the pretty lighting and flooring had a price, and that price was reflected in their grocery bill. In the era of Vietnam protests and feminist consciousness raising, politicized shoppers started boycotting chains they suspected of price gouging.

Suddenly, flashy buildings were out. No-nonsense boxes were back in. It would take until the mid-1980s before interest in flashy rooflines and enticing decor really returned.

### Blind them with science

It wasn't only the architecture of the supermarket that was getting more sophisticated. An influential book published in 1963, Edward A. Brand's *Modern Supermarket Operation*, advocated such now-standard practices as building continuous gondolas (so shoppers couldn't wander haphazardly around the store), placing meat counters at the back to draw people through the store, and putting high-margin goods at the ends of aisles. Those prize spots, or end caps, are prime places for people to make impulse buys.

Other hot spots for profitable goods are the shelves next to the checkout stands and the aisles on the edges of the store, which get more traffic than other areas. Also, since stores are designed to funnel shoppers through them in a predictable pattern, designers can tell which way we're likely to travel down any particular aisle; since most of us are right-handed, the impulse-buy products are usually on the right side of the aisle.

In the 1960s, aisles became wider to accommodate bigger grocery carts. All those booming families needed more groceries than Sylvan Goldman's original shopping cart could hold. And in those aisles, grocers were placing products more strategically. High-profit items got eye-level shelf space, although "eye level" varied with the target market. The next time you're in the cereal aisle, you'll probably notice the relatively wholesome Raisin Bran and granola in your direct line of sight. But look down. There, at the perfect height for a child, are the sugar-laden treats promoted on Saturday morning TV.

Technologies evolved as well, since bigger stores needed to be more efficient. Incredibly, prices weren't marked on individual items in most stores until the late 1940s and, even then, staff had to write the price on every item one by one. In the 1950s, price stamps took the drudgery out of this chore. To speed up checkouts, cashiers were trained to look at these price stamps, not at the cash register keys, when punching in sales. And, for the first time, customers' receipts included an itemized list of everything they bought.

The first supermarket UPC scanner went into service on June 26, 1974, in a supermarket in Troy, Ohio; the first product across its little glass window was a pack of Wrigley's gum. The UPC scanners became so common that then-President George Bush became a national laughingstock in 1992 when a newspaper article erroneously made it seem as though he had never seen one.

The average checkout clerk can scan 20 items a minute with one of these gizmos. Even so, it turns out that automation isn't perfect. The Arizona Department of Weights and Measures found that retailers failed to scan items accurately in 60 percent of the 2,255 UPC inspections the department conducted in the first 10 months of 2001.

Happily, most of the scanning mistakes were in the consumer's favor. Nevertheless, the department urged shoppers to write down prices, keep an eye on the register, and check their receipts closely to avoid being overcharged.

If all this caution strikes you as rather defeating the purpose of automating the checkout process in the first place, you're not going to like this next bit. Stores have started installing lanes where customers run their own purchases over the scanners. By early 2003, almost 30 percent of American grocery retailers had self-scanning checkouts in at least one store.

You can imagine what those turn-of-the-century shoppers would say. "Not only do grocery stores make us shove our food all over the store, pack our own bags, and haul the booty out to the car. Now we're expected to be our own checkout clerks too!" Nevertheless, you can't argue with progress, even if (at least in Arizona), it gets things wrong more than half the time.

## Meanwhile, elsewhere in the English-speaking world . . .

The galloping success of American supermarkets did not go unnoticed in other parts of the world. During World War II, a GI on leave in England might have been flummoxed by the fact that he couldn't walk into a grocery store and just help himself to the goods. The first self-service grocery store in Britain, a branch of the London Co-operative Society, didn't open until 1942.

That didn't mean grocers weren't interested in the concept. By the late 1940s, retailers such as Jack Cohen of Tesco and Alan Sainsbury had made pilgrimages across the pond to study supermarkets. They were eager to transplant the idea to Britain, but several factors made it difficult for a few years. Food rationing, which lasted from 1940 until 1954, made it hard to fill the shelves with the range and quantity of products that made American supermarkets so appealing. And, like some of the shoppers who had turned up their noses at the Piggly Wiggly concept in the U.S. in 1916, upper-class customers in Britain's more class-conscious society were unenthusiastic about carting their own groceries around the store.

But retailers pressed on, realizing that self-service offered huge cost savings for them and convenience for most customers. Tesco opened its first self-service grocery store in 1947; Sainsbury's followed suit three years later. The latter claims the distinction of opening Britain's first supermarket, in a London suburb, in 1955.

Perhaps as a result of a longer tradition of deferential clerks in Britain, counter service lingered much later in the U.K. than it did in the United States. Well into the 1950s, many British shoppers continued to buy their provisions in counter-service stores.

Working-class shoppers were more excited about self-service than their richer compatriots, but even they felt a bit uncomfortable in this new environment. As a Sainsbury's publication noted: "The customers came in a little bewildered and in need of guidance. They were helped around, shown where to find what they wanted and told where to pay."

California-based Safeway saw Britain as a market opportunity. It began buying up small grocery stores, and opened its first British supermarket in 1963. The company tried to lure shoppers with various "American style" perks, from post offices to coin-laundry facilities. Most of the perks didn't work, but the supermarket idea itself continued to rise in popularity across the U.K.

Like the British, Australians were reluctant to give up counter service. Chains there began to open self-service stores in significant numbers in the 1950s, but counter service and self-service stores coexisted throughout the decade. Supermarkets didn't really take off there until the 1960s.

A new self-serve grocery store called McEwan's distributed a flyer to its customers in 1953, trying to ease shoppers' discomfort with the process. Under the title "How to Shop," it gave newbies the following instructions.

1. You will find here all types of Grocery, Hardware, etc. neatly arranged on shelves, where all prices are indicated in a clear and easily readable manner;
2. At the entry of the store, you leave your own basket and other purchases with the cashier;
3. You will take a "McEWAN" shopping basket;
4. Move freely in the store, completely at your ease;
5. If you need advice, just apply to the staff;
6. "Serve yourself"—if you see something you like, just "take" it and put it in your "McEWAN'S" basket;
7. **Serve yourself** just means quick service, and **lower prices**, thus saving you time and money;
8. For delivery, follow directions as above, and attach an address label to a McEWAN'S basket and when your shopping is complete, leave with the cashier.

It seems a long time since we needed an invitation to help ourselves, doesn't it? And as the range of products has grown, so have the temptations.

### New and improved!

A couple of years ago, I stumbled on what I thought was a cool new product in the laundry detergent aisle of my local supermarket. It was the perfect thing for a lazy housekeeper like me: Downy Wrinkle Releaser. It came in a squirt bottle like glass cleaner. You sprayed it on your unironed clothes, pulled and smoothed the fabric, and *voilà*—a less wrinkled garment. You might not be ready for the catwalk in Milan, but your chinos could pass muster at the average business meeting.

I used it probably more than I should admit in public, as my iron gathered even more dust than usual. After a few months, I trotted back to the laundry aisle for more, only to discover that—horrors!—there were no bottles on the shelves. Assuming the store was just out of stock, I tried another grocery store a few days later. No luck.

You know where this story is going, don't you? You've been there yourself. My beloved new product had been discontinued, just like a TV show that is canceled as soon as you've become interested in the characters.

Up to 80 percent of all new products launched in the United States meet a similar fate within about a year of their release, according to a barrage of studies. Some, like New Coke, fail spectacularly. Others just fade away.

In a way, it's not surprising. The average American grocery store covers 44,000 square feet and stocks 30,580 items. In the visual din, it's getting harder and harder for distributors to catch our attention and convince us to spend our hard-earned bucks for their latest products.

Perhaps that's why new products seem to be getting weirder by the day. Writer and academic Robert McMath studies product failures and has collected more than 70,000 disastrous examples, which are now housed with a company called NewProductWorks in Ann Arbor, Michigan. Some of these things are like Ed Wood movies—so bad, they're good. You've gotta love the chutzpah of the people who came up with Thirsty Cat, the bottled water for pets. Or how about Maalox Whip, which sweetens your apple pie *and* reins in nasty diarrhea? You might need that after sampling another loser, garlic fruitcake, which should be the poster product for McMath's 1998 book, *What Were They Thinking?*

Not all of these oddball products are safely confined to a museum, either. The other day, while browsing in a convenience store in Gatineau, Quebec, I spotted a package of cocktail peanuts coated with dill pickle-flavored potato batter.

What were they thinking, indeed.

Well, it's easy for me to sit here and giggle—I bet the folks who came up with the idea of putting potato chips in a tennis ball can had their fair share of detractors. But those Pringles folks sure got the last laugh.

## The fight for shelf space

One way distributors try to ensure success is by paying grocery stores a fee to stock their newest products. These "slotting allowances"—introduced in the 1980s—are designed to cover the costs a grocer has to pay to add a new product to the shelves. A store needs to go through up to 24 steps to put a new product on the shelf—everything from reprogramming checkout scanners to reconfiguring space in the warehouse and on the shelves. A 1995 study estimated that food retailers spent almost $1 million *per store* every year to add new products that would ultimately fail. To mitigate this risk, they started asking distributors for slotting allowances on some products. Distributors sometimes offer allowances without being asked. It's a dance of mutual fear.

And sometimes it's not the manufacturers who try to tempt us with new products. It's the stores themselves.

In the late 1970s, North American grocery chains imported a money-saving idea developed in France in 1976: generic products. With their plain labels and low prices, these humble products screamed "value" to shoppers battered by inflation and recession throughout the 1970s. By 1980, some 14,000 supermarkets across the U.S. were selling generic products. In many markets, their success was short-lived, a victim of the 1980s yuppie mentality. The economy improved and people didn't want to scrimp on plain-looking products.

Grocers rolled with the punches. Store-brand products had been around since the nineteenth century, when A&P first marketed Eight O'Clock Coffee. Stores pushed their nongeneric brands as high quality alternatives to national brands—similar products that cost much less than the widely advertised ones.

But some stores weren't content with simply matching the quality of national brands. Just as the whole *Dallas/Dynasty/L.A. Law* me-mentality was kicking into high gear, they rolled out *premium* store brands that were actually *better* than the products consumers were used to buying. One of the first products in Loblaws' premium President's Choice line— and still its most successful—was the Decadent Chocolate Chip cookie, which boasted that it had more chocolate chips than any competing brand.

Store-brand products aren't the only way that your local supermarket reflects the ups and downs of the economy. The variety of products also changes with the market. When times are good, there are lots of choices, because in Western societies (particularly in North America) we're conditioned to value choice highly—even if the "choice" involves selecting one of six brands of ketchup that are very, very similar. However, when the economy slows, the range of products in the grocery store contracts as well. By buying greater quantities of fewer products, retailers get greater volume discounts, which mean lower prices for the consumer. Simply put, when times are good, we value choice. When money's tight, we value price.

(Of course, like most simple formulas, this one doesn't apply perfectly in all situations, particularly outside the wealthy Western world. Palestinian journalist Rami Khouri has been conducting an interesting market study since 1995: she goes to the shampoo and hair conditioner aisle of a Safeway in Amman, Jordan, and counts the varieties of products on offer, with each different size and formulation of a particular brand counting as a separate variety. In 1995, when the average per capita income in Jordan was $1,807, there were 125 varieties in the shampoo/conditioner aisle. Five years later, when per capita income had dropped by 16 percent to $1,516, the number of hair goop varieties had almost tripled, to 354. How could this be? As Khouri explains it, trade liberalization and globalization have increased both imports of shampoos and domestic manufacturing of international brands, skewing the usual relationship between prosperity and choice.)

Economic times in North America and Europe have been pretty good, overall, for the last decade or so, despite terrorist attacks and the dot-com bust. The results are plain to see on the outskirts of just about any city from Manchester to Miami: giant supermarkets stuffed with choices. But are we *happy*?

## Too big for our own good?

Certainly, not everyone is thrilled with the trend toward gargantuan grocery stores. In Ottawa, where I live, a rapidly gentrifying neighborhood called Westboro was recently convulsed in controversy for four years over Loblaws' proposal to build a 94,600-square-foot store on the site of an abandoned printing plant. Some residents, less than thrilled with their existing choice of supermarkets—several smaller, aging stores run by competing retailers—were excited about the idea of so much choice just a walk or short drive from home. Others, afraid the massive store would kill local retailers and bring choking waves of traffic into the neighborhood, fought the proposal tooth and nail.

It got ugly. Supporters of the store were branded as crass commercialists with no feeling for urban character and livability. Detractors of the store were called yuppie BANANAs (Build Absolutely Nothing Anywhere Near Anythings) who couldn't see that the store would be a wonderful asset for people in the neighborhood who didn't have cars and thus didn't have access to the mega-stores in the suburbs.

The debate dragged on so long that Loblaws' application expired and the company had to resubmit it. The grocer changed the design of the store in an attempt to make it fit better into the streetscape. Boutiques selling cards, wine, and other specialties—accessible only from inside the main store in Loblaws' other Ottawa locations—now have doors opening onto the street. The store is flush with the sidewalk along Richmond Road, with the massive parking lot stashed behind. Parts of the store are clad in brick rather than the chain's trademark green metal. There's even talk of installing some sort of public art.

So the Westboro Loblaws will be less intrusive on the outside. But skeptics of the big-box concept remain. Describing the larger College Square Loblaws—the behemoth I visited at the beginning of this chapter—*Ottawa Citizen* reporter Kelly Egan compared the cavernous space to an airport terminal and asked readers plaintively, "Will you join me in screaming 'BITE ME!' to this kind of retailing?"

From the hordes that descended on College Square when it opened in November 2002, it seems Egan may have been a voice crying "bite me" in the wilderness. By the end of the store's first day, security guards had to be dispatched to the parking lot to control traffic.

Egan and others are mourning the passing of the small, street-scale grocery shop, and the urban enthusiast side of my brain agrees with them. And yet, when confronted with the opportunity to buy frozen dinners, jeans, and towels all in one handy place, I'm seduced. Even critic Egan admits he self-scanned an order of groceries at the College Square store the week before he wrote his column.

## When bigger isn't better

The average size of American grocery stores has mushroomed in the last decade, from 31,500 square feet in 1991 to 44,000 square feet in 2001, pushed ever upward by the growing popularity of supersize store formats.

But there's one small sign that North Americans' obsession with size may be waning, at least when it comes to grocery stores: the poor performance of the hypermarket.

For all those who think everything gigantic in corporate culture originates in the U.S., it's interesting to note that this mother of all supermarket formats is an import from France. Although it builds on lessons from the U.S. discount-store industry, the idea of combining a discount store and a supermarket under one massive roof was a French one. A company called Carrefour opened the first hypermarket in St. Genevieve-de-Bois, near Paris, in 1963—a decade before the first such store in North America (a failed project in Montreal) and two decades before the first U.S. hypermarket opened in Batavia, Ohio, in 1984. These stores have about 180,000 square feet of retail space, with about 60 percent devoted to grocery products and the rest to nonfood items. They're like the Westboro and College Square Loblaws outlets . . . on steroids.

Early on, U.S. experts were skeptical about the concept. In a 1990 report, a Salomon Brothers analyst, Debra Levin, predicted that hypermarkets would never succeed widely because they needed to draw from a huge market area in order to turn a sufficient profit, and customers would be reluctant to drive up to 30 miles to shop at a store that was tiring to walk around and didn't offer a significant price advantage.

In the short term, at least, it appears that the experts were right. As of 2001, there were only nine hypermarkets in the entire United States, accounting for just 0.1 percent of Americans' grocery spending. Neither of those numbers is expected to increase by 2006.

Maybe our fascination with size has finally come to a halt. So if "thinking outside the box" doesn't just mean bigger boxes, where do the always-competitive retailers go from here?

### Giving George Jetson a second chance: Tomorrow's supermarket

As consumers get more discriminating and demanding—as retail history leads us to believe they will—what's next for the humble grocery store?

Retail expert Phil Lempert, nicknamed "The Supermarket Guru," thinks the time is ripe for a revolution at the checkout stand. It's illogical, he argues in his book *Being the Shopper*, for stores to provide express lanes as a perk for the least profitable shoppers without doing anything to pamper and reward the folks who spend much more: families pushing packed shopping carts. He suggests some savvy retailer should set up "full cart" lines with the store's fastest checkers and two bag clerks per cashier. Antsy shoppers would be offered a free soft drink while their purchases were rung up. I'd go for it.

Meanwhile, over in the U.K., Tesco is trying to cater to people who often *don't* like to buy groceries: men. Despite Gloria Steinem, grocery shopping is still largely Mom's job. In 2001, the "female head of household" did 69 percent of the grocery shopping for America's households. The picture is a little less unbalanced in the U.K., where a survey a few years ago showed that half of all couples at least claimed to share responsibility for grocery shopping.

But even in such an apparently liberated society, men still seem to dislike the experience. In 1999, the British Tesco chain tested a men's retreat room in one of its superstores, complete with easy chairs, sports magazines, pinball machines, and big-screen TVs. The theory was that women could buzz around the store doing their thing, then collect hubby to help them haul the groceries out to the car. The jury's still out on this one, but if you ask me, the missing ingredient in making this concept a success is probably beer.

Some stores are starting to get imaginative with their design again. A Florida chain called Kash 'N Karry is opening "round stores," with 40-foot ceilings and a semicircular layout, to differentiate themselves from the competition. They'd better hope there are no Piggly Wigglys nearby—in 2001, that chain opened a new flagship store in Sheboygan, Wisconsin, that replaced the hard right angles and harsh illumination of the standard grocery store with curved walls and lots of natural light, to create a more relaxed space. Halfway across the state in Madison, a remodeled Sentry Foods store is using theatrical lighting techniques to add drama and excitement to the displays. In the seafood department, for example, lighting on translucent panels behind the counter looks like waves.

Around the same time these stores opened their doors, readers of a trade magazine called *Progressive Grocer* were learning how to use the Chinese design philosophy of *feng shui* to ensure their stores were in harmony with the natural environment. According to the article, the store's location and orientation should attract positive energy (*chi*) and deflect negative energy (*cha*). For example, the front entrance should include a water feature (which conserves *chi*) and face south, but there shouldn't be a tree nearby: trees obstruct profits.

The article did note that factors such as zoning laws and real estate prices could make it hard for retailers to incorporate some of these principles, and somehow I just can't see the manager of the Piggly Wiggly in Peoria going mad for *feng shui*. But then again, what do I know? I thought Downy Wrinkle Releaser would be a hit.

# 5 From Mesopotamia to Minneapolis: It's a Mall World

*If you were looking for an analogy for the modern mall you would have to go back to the walled cities of Italy and France. Like San Gimingnano or Les Baux de Provence, the mall offers the ancient trifecta of enclosure, protection, and control. The analogy is not with a well-policed downtown but with a small, thoroughly fascist medieval city-state.*

—James B. Twitchell, *Lead Us Into Temptation,* 1999

It's three weeks before Christmas, and I'm trying to capture the attention of harried shoppers at Bayshore Shopping Centre in Ottawa's western suburbs. Given my competition—brightly lit clothing shops, kiosks with noisy flying toys, Madonna's latest hit thundering from a nearby music store, Santa in his castle down the hall—it isn't easy.

I'm doing a book signing, which most people picture as the purest form of ego gratification, with hordes of adoring fans waving pens. That's probably what it's like for Stephen King. When you're a somewhat shy author flogging a local guidebook and a Regency romance novel, the experience feels more like, well, hell.

From my tiny table in front of the Coles bookstore, I'm trying to convince what appears to be half the population of metropolitan Ottawa that two books whose creation consumed immense amounts of my waking hours are worth a total of C$22—less than the price of two tickets to the latest disaster flick.

My smile is bright, encouraging, and frozen. If someone has the bad judgment to actually stop, I try to interest him or her in one of the books on display. "It's set in Jane Austen's time period," I say to the stylish middle-aged woman peering at my romance novel. With luck, she saw the TV version of *Pride and Prejudice.* No luck. She has her shopping blinders on.

I've worn such blinders myself: in the cacophony of the modern mall, you have to focus. You're on a mission, and if you let something as trifling as a desperate author distract you, you'll be in the mall all night. She nods politely and sidles away.

That's OK. Two twentysomething guys are looking at my guidebook. "It's about Ottawa's offbeat sites," I tell them in a hopeful voice. At Christmastime, I find men are more likely to make impulse purchases than women are. They're buying gifts, and they want all the help they can get.

A debate between the two guys ensues. "You know how often we sit around saying, 'What do you want to do?' 'I don't know. What do you want to do?'" one says. The other one nods, examines the book again. In the end, they don't buy the guidebook, but they do walk away with a copy of the romance novel as a "Mom" present. I sell a surprising number of romances to men.

My little table goes quiet once again, giving me ample opportunity to people-watch. The modern mall at Christmastime attracts a larger cross section of humanity than you're likely to see in any other quasi-public place: a Baby Boomer man with his mother, couples with toddlers, solitary power shoppers. The squads of teenage girls, with their cell phones and long, shiny ponytails, along with a smattering of *GQ*-ish young men, are the best-dressed folks in the place. They've obviously decided to treat shopping as an event, and they've dressed for the occasion. Just about everyone else is in jeans, the universal outfit of errand-runners everywhere.

### I came, I saw, I bought everything

We tend to think of malls as modern creations, spawned by the same postwar wave that gave us Levittown, transistor radios, and Tang. And, yes, America's first fully enclosed, climate-controlled shopping mall *was* an invention of the Eisenhower era: the Southdale Shopping Center opened in suburban Minneapolis in 1956. However, it wasn't the world's first building to shelter a number of retailers under one weatherproof roof—not by a long shot.

Like so many things about city life, the mall as we know it evolved in stages. By about 1600 B.C., in the Mesopotamian city of Ur, someone had come up with the idea of separating a street of shops from the rest of town with doors that were closed at night. Historians think that shoppers may have been able to take shelter from the elements under a series of awnings as well.

That's pretty much as far as the enclosed shopping promenade evolved for more than a millennium. But then the ancient Greeks came along, with their penchant for marketplaces. Unlike today's malls, where political rabble-rousing is very strongly discouraged, these marketplaces were centers of debate and discussion. In fact, one of the major Greek schools of philosophy, stoicism, was named for the *stoa*, a large roofed structure that was open to an outdoor square on one side but walled on the other three. Stoas served various functions, but many were used as marketplaces. By the fifth century B.C., the Greek city of Miletus (now in Turkey) boasted an L-shaped market stoa fronting on the harbor, its prominent placement proof of the importance residents and visitors placed on trade.

Flash forward 500 years to the days when Trajan was emperor of the Roman Empire (A.D. 98–117). In a move that sounds eerily like the activities of the urban renewal zealots of the 1960s, Trajan decided that Rome's crowded jumble of streets and small buildings should be replaced with grand buildings and a more formal plan. Down came thousands of homes and shops, and up went the massive forum.

Just as shopping malls and major sports stadiums tend to sprout next to each other today, a series of markets was built next to the forum. The ones nearest the stadium were multistory buildings wedged into the side of the Quirinal hill. But just beyond them was the Aula Traiana, a two-story market with a vaulted roof. The ruins today look oddly familiar, with large square shop doorways marching methodically down each side of a central corridor, and a second story of shops lining a gallery that runs the length of the hall. Add a Sunglass Hut kiosk and a food court, and you could be in a very early prototype of your local shopping center.

## That's, like, totally bazaar, dude

The next move in "mall" development would take place in the Middle East, where some unremembered shopkeeper hit on the idea of building a roof between his shop and the one across the street. Others followed suit, sometimes covering multiple connected streets. The result was called a bazaar or souk.

One twelfth-century observer described a Jerusalem souk known as the Street of Herbs, which had divided itself into sections by commodity. "At the top of the street is a place where they sell fish. And behind the market where they sell the fish is a very large place on the left hand where cheese, chicken and eggs are sold. On the right hand of this market are the shops of the Syrian gold workers."

These souks shared a few traits with their modern, enclosed counterparts, such as a labyrinthine floor plan, and diverse but segregated uses. In the fifteenth century, builders in Constantinople (today's Istanbul) would begin building the mega-souk, the Mall of America of its day: the Grand Bazaar, also known as the Covered Market.

The bazaar started as a small warehouse and evolved along a series of actual streets, which were gradually roofed. Today, more than 3,300 shops line the 60-odd "streets" of the Grand Bazaar. While some of the historic divisions of individual streets have been superseded by new types of commerce (I doubt that souvenir T-shirts, for example, were a big seller during the reign of Suleyman the Magnificent in the 1500s), you can still find gemstones on Jewelers' Street, and silver teakettles, carpets, and leather goods in their own domains.

Even though the bazaar is now a massive tourist trap, alive with touts and pickpockets, I discovered on a trip in 1999 that it has a charm the average North American mall can't match.

The vaulted roof shimmers in jewel tones of blue, red, and gold through the rather gloomy lighting. An old man sits cross-legged in a courtyard in front of his carpets. Stall after stall displays open bowls of fragrant cardamom and cinnamon. And instead of neon signs and blaring loudspeakers, most shops have a personable young man (and they are almost always men) whose sole job is to engage shoppers in conversation, using some of the most transparent ruses ever devised.

"You are going the wrong way!" one cried out as I passed him. I stopped, startled. It was entirely possible that he was right. I'd been wandering the twisty interior streets for half an hour, fascinated and utterly lost.

Seeing that he had caught my attention, he crowed, "This is the right way for you!" Delightedly, he pointed toward his small shop, and I couldn't resist taking a peek. Years later, it occurred to me that I could have used the services of someone like him when I was trying to funnel people to my book signing. Maybe there is something to this Wal-Mart greeter business, after all.

### Throwing good shillings after bad

For centuries, the vast majority of customers shopped on streets that were by turns muddy, windy, rainy, and dirty. But retailers across Europe were beginning to discover the advantages of setting up shop inside large buildings that already attracted crowds of the wealthy and powerful, such as castles, palaces, and merchants' exchange buildings. In the 1500s, the nave of Saint Paul's Cathedral in London was home to a number of small entrepreneurs, and it was a popular place for wealthy townspeople to show off their new clothes. Visitors to such public buildings could usually buy toys, books, sewing supplies, and other small items from makeshift stalls.

More established shopkeepers were initially wary of setting up businesses in communal buildings. When Sir Thomas Gresham, a London financier, built the Royal Exchange between 1566 and 1568, he designed it as a facility for both traders (on the main floor) and shopkeepers (in the two upper galleries). However, shopkeepers who were used to living above their stores—where they could keep a close eye on the premises and thwart attempted burglaries—were not thrilled about the idea of shops they couldn't guard overnight. Moreover, the thought of sharing the same building with so many competitors made them nervous.

The retail areas of the building were virtually empty for three years, until Gresham offered tenants a year's free rent if they agreed to move in. The shopkeepers who took him up on his offer wouldn't regret it; once it was full, the exchange prospered and spurred many other rich men to open similar enterprises. The Exeter Exchange on the Strand in London was built solely to house market stalls.

## The Palais Royal: Flush with shopping

Early exchanges had some things in common with the modern mall, but shopping trends would soon take another turn that would send shoppers back outdoors.

Glazing techniques in the eighteenth century allowed shopkeepers to build large store windows, where they could set up elaborate displays that customers could not easily disturb (unlike a pile of goods on a market stall table). London streets such as Pall Mall and the Strand, with their spacious sidewalks, were soon lined with bow-fronted shops, which shoppers found much more enticing than simple stalls.

By the late 1700s, visitors from all over the world were marveling at the pleasant, organized nature of London's shopping streets. "A stranger . . . appreciates the sidewalks made of broad stones, running down both sides of the streets, whereon he is safe from the terrifying rush of carts and coaches as if he were in his own room; for no wheel dares to encroach even a finger's breadth upon the footpath," wrote Carl Philip Moritz, a German who visited England in the 1780s. "Especially in the Strand, where one shop jostles another and people of very different trades often live in the same house, it is surprising to see how from bottom to top the various houses often display large signboards with painted letters."

However, one problem remained: shoppers didn't like browsing in the wind, rain, and hot sun. The solution to that problem would come from a city that had more pressing reasons than most others to solve it: Paris.

Unlike London, late eighteenth-century Paris was not a pleasant place to stroll. The streets—long before Baron Haussmann would develop the city's famous boulevards—were narrow, and few had sidewalks. Window-shopping was a muddy and rather dangerous pursuit.

Then, in 1780, the Duke of Chartres had an inspired idea. Like modern English lords, who open their homes to tourists in order to pay their taxes, the duke needed money and decided to commercialize his residence. Luckily, he lived in the Palais Royal, so he had a prime bit of real estate to play with.

On the surface, his plan wasn't terribly revolutionary: he decided to enclose the palace's back garden on three sides with residential buildings, each with a colonnaded row of shops on the ground floor.

Similar squares existed throughout Europe, from the Piazza San Marco in Venice to Covent Garden in London. But the Palais Royal—with its prestigious location in the heart of Paris, and its use of the latest building materials and techniques—brought together the right elements at the right, prosperous time.

Instead of market stalls, the colonnades sheltered permanent, elegant shops. Each shop had a glazed window, perfect for displaying the luxury goods that the growing middle class coveted and the rich upper class could afford. The covered walkway in front of the shops opened not to a square full of traffic, as in Covent Garden, but to a festive park.

Like the Greeks' L-shaped stoa overlooking the harbor at Miletus, the colonnade of the Palais Royal allowed shoppers to move easily from outdoor space to enclosed space. It protected them from rain and snow, while allowing breezes to cool them in the heat of summer. In the garden court, fountains, trees, and concerts provided diversion for weary buyers.

The place was an immediate hit.

Like today's largest malls, the Palais Royal boasted many amenities besides shops, including cafés, social clubs, a currency exchange, hotels, concert rooms, theaters, and a waxworks. The three stories of apartments above the shops attracted the equivalent of today's loft owners—artists and single men—as well as a fair number of prostitutes, who had the sense to live where society gathered.

### Sex and bloody revolution: at a mall near you!

The Palais Royal was not a cheap place to shop, which only added to its allure. Unlike people who browsed for ribbons and toys in the make-shift stalls of the previous century's exchanges, shoppers in the purpose-built Palais Royal chose largely from luxuries: jewelry, finely tailored clothes, marble objects, furniture, paintings, and similar items. In addition, they could avoid the hassle of bargaining, since the shopkeepers were the first in Paris to adopt fixed prices for their goods. Perhaps because the resulting prices were so high, the fixed-price trend wouldn't take wide hold in Paris for another six or seven decades.

The high prices didn't stop the crowds from coming. The Palais was *the* place to shop, flirt, gamble, and discuss big ideas. In fact, in a bit of brutal irony for the Palais' noble developer, the complex was one of the flashpoints for the French Revolution. On July 12, 1789, a riot against the city's royal troops began in the Palais' gardens and engulfed the city; two days later, a mob stormed the Bastille.

But even the intrigues and danger of the Revolution couldn't shake the hold the Palais had on the people of Paris. It remained a hotbed of gossip and social life. In 1790 a Russian visitor, N.M. Karamzin, observed:

> Everything that can be found in Paris (and what cannot be found in Paris) is in the Palais Royal . . . Here are assembled all the remedies for boredom and all the sweet banes for spiritual and physical health, every method of swindling those with money and tormenting those without it, all means of enjoying and killing time. One could spend an entire life, even the longest, in the Palais Royal, and as in an enchanting dream, dying, say "I have seen and known all."

What wouldn't the developers of today's malls give for that kind of press?

However, success was a double-edged sword for the Palais Royal. During and after the Napoleonic Wars, its colonnades were magnets for off-duty soldiers looking for amusement. Customers became more interested in gambling and amorous liaisons, and less interested in buying goods. When the Duke of Chartres's son, Louis Philippe, outlawed both prostitution and gambling on his property in 1837, the Palais' fortunes tumbled.

### Arcades uneaten by Pac-Man machines

What the duke and his son had failed to foresee were the advantages of a completely enclosed shopping space. Colonnades let in light and fresh air, but they also admitted dirt and snow. Future developers would solve these problems with an innovation that was at once both obvious and ingenious.

In London and Milan, in Naples and in Paris itself, architects simply replaced the outer pillars of the colonnade with a solid wall or with a second row of facing shops. By doing so, they cut off the colonnade's extensive, permeable access to the outdoors. But while that meant that shoppers had fewer entry points, it also meant better protection from the elements—and better control over the resulting space. The result was the instantly popular shopping arcade.

English architectural critic Ralph Redivivus, writing in 1839, was as excited about the arcade concept as Karamzin had been about the Palais Royal half a century earlier:

> As far as possible convenience is concerned most assuredly nothing could be devised more suitable to such a climate as ours . . . than a covered street which bids defiance to the humours of the atmosphere, and where one may lounge and look at shop-windows, though the rain should come down in torrents, or though an August sun should broil people as they walk along in the open streets.

Generally, in these days before electric light, arcades had glass roofs or skylights to decrease the need for candles or gaslight—a design element that caused maintenance headaches for the arcades' owners until glass technology improved in the late nineteenth century.

Some arcades, following the pattern of the Grand Bazaar in Istanbul, were merely roofed versions of existing streets. Many others, such as London's Burlington Arcade, were enclosed spaces from their inception. Like the colonnades that had preceded them, these planned arcades drew heavily on classical ideas of regularity and order. Unlike the typically chaotic city street, they presented shoppers with a tidy environment of uniform windows and doors. And although they were enclosed, they were conceived as "streets" of a sort, often built between existing buildings and giving pedestrians an additional route between two other thoroughfares.

### Snooty shopping, U.K. edition

Arcades were the last major form of enclosed, multiple-vendor shopping space to take root before the climate-controlled mall burst onto the scene in the twentieth century. But both arcades and their cousins, the colonnades, continued to evolve in the intervening years.

The fortunes of arcades rose or fell based on the fortunes of the streets that surrounded them. Closed off as they were, they usually withered if commerce moved elsewhere. Some of those that survived, such as the Burlington Arcade, pinned their hopes on the carriage trade.

From the day it opened in 1819, the Burlington Arcade has positioned itself as an elegant and exclusive shopping destination. Critics, of course, have always found its wares foolish. As journalist Augustus Sala noted dryly in 1859: "I don't think there is a shop in its *enceinte* where they sell anything that we could not do without. Boots and shoes are sold there, to be sure, but what boots and shoes? Varnished and embroidered and be-ribboned figments, fitter for a fancy ball or a lady's chamber, there to caper to the jingling melody of a lute, than for serious pedestrianism." Harsh words from a man whose love of fine china and rare books often led him into debt.

In the intervening years since Sala's era, the arcade has maintained its image as an upscale destination. In early 2003, its Web site fairly radiated snooty class.

"The Burlington Arcade provides a fashionable destination for wealthy domestic and overseas visitors to London and is a focal point amongst some of London's most famous retailing names," it proclaimed. "Fortnum and Mason, Simpsons and Aspreys together with an exciting selection of restaurant, café and food emporiums are all within close proximity providing a rare opportunity for retailers in Burlington Arcade to access a broad range of affluent custom."

Hey, it takes a lot of profit to maintain a Grade II heritage property.

### Snooty shopping, U.S. edition

The Burlington Arcade is neither the first nor the last shopping enclave to appeal to customers' sense of status. But the next buildings to do so successfully would not be built in the old world. For the next stage in the mall's evolution, it's time to cross the Atlantic.

The first planned shopping area in the United States was Market Square, built in the Chicago suburb of Lake Forest, Illinois, in 1916. Like the Palais Royal, it consisted of three low buildings surrounding a central park, although in this case streets rather than colonnaded walkways fronted the buildings.

Six years later, a developer in Kansas City, Missouri, took this idea one step further. Country Club Plaza was billed as the first major shopping development in the world to focus specifically on shoppers arriving by car. Developer J.C. Nichols didn't have much choice: the city's rail line didn't reach as far as his site on a largely undeveloped swamp.

Locals called the place "Nichols' Folly," but the developer had the last laugh—he had correctly hedged his bets on America's burgeoning love for the automobile. Rather than a park, the Spanish-themed plaza with its red-tile roofs was built around a series of parking lots. But, like Market Square, it was a three-sided structure of low-slung buildings, and each shop had an external entrance.

Similar structures sprang up across the United States in subsequent decades, particularly in California. Efforts to promote the centers grew more flamboyant as the competition increased. In 1950, the Campus Drive-In shopping center in San Diego opened with a 50-foot neon majorette marking its entrance; the previous year, the new Town & Country Shopping Center in suburban Columbus, Ohio, had promoted night-time shopping by hiring a woman named Grandma Carver to dive 90 feet into a four-foot pool of flaming water set up in the parking lot.

While they often offered drivers advantages over congested downtown shopping streets, these early malls shared one major disadvantage with their more traditional competitors: exposure to the elements. However, builders didn't have easy access to the technology needed to easily heat and cool a large, enclosed mall until the 1950s.

### Oofta, by golly! Cold-weather shopping in Minnesota

Weather wasn't such a major problem in sunny California and Texas, but in the cities of the Midwest, humid summers and icy winters discouraged shoppers from coming out to spend. It's no accident that America's first fully enclosed, climate-controlled shopping mall sprang up from the prairie in suburban Minneapolis.

To avoid building boilers for the 800,000-square-foot Southdale Shopping Center, architect Victor Gruen's Los Angeles-based firm developed a new kind of heat pump to heat and cool the mall, which opened in 1956. Like the developers of European arcades a century earlier, Southdale's builders realized that their enclosed space gave them a major advantage over their competitors, an advantage they promoted in a fact sheet published for the mall's opening:

In a region which is often beset by inclement weather, the fact that
Southdale [shoppers] will enjoy a perpetual springtime looms as
an important drawing card. Every foot of the Center, including
all shops, arcades and public areas, will be air-conditioned, completely free of snow, soot, or wilting heat.

Another advantage the center had over many older malls was the
fact that it boasted two department stores, Dayton's and Donaldsons. In
a situation reminiscent of Thomas Gresham's struggles with the Royal
Exchange four centuries earlier, it took the developer more than a year of
negotiations before the two companies agreed to open under the same
roof.

### Malls, kudzu, and other creeping menaces

In less than half a century since Southdale was built, malls have changed
and expanded beyond most developers' wildest dreams—and most critics' direst nightmares.

Eight years after Southdale opened, the U.S. boasted some 7,600
malls. By 1972, the total had jumped to 13,174. But it was the greedy 1980s
that were the golden age of the mall developer: more than 16,000 malls
were built in that decade.

By the end of 2001, there were more than 45,000 malls in America—
6,086 in California alone. And even though 95 percent of these centers
were strip malls—structures in which a line of stores opens onto a street
or parking lot—it was clear that Americans had embraced the concept
of planned shopping centers with a vengeance.

However, the statistics hide another story: the bloom had started to
fade from the shopping center rose, at least in the United States. The
savings and loan crisis knocked the development industry for a loop in
the early 1990s, and analysts began muttering nervously that many areas
of the country had more retail space than they needed.

As a result, many developers changed their approach in the 1990s.
Instead of building "ordinary" new malls, they either built over-the-top
extravaganzas, or focused on upgrading and expanding their existing
properties.

## Mega-oofta: the Mall of America
## and its Canadian cousin

Southdale's original 800,000 square feet—considered enormous at the time—would make the complex simply an average "regional center" these days, according to definitions published by the International Council of Shopping Centers. Perhaps that's why Southdale has ballooned to 1.7 million square feet. The most recent expansion added restaurants, a 16-screen movie theater, and a third-floor wing of teenybopper stores called Trendz on Top.

Of course, Southdale is in a peculiar situation. It's competing for customers with the Godzilla of U.S. shopping centers: the 4.3-million-square-foot Mall of America, which opened in 1992 just six miles to the east. So much ink has been spilled on that complex that I won't add much to it here. You probably already know most of the mind-boggling details, such as the fact that the mall logs 600,000 to 900,000 visits *every week,* and that over a third of its customers come from more than 150 miles away. More than 2,500 couples have been married here. And apparently, if you took off the roof, nine Eiffel Towers could be crammed inside.

Even those facts pale beside the vital statistics of Mall of America's mother ship, the West Edmonton Mall. Built in four phases (so far) between 1981 and 1998, the 5.2-million-square-foot mall is home to more than 800 stores, a bungee-jumping facility, a submarine, an ice rink, a chapel, several aquariums, a hotel, the world's biggest indoor theme park . . . when you have a reputation to uphold as the world's largest mall, the list of attractions just keeps growing.

My first and last visit to WEM, as its developers call it, took place in the summer of 1986, just after the third phase opened. Along with other attractions, that expansion added the water park and two "theme streets," Bourbon Street and Europa Boulevard.

I was in Edmonton for a wedding. As the bride-to-be and I floated in the wave pool, waiting for the next artificial roller to crest over us, I thought about the mall and what it all meant. Of course, I was only 21 at the time, so I didn't think terribly hard.

I remember being both fascinated and appalled by the sheer size of the place. As a third-year university student in the middle of acquiring a traditional liberal arts education, I felt compelled to be at least somewhat dismayed. But as a young woman with a little money saved up from a summer job, I couldn't help but be transfixed by the number of opportunities to splurge.

What sticks with me to this day, however, was the unabashed artificiality of WEM. The developers had no compunctions about claiming that a visit to their Bourbon Street was just as good as—or better than—a trip to the real New Orleans. Better, of course, because it was safer, more predictable, and climate controlled.

### The theme park mall

Safety and artificiality have come to be the defining qualities of malls around the world. As city cores fell into scary disrepair, mall managers around the world touted the fact that their spaces were enclosed, patrolled, and secure. Look around any mall today, and within minutes you'll likely spot a security guard in quasi-police garb. Read promotional materials and you'll see frequent references to well-lit parking lots. Some shopping centers have capitalized on this aura of security to bring formerly public events, such as Halloween trick-or-treating—now known as "Malloween" in some malls—into their sanitized confines.

This focus on control annoys critics of shopping centers, and even makes shoppers who appreciate safety slightly uneasy. As I did at West Edmonton Mall, many others wonder whether this theme park atmosphere is healthy for us. As Daniel Miller and his British coauthors put it:

> When people yearn for a return to "personal service" or support current trends for opening up enclosed shopping centers to "natural light", we suggest that they are at least as concerned about the increasing artificiality of their social relationships (and in particular the perceived materialism of their children) as they are about the physical environment itself.

If this sort of artifice is enough to bring people into the mall, getting them to stay requires an array of psychological trickery that would have amazed the Duke of Chartres.

## You can head for the checkout, but you can never leave

Have you ever wondered why most malls have no windows to the outside world? That's easy. The architects want you to forget any other world even exists. The sight of trees, sunshine, and birds might encourage you to *leave the mall*. And, not surprisingly, shopping mall owners don't want you to do that.

Instead, they want you to stay inside as long as possible. The idea is to replicate the artificial feeling of a theater or a Hollywood sound stage, where shoppers can be the stars of their own show. The shopping center industry has even coined a term for the idea of shopping as theater—the "retail drama"—which William Severini Kowinski popularized in his landmark 1985 book, *The Malling of America*.

In the retail drama, we are all actors treading the shopping mall boards. The sales clerks and the other shoppers are part of the cast. In the mall, the large rectangular doorways of each store, shaped like the proscenium arches of a traditional stage, add to the fantasy. We can enter a variety of stages, try on new "costumes" and touch new "props," which we can ultimately buy to fulfill our fantasies of who we are and who we want to become.

Blank, windowless walls aren't the only technique developers use to keep us immersed in our fantasies. Builders also do their best to ensure that we can't find our way out. Most of today's successful malls are designed more like ancient labyrinths than like the long, straight corridor of the Burlington Arcade.

If you've ever become hopelessly lost in a mall, take comfort in the fact that you've been purposely led astray. It's known as the "Gruen effect," named after Southdale's architect. Basically, the intent is to force serious shoppers—the blinkered, intent folks who come to the mall with a shopping list and attitude—to see stores they wouldn't otherwise visit. Straight hallways and clear sightlines make it too easy to find your store, buy what you came for, and get out.

It's a peculiar concept. Many shoppers—like my husband, for example—find the idea of trolling through endless, confusing corridors so annoying that they avoid malls completely. Others, like me, spend half their time sighing in frustration as they try to decipher the rare mall maps.

I remember the first time I learned that the confusing nature of malls was no accident. I was taking a press tour of Bayshore—the very mall where, 16 years later, I'd be doing my book signing—and I noticed an escalator that ran from the ground floor directly up to the new third story. I naively asked why there weren't two sets of escalators: an up-and-down set between the first and second floors, and a second pair between the upper two stories.

The PR person giving the tour explained, without shame, that the one-way express escalator was designed to keep shoppers moving around the mall, even if they didn't really intend to.

I can testify that the escalator fulfils that function admirably. I've lost count of the times I've stepped onto it by mistake and watched the second-floor store I had hoped to reach pass me by like a desert mirage. As a result, I have to hike across half the mall to find a staircase, escalator, or elevator that will actually take me where I want to go.

This design strategy seems counterproductive. Yes, it makes me pass stores I didn't plan to see. But, trust me, I'm in no frame of mind to buy. Usually, I'm muttering unpleasant words under my breath as I hotfoot it down the corridors. Until, of course, I sprint by a display of discount books and something catches my eye.

All right, I admit it. I'm annoyed, but I still buy. With luck, though, this mall-as-maze idea will be one of the design trends to lose favor among shopping center architects. Such miracles do happen.

There are encouraging signs that change is in the wind. For instance, the wisdom of sealing off shoppers from the real world is now being questioned in Broomfield, Colorado. There, a mall called FlatIron Crossing features "window walls" of clear glass that can even be rolled back to let in light and air when the weather permits. "We're trying to blur the lines of where [outdoors] and indoors start and stop," David Scholl, one of the mall's developers, told a newspaper reporter in 1999.

The builders of the stoa at Miletus, and the Duke of Chartres's architect at the Palais Royal, would recognize this idea. Just like the fashions sold in mall stores throughout the world, everything old eventually becomes new again in the world of shopping center design. And if bell-bottoms and platform shoes can be revived, nothing's impossible.

# 6   On the Road Again: From Peddlers to Avon Ladies

*For a salesman, there is no rock bottom to the life. He don't put a bolt to a nut, he don't tell you the law or give you medicine. He's a man way out there in the blue, riding on a smile and a shoeshine.*
— *Death of a Salesman*, Arthur Miller, 1949

I was probably the worst Avon lady in recorded history.

Most of my acquaintances didn't even know about my brief career selling blush and lipstick in 1990. That's how circumspect I was. I'd occasionally say to really close friends: "Hey, if you've ever kinda thought of maybe buying something from Avon, I could give you a catalog. But only if you're interested."

The idea of approaching colleagues at work made me queasy. Approaching neighbors or total strangers was out of the question.

I got into the business in the first place as a favor to a friend, who was also an Avon lady and a darned good one. She was going to win some kind of prize if she signed up another rep, and she assured me that I didn't really have to *do* anything if I didn't want to. And there were perks: I'd get discounts on Avon products.

But I wasn't even a good customer to myself. I missed the whole girly-girl "let's put on makeup and do each other's hair" thing in high school—I think I was off developing photos in the camera club's darkroom that day—so most cosmetics are completely lost on me.

In the end, I bought several gallons of bubble bath and Skin-So-Soft before I finally raised the white flag and bailed. As others have remarked, I couldn't sell air conditioners in Florida. Perhaps that's why I've always had a sneaking admiration for people who can.

### Dingdong, Avon calling

The first Avon lady was not from Stratford-upon-Avon, nor was he a lady. His name was David McConnell, and he sold books door-to-door in suburban New York City. McConnell gave away perfume samples to get his foot through the housewife's door. When he found out his customers preferred fragrance to literature, he switched gears and opened the California Perfume Company in 1886. (McConnell chose the name "California" for its romantic appeal; his son changed it to "Avon" in 1939 to call up pastoral images of Shakespeare's birthplace.)

Almost immediately, Mrs. P.F.E. Albee of Winchester, New Hampshire, became the company's first sales rep. Today, Avon gives out porcelain figurines called Albee awards to the firm's top-selling Avon ladies.

The 1880s was the right time to start a door-to-door sales company. Few middle-class American women worked outside the home, so they were in residence and looking for a little grown-up company when the Avon lady came knocking. They were also used to buying at home; the grocer, the milkman, the brush salesman, and a host of other retailers were already familiar figures at their kitchen doors. But cosmetics were a lot more fun to buy than brooms and vegetables, especially when you could share a cup of tea and a chat with your Avon lady.

The Avon ladies loved it too. Despite the predominant stereotype of the man who brought home the bacon and the woman at home who cooked it, there were many women who wanted, or financially needed, to be part of the workforce. "Avon lady" was one more addition to the tiny roster of acceptable female occupations, and a useful one for women who didn't have the stomach for nursing, the patience for teaching, or the ability to spend large chunks of time away from home in any capacity.

The company expanded into Canada in 1914, but it would be another 40 years before Avon made its next two international forays (to Puerto Rico and Venezuela). Once that round of expansion started, though, it continued at a breakneck pace. Today, you can buy Skin-So-Soft in

Taiwan and Anew in Argentina. Avon ladies in canoes will bring your purchase down the Amazon—there are more Brazilians working as Avon sales reps than serving in the country's army and navy combined.

"The Avon Opportunity is open to all," trumpets the company's Web site. Quite a few people have taken Avon up on that invitation. Since 1886, there have been some 40 *million* Avon ladies—or, as the company now prefers to call them, sales representatives. As of early 2003, there were 3.9 million Avon ladies in 143 countries. Think about that. That's more than the 2000 population of the city of Los Angeles. It's higher than the estimated 2002 population of Ireland. Combined, they rack up one billion sales transactions a year. That's one transaction for every six human beings on the entire planet, including children and men.

### You have e-mail—from Avon

It's a good thing that Avon began expanding seriously in the 1950s. As North American and European women started entering the workforce in droves in the 1960s, there were suddenly fewer and fewer women at home to answer the famous dingdong Avon doorbell. Today, two-thirds of the company's revenues come from outside the United States.

It doesn't help that Avon's image has taken a bit of a beating domestically in the last few decades. It's not that Avon ladies have been out trash talking and nicking silverware from customers' houses—far from it. Rather, the problem is that the firm's products are considered, well, a little frumpy. Your sweet Great-Aunt Flossie might buy from Avon, as might the woman in front of you in the grocery store line in sweatpants and curlers.

But if you see yourself as more of a corner office woman, you're probably trotting off to an upscale department store to enhance your image with Calvin Klein perfume and Estée Lauder lipstick. Besides the fact that you don't think that Avon's products are *you*, you don't have time to sit around munching homemade fruitcake with the kindly Avon lady. You have places to go, things to do.

The folks at Avon are all too aware of all this. Throughout the 1990s, when a smoking-hot economy sparked record sales for many retailers, Avon's sales grew at a relatively sluggish average pace of four percent a year.

Obviously, it was time to bring the company into the new millennium. And Avon's CEO, Andrea Jung, has been doing so with a vengeance. The company's Web site has been updated so that customers can order products directly, a potentially explosive strategy that the company has been pursuing very, very carefully. Avon ladies are concerned that head office will cut into their profits by selling over their heads, and the last thing head office wants to do is annoy 3.9 million women armed with perfume atomizers. Happily, the company knows that the sales representatives are the only factor that makes Avon stand out from the competition, and it wants to keep them on board.

"If we don't include [sales reps] in everything we do, then we're just another retail brand, just another Internet site, and I don't see the world needing more of those," Jung told *Business Week* in 2000.

In fact, in an intriguing move, Avon recently launched a major effort to lure a whole new generation of women into the Avon fold. The annoyingly named "mark." (yes, lower case, with a period) line of products has been designed specifically to appeal to shoppers aged 16 to 24. Not only are they funkier than the usual Avon products, they're also a bit more expensive. Image is everything in high school, and no cheerleader worth her salt wants her friends to think she's skimping on primping.

The line's moniker has a cloying little story behind it. According to an Avon news release, "The name 'mark.' reflects the brand's positioning of celebrating young women who are making their mark in the world."

As my nieces would say, "Whatever."

The interesting part of this whole enterprise is that current Avon reps won't be the only people selling the line. Avon has plans to recruit a whole team of reps aged 16 and up who will sell *only* the mark. line. The beauty of this strategy—pardon the pun—is that young women in this age group (who aren't nerdy bookworms like I was) already spend a lot of time trading makeup tips and giving each other makeovers. Avon calls such activities "Social Beauty." I swear I'm not making this up.

The company hopes that the 10 million young women who already know an Avon representative—such as the daughters and sisters of current Avon ladies—will be ushered into the fold and become long-term reps themselves. With this hope, the history of itinerant retailing has come full circle. Centuries ago, most people who sold fruit on the street or silk from a knapsack were born into the trade.

## Hey, Ma! Here comes the peddler!

In Europe from the Middle Ages until the end of the nineteenth century, peddlers (also called petty chapmen) were an invaluable source of fabric and other manufactured goods for people living outside major cities. Many of them learned the business from parents, siblings, or cousins, and one family might have a corner on trade in a particular region for generations.

And I do mean generations. Peddling is right up there with prostitution as one of the world's oldest professions. The mythical Ulysses once posed as an itinerant merchant, and the Code of Hammurabi from ancient Babylon included measures to protect and properly compensate peddlers.

Peddlers needed protecting because they filled an important niche in an economy where people were relatively immobile and couldn't exactly drive out to Wal-Mart whenever they ran out of—well, whatever ancient Babylonians were wont to run out of.

But back to medieval Europe. What were people there buying from peddlers? The customers of one Jean Bernard, who plied his trade in late-seventeenth-century France, could choose from a wide variety of fabrics whose very names seem exotic today, including cordillat, ratine, and drugget. Bernard also proffered shoes, haberdashery, braid, sewing silk, and ribbons.

Poor peddlers often specialized in portable luxury goods that they could carry on their backs and mark up significantly, such as lace, jewelry, eyeglasses, and spices. More prosperous competitors with a horse and cart could bring a miniature general store to far-flung farms and villages.

The stock varied by peddler and by country. One group of three French peddlers sold the usual fabrics and sewing goods, but also hawked cutlery, wine, rosary beads, mirrors, sugar, tobacco, and writing cases. In the Italian Alps in the early nineteenth century, peddlers often added soap, knitting needles, pipes, and clock keys to their portable stock of fabrics. Across Europe, many peddlers sold gloves, socks, belts, hats, and other fashion accessories.

Despite their ubiquity, peddlers didn't inspire a lot of trust, perhaps because they lived outside the easily comprehensible social structure of the day. They were neither town citizens nor country folk, but inhabited a shadowy realm in between (like the modern-day carnies who try to convince us to toss rings over dowels at fairs, all for the dubious privilege of winning a giant stuffed panda).

Contemporary literature often refers to peddlers as tricky thieves who sold shoddy goods. In *The Winter's Tale*, Shakespeare characterizes the peddler Autolycus as a "snapper-up of unconsidered trifles" who boasts that "my revenue is the silly cheat." A book published in France in 1596 claimed that peddlers had to swear the following oath to be admitted to the business: "I will steal at any opportunity."

## Saintly peddlers

There is, however, at least one instance of a saintly peddler: Saint Godric. Of course, he only got to be a saint after selling off all his stock, giving the money to the poor, and becoming a hermit, but it still shows they weren't all bad folks.

Godric lived in the twelfth century, but that doesn't mean he was the kind of guy you could keep down on the farm. Even as a boy, he wanted to be a chapman. He started off selling inexpensive items in the villages near his home, until he had acquired enough capital to make him a worthwhile business partner for some city merchants. For the next few years he wandered around the countryside, hitting all the big shopping hot spots: fairs and fortresses, cities and towns, and anywhere else where there were people who might be interested in his growing range of merchandise.

He traveled frequently to Scotland and made his first trip to Rome. Sea voyages weren't particularly safe in those days, and when he started getting through a few of them without mishap, he became increasingly convinced that God was looking out for him. He began adding visits to noted holy places to his itineraries. A contemporary relates that his pure thoughts led to financial success, too: "Thus aspiring ever higher and higher, and yearning upward with his whole heart, at length his great labours and cares bore much fruit of worldly gain." (Interestingly, this combination of religious fervor and earthly riches would show up time and time again in the stories of successful retailers as the centuries went on. John Wanamaker, a Philadelphia department store magnate, was famous for his dedication to the Presbyterian Church. Although Godric was a Catholic, he seems like the perfect poster child for the Protestant work ethic.)

The more Godric prospered, the more he traveled. Off he went

> . . . to Denmark and Flanders and Scotland; in all which lands he found certain rare, and therefore more precious, wares, which he carried to other parts wherein he knew them to be least familiar, and coveted by the inhabitants beyond the price of gold itself; wherefore he exchanged these wares for others coveted by men of other lands; and thus he chaffered most freely and assiduously. Hence he made great profit in all his bargains, and gathered much wealth in the sweat of his brow; for he sold dear in one place the wares which he had bought elsewhere at a small price.

"Buy low, sell high" works as well for saints as it does for sinners, apparently.

Godric's travels continued, but he was focusing more and more on holy places: Lindisfarne, Jerusalem, Santiago de Compostela in Spain. When his mother came with him on a trip to Rome and insisted on traveling barefoot, he ended up carrying her part of the way back to London, a feat which may in and of itself have qualified him for saint-hood. Eventually, he sold all his goods and hit the road once more, but this time as a hermit rather than a salesman.

Oddly, though, for all of his peddling, he didn't manage to get named patron saint of peddling. In fact, he doesn't seem to be patron saint of anything at all. Instead, peddlers had to share Saint Lucy of Syracuse with cutlers, glaziers, peasants, saddlers, and anybody having a hemorrhage. Most importantly, though, Lucy is the patron saint of people with eye problems, as she had her eyes plucked out after she refused to enter a life of prostitution. How this relates to peddling is unclear and probably not worth thinking about too hard.

### Dim lights, small city

Beginning in the late seventeenth century, the English government got a slice of the itinerant trade by licensing peddlers and hawkers. As fixed shops became more common throughout the country in the eighteenth century, shopkeepers placed increasing pressure on Parliament to control peddlers. After all, argued the retailers, shopkeepers paid town taxes, so they should have a greater right to the townspeople's custom.

There are shadows of this, even today. Many taxpaying restaurateurs object vociferously to the French fry trucks that appear like mosquitoes in the summer, selling cheap, quick, convenient snacks to passersby who might otherwise come inside for a full meal, with beverage, coffee, dessert, and tip. Some cities even regulate buskers, the street musicians who play for spare change, and many places bar street trade altogether as a way to combat "squeegee kids." But for every effort to ban itinerant sellers comes a protest from people who enjoy doing a little al fresco shopping.

Outlawing street traders wasn't a universally popular idea in preindustrial Britain, either. Not all cities and towns developed a similar range of shops at the same time. By outlawing peddlers all over the country, Parliament would deprive people in many rural villages of a significant source of goods. Various governments seesawed back and forth on this issue until the late 1790s, when Parliament finally told shopkeepers to stop agitating for action; Parliament had decided to let the peddlers alone and that was that. Many towns and cities passed local bylaws controlling peddlers and street traders, but these varied from locale to locale.

Peddlers continued to prosper during the Industrial Revolution, because people who moved to cities from the countryside felt more comfortable dealing with peddlers than with shopkeepers, at least initially. As historian David Alexander points out, "The newly urbanized encountered enough bewildering experiences without adding such a vital function as shopping to the list." He adds that new city dwellers in Industrial Revolution England weren't unique in this regard; Puerto Ricans and African-Americans from the U.S. South also preferred to deal with itinerant sellers in 1960s New York, at least until they became acclimated to their new surroundings.

Another reason that peddlers persisted in Victorian England was that cities were expanding so rapidly that houses were often built before sufficient shops were available and before mass transit could efficiently move people to stores in the city center. Shoppers who bought food from a suburban street seller were often very grateful for the privilege—the nearest market (where the peddler bought the goods) might be up to 30 miles away. Also, street selling was an easy trade to enter for unskilled workers with little ready money. With labor in such flux at this point—rural people moving to the city, factories laying off people with no safety net during slow times—street selling was a moderately attractive job option, at least for the short term.

Most street sellers carried their goods in trays, baskets, or barrows; only the really successful ones could afford an animal-drawn cart. The poorest street sellers sold snacks such as oranges and nuts, and inexpensive small goods such as brushes and toys.

Hawkers bought their stock from a variety of sources, including fishermen, wholesale markets, gardeners, neighbors, and small-scale manufacturers. Some bought directly from fixed shops; retailers who worried that having a bunch of street sellers milling about their establishment would repel well-heeled shoppers asked sellers to come early in the morning, or directed them to a back entrance. "Swag shops" wholesaled goods such as jewelry, pencils, cutlery, and dishes to street traders and small-scale shopkeepers.

However, many shopkeepers still resented street sellers for their low overheads. (The fact that hawkers had to ply their trade outside on cold, scorching, rainy, or windy days didn't seem to trouble the merchants a whit.) And Victorian shopkeepers were slow to realize a principle that is at the foundation of today's modern malls: the more retailers you can bring together in one place, the greater the number of customers you can attract.

At a time when not all goods were available in shops, customers wanted both shops and street sellers in the same vicinity. Otherwise, they would need to go to one neighborhood to buy meat, fish, and cheese (from shops) and another to buy fruit and vegetables (from street sellers). Many shoppers were also convinced that food was more expensive in stores than on the street. They were quite likely right; not only did shops cater to the middle classes rather than the working classes, and so likely set their prices accordingly; shopkeepers also had to cover those aforementioned overhead costs.

Finally, some shoppers preferred dealing with street sellers when they could because they saw it as a way of helping the poor. Street sellers were usually much closer to the edge of starvation than shopkeepers were.

## What the heck is a costermonger?

In the mid-nineteenth century, journalist and social reformer Henry Mayhew conducted a fascinating study of London's urban poor, including many street sellers. So concerned was he with the fate of street sellers that he tried to found a mutual benefits society for them.

His reports were published periodically in newspapers and in two-penny weekly installments between 1849 and 1862. It was a particularly tumultuous time for the city's street vendors. As a result of the potato famine, desperate Irish families had flooded into the English capital, willing to work for a pittance. They had to fight for the street shoppers' pennies with unemployed railway workers, who were victims of a recent reorganization of the industry that left many out of work and considering street selling as the last alternative to the dreaded workhouse. Unfortunately, just as more people were trying to make a living as street sellers, a cholera epidemic swept the city, making consumers hesitant to buy food from anyone but their most trusted vendors.

Mayhew estimated that 43,600 hawkers were plying their trade in London in the 1850s. Almost three-quarters of these were costermongers, who sold fish, fruit, vegetables, game, poultry, and flowers. (The peculiarly British word *costermonger*, dating from the early sixteenth century, comes from the even older word *costardmonger*, meaning an apple seller.)

Most vendors sold only one or two types of products, but these included just about anything portable. Goods on offer ranged from birds' nests and squirrels to sheet music and seashells. A Victorian shopper could buy salt, matches, spot-removing compounds, books, second-hand clothes, nutmeg graters, tortoises, dishes, or dogs on the street.

The variety of prepared food available on London's thoroughfares was particularly varied. Pub entrances were lucrative locations for food sellers. Then, as now, drinkers got hungry and, as the night went on, they cared less and less about the prices of things. Shellfish sellers boiled live lobsters and crabs over grates in yards, and the going rate for hot oysters was four for a penny.

Chilled pub patrons could also avail themselves of a warm snack from relative newcomers to London's street traders: the hot potato men, or "baked taties." Many of these sellers were disabled tradesmen and laborers, and they began wheeling their portable tin stands, called "cans," through London's streets in the 1830s. The baked potato season ran from mid-August until the end of April. Many passersby bought them to warm their hands as much as to eat.

### Hopped up on java: Victorian caffeine pushers

One business that took off in the 1830s was the coffee stall—not what we think of as a permanent "stall" at all, but a portable cart equipped with large tin urns, warmed by charcoal fires. The most elaborate ones had brass oil lamps and oilcloth roofs, and their owners sold bread, cakes, and sandwiches as well as coffee.

Before the popularity of coffee, the main hot beverage sold on London's streets was saloop, an unappetizing-sounding concoction of boiled sassafras wood laced with sugar and milk. But after the duty on coffee dropped in 1824, English consumption of coffee almost tripled in the subsequent seven years. When the duty declined again in 1842, the number of coffee stalls doubled within a year.

Just like Starbucks franchisees today, coffee stall vendors staked out prime corners (or "pitches") for their businesses. Busy streets and entrances to markets were popular venues. People on their way to work would line up, cup and saucer in hand, even if there was a strong possibility the beverage they'd receive would be doctored with saccharine root and carrots.

### Ethnic turf

Some commodities were closely associated with particular ethnic groups. By the 1850s, most London orange sellers were Irishwomen. Since orange selling was one of the least lucrative street vending jobs, the untrained immigrants faced less competition from established street sellers and from men.

In another instance of ethnic specialization, the itinerant spice and rhubarb trade in the city had been the province of a group of Moroccan Jews since the late 1700s. New immigrants apprenticed with their countrymen, and so the trade remained in the community. But, unlike the Irishwomen, whose ethnicity had no relation to the goods they sold, the Moroccans seem to have become spice sellers because shoppers thought their exotic accents and dress increased the chances that the spices were genuine. As one spice seller explained the success he and his country-men enjoyed in this line of work, "I can't tell what first make dem sell de rhubarb and de spice; but I tink it's because people like to buy de Turkey rhubarb of de men in de turbans."

### "Who'll buy a bonnet for fourpence?"

One of the only ways street sellers could attract attention and customers was through the skillful use of their voices. Mayhew captured a few of the cries that echoed through the streets of London:

> "Chestnuts all 'ot, a penny ascore," bawls one, "an 'aypenny a skin, blacking," squeaks a boy. "Buy, buy, buy, buy—bu-u-uy!" cries the butcher. "Half-quire of paper for a penny," bellows the street stationer. "An 'aypenny a lot ing-uns," "Twopence a pound grapes." "Three a penny Yarmouth bloaters." "Who'll buy a bonnet for fourpence?" "Pick 'em out cheap here! three pair for a halfpenny, bootlaces." "Now's your time! beautiful whelks, a penny a lot." "Here's ha'p'orths," shouts the perambulating confectioner. "Come and look at 'em! here's toasters!" bellows one with a Yarmouth bloater stuck on a toasting-fork. "Penny a lot, fine russets," calls the apple woman . . . the girl with her basket of wal-nuts lifts her brown-stained fingers to her mouth as she screams, "Fine warnuts! sixteen a penny, fine war-r-nuts."

To our modern sensibilities, the number of children selling goods on London's streets would have been disturbing. Children as young as seven worked to support themselves and their families, selling water-cress, flowers, matches, and other small, inexpensive items.

Flower sellers could do a brisk business in well-off London neigh-borhoods such as Hampstead and Saint John's Wood, since shoppers believed that people who kept flowers in their home were clean, respect-able, and inarguably middle class (even if, in their minds, the people selling the bouquets were none of those things). A typical posy might include violets, primroses, carnations, wallflowers, lilies of the valley, or roses, wrapped in paper and tied with rushes.

The flower girls' typical sales pitch was designed to appeal to Victorians with a soft spot for the "deserving poor": "Please gentleman, do buy my flowers. Poor little girl! Please, kind lady, buy my violets. O, do! please! Poor little girl! Do buy a bunch, please, kind lady!"

And there really were poor little match girls—although people of all ages sold matches, young girls were particularly associated with the trade. Before 1820, match sellers used to make their own merchandise by dipping wooden splints into a ladle full of melted brimstone. The resulting matches weren't easy to use; one had to light them from a flame created with steel, a flint, and a tinderbox. But around 1820, someone invented a match you could light by sweeping it across a strip of sandpaper. These matches were originally called "instantaneous lights" or "Congreves," but by the 1850s they'd acquired the name "lucifers."

### Caveat emptor: You get what you pay for

As many shoppers learned to their dismay, not all the little match girls were exactly honest. An 1862 article warned readers against the tricks of "lucifer droppers." Their usual targets were kindly looking gentlemen. After approaching the man to offer the matches, the child would purposely drop the boxes in the mud and start crying loudly. The embarrassed gentleman, anxious to ease the child's tears, would often buy the whole lot for much more than they were worth.

The temptation to cheat customers was great, because the profits involved in street selling were so small. As an 18-year-old street seller explained to Mayhew:

> If we cheats in the streets, I know we shan't go to Heaven; but it's very hard upon us, for if we didn't cheat we couldn't live, profits is so bad . . . Why, look at apples! customers want them for less than they cost us, and so we are forced to shove in bad ones as well as good ones and if we're to suffer for that, it does seem to me dreadful cruel.

Relations between shoppers and street sellers weren't always cordial. A baked potato seller told Mayhew that rich customers were particularly apt to complain. "Gentlemen does grumble though, for I've sold to them at private houses when they've held the door half open as they've called me—aye, and ladies too—and they've said, 'Is *that* all for 2d.?' If it'd been a peck they'd have said the same, I know."

And remember the pieman Simple Simon met, going to the fair? I always thought piemen sold fruit pies. But their wares were meat filled, and the piemen came in for particularly bad treatment from customers. People skeptical of the often-dodgy contents of the pies would mew and bark at the piemen.

Bored shoppers could take advantage of the custom of "tossing the pieman." Instead of bargaining normally for a price, costermonger boys and gentlemen on their way home from the pub would toss a coin. The pieman would call heads or tails. If the pieman called right, the customer would give him a penny but wouldn't get a pie in return. If the pieman lost, he had to give the customer a pie for free. In many cases, gambling rather than the pie was the point of the whole exercise, as one pieman explained to Mayhew: "Gentlemen 'out on the spree' at the late public-houses will frequently toss when they don't want the pies, and when they win they will amuse themselves by throwing the pies at one another, or at me."

### If you can make it there . . .

A decade after Mayhew finished publishing his crusading reports, journalist James D. McCabe, Jr., wrote about the street sellers of New York City. For the most part, the same sorts of people were involved in the same sorts of trades on this side of the Atlantic. "Watches, jewelry, newspapers, fruits, tobacco, cigars, candies, cakes, ice cream, lemonade, flowers, dogs, birds—in short, everything that can be carried in the hand—are sold by the Street Venders," McCabe wrote. Irishwomen in ragged caps sold food, while men ran newspapers stands on Broadway, on Wall Street, and near the ferries.

In England, a man selling apples would be considered a layabout, as selling fruit was seen as a woman's job. In New York, that disdain was reserved for men selling toys. "The dealers in these articles are strong, ablebodied men, who prefer to stand on the side walks pulling the strings of a jumping jack, or making contortions with a toy contrived for that purpose, to a more manly way of earning their bread," sniffed McCabe.

The question remains: why did people shop on the street? And, more to the point, why do we continue to do so today? Where I live, you can buy tie-dyed shirts and woven Guatemalan purses on the street in the summer. Year round, you can stop at a chip wagon to buy poutine, a cholesterol bomb in a box involving fries, cheese curds, and hot gravy.

Other cities have their own street treats, from hot cashews in Toronto to giant pretzels in New York. (And yes, I know there are all sorts of other things you can get on the street, but I'm only talking about legal stuff here. This is a law-abiding book, so it is.)

So why do we like lining up in the cold and the rain, when we could just as easily be in a shop? McCabe provided a very persuasive answer to this question. Street vendors' goods are usually inexpensive treats, he explained, and when you're hurrying along the sidewalk, sometimes you just need one.

> When the day is wet and gloomy, and the slush and the mud of Broadway are thick over everything animate and inanimate, and the sensitive soul shrinks within itself at the sight of so much discomfort, the flower-girls do a good business . . . On such days you may see hundreds of splashed and muddy men on the great thoroughfare, utterly hopeless of preserving any outward semblance of neatness, but each with his nosegay in his buttonhole; and as he glances down at it, from time to time, you may see his weary face soften and brighten, and an expression of cheerfulness steal over it, which renders him proof against even the depressing influences of the mud and the rain.

### The little match girl goes high tech

Mixed in among the people selling hot dogs and copies of *The Watchtower* on modern Western streets is a relatively recent interloper that may, in fact, be the future of street retail: the vending machine.

Well, OK, vending machines aren't exactly "new." In 215 B.C., a mathematician named Hero of Alexandria described devices in Egyptian temples that dispensed holy water in exchange for a coin. But modern vending machines wouldn't hit the United States until 1886, when the

Adams Gum Company set up penny vending machines on New York train platforms.

But these days, the vending machine industry is big business. According to the latest industry census published by *Vending Times*, a trade publication, Americans bought $15.7 billion worth of canned cold drinks alone from the things in 1999.

Machines are popping up in untraditional places, selling an ever-widening range of goods. In North America, you'll find gizmos that sell telephone calling cards, car license renewal stickers, perfume, and CDs, among other things. But the cornerstones of the industry are food and beverages, such as coffee, snacks, and ice cream bars.

For sheer inventory inventiveness, one needs to look to Japan, where the devices are known as *jidou hanbaiki or jihanki*. The entire U.S. vending machine industry, which also includes video games, jukeboxes, and foosball tables, was worth US$36.6 billion in 1999. In Japan—with just 40 percent of the population of the United States—vending machine sales toted up to $57.7 billion in 2001. That's $542 for every Japanese man, woman, and child.

That's a lot of Coke, I can hear you thinking. It's true that pop sales originally drove the Japanese industry, and drinks are still a popular *jihanki* item. The number of beverage-dispensing *jihanki* doubled between 1998 and 1999, and by 2002 there were about 2.7 million of them in Tokyo alone. But the *jihanki* ranks include much more imaginative appliances than mere Coca-Cola machines. Passersby can avail themselves of everything from fresh flowers and disposable clothing to live insects and adult videos.

Why are vending machines so popular in Japan, where their total revenues outstrip those of convenience stores? According to Calvin Campbell, writing about *jihanki* in the *Globe and Mail*, the answer may lie in the stereotypical Japanese penchant for discretion. "Been out on the town and require a discreet change of underwear?" he asks. "The *jihanki* shall provide, and without the accusatory glances one might receive from a nosy convenience store clerk."

## Door-to-door "peddling"

Some street sellers in London, as we've seen, came right to their customers' homes. The home sales industry became an even bigger business around the turn of the last century, when the prototypical Avon ladies were making their rounds.

Business was good because people were already used to the idea of stores such as grocers bringing goods to the door. But when American grocers started cutting back on home delivery service in the 1910s, firms such as the Jewel Tea Company decided to bring the whole grocery store to Harriet Housewife.

These companies usually offered a range of between 100 and 200 lightweight, nonperishable goods, some of them items that the customer couldn't buy elsewhere. There were cake mixes and cleansers, coffee and candy, and a variety of other products. Customers would place their orders and two weeks later the salespeople would deliver them. There was usually time for a bit of chat; reps would even demonstrate unfamiliar products. The strength of home selling has always been this personal touch. After the socializing, the sales rep would take the next order.

These delivery companies had an ingenious way to hook their home shoppers and keep them spending. Most grocery stores allowed customers to save up trading stamps that they could exchange for a gift. Home delivery companies gave them the gift first, and then required them to buy a certain amount of groceries in the future to "pay off" the premium. This type of promotion encouraged shoppers to keep using the service, and once they'd developed the habit it was harder to break. (Half a century later, mail-order record and book clubs would start using the same trick to their advantage.)

Once cars and trucks became more affordable, one enterprising company tried to take the home grocery idea one step further. The W.K. Hutchenson Company of Massachusetts invented the Roly Poly—basically, a mobile grocery store that could be driven around a suburban neighborhood. The "store" would pull up to the curb, the driver would ring a bell, and shoppers could come out and peruse the goods on the shelves. But these mobile stores couldn't get the volume discounts that the chain stores could, and they didn't use the premium gift gimmick that worked so well for the home delivery companies. The "mototeria" soon disappeared.

## Party on, ladies

The next step in the ongoing efforts to turn consumers' homes into stores came about almost by accident. While making plastic parts for gas masks during World War II, Earl Tupper also developed a new consumer product: plastic food storage containers. After the war, he tried to flog them through stores, but customers weren't keen on the newfangled bowls. They also didn't understand the whole burping-lid thing.

Then a single mom from Detroit named Brownie Wise started selling the products as an independent representative. Her sales figures went through the roof, and Tupper wanted to know why. Wise explained that she sold the containers through "home parties," where women in the booming new suburbs could trade recipes and child-care tips while Wise demonstrated the benefits of Tupperware.

She'd sold America's housewives, and she sold Tupper. In 1951, he yanked Tupperware from retail shelves and hired Wise to develop a home party program and train a veritable army of Tupperware ladies.

Yeah, sure, we joke about Tupperware parties now. But in the early postwar days, women were told to give up their factory jobs so returning vets could have them. Like Avon, Tupperware gave women the opportunity to earn a bit of cash and independence, while getting to know their neighbors.

In the years since, study after study has shown that women buy more when they shop together than when they shop alone. Marketing analyst Paco Underhill, who studies shoppers in stores, found in one study of a national housewares chain that women shopping with a female companion stayed in the shop for an average of eight minutes and fifteen seconds. Those shopping alone stayed five minutes and two seconds. "When two women shop together, they talk, advise, suggest and consult to their heart's content," Underhill concluded in his 1999 book, *Why We Buy*.

Long before Underhill conducted his study, Brownie Wise understood that fact intuitively. She also understood, from the example of the Avon lady and the Fuller Brush man, that people like to touch products and see them demonstrated in a nonstore setting. But, unlike a visit from the Avon lady, a Tupperware party was an *event*. There were probably handwritten invitations. Sausage rolls and punch were likely involved.

Under Wise's extroverted tutelage, Tupperware ladies conquered the bungalows of America, and the company boomed. Wise would be the first woman ever featured on the cover of *Business Week* magazine.

Of course, the party didn't last forever. Tupper, by all reports a rather dour Yankee, rarely saw eye to eye with the ebullient Wise, and he fired her in 1958. And once, inevitably, competitors like Rubbermaid started making similar products and selling them in stores, Tupperware's edge dulled. But, like Avon, the company is soldiering on. Every 2.2 seconds, somewhere in the world, a group of women is sitting down to hear about the wonders of FridgeSmart containers and Shape-O toys. But, also like Avon, Tupperware has found greener pastures abroad; 85 percent of the company's sales come from outside the United States.

In Tupperware's wake has come a deluge of salespeople eager to make your home their shop. About three-quarters of these heirs to the peddler's ancient trade are women.

There's PartyLite, based in Hyannis, Massachusetts, which now sells its upscale candles through home parties in ten countries. The company's slogan perfectly captures the zeitgeist of frazzled women who come to these events in the hope of salvation, or at least a little peace and quiet: "*Decorate* your home, *Celebrate* your life, *Illuminate* your spirit." (All italics courtesy of PartyLite.)

Then there's the Pampered Chef, launched in 1980 by a home economics teacher from Chicago who wanted to turn the world on to the joys of professional kitchenware. Today, 67,000 "independent Kitchen Consultants" in four countries rack up total annual sales of $740 million.

In countless living rooms in countless houses around the world, women are gathering around a coffee table getting mildly hammered on chardonnay and buying lingerie, jewelry, sportswear, or—believe it or not—"adult toys." Clearly, there's still a lot of money to be had just by knocking on the kitchen door.

### Why does it work?

One of the keys to the home party phenomenon is that it relies on two basic human instincts: desire and guilt. The desire arises not only from the guests at the party, but even more strongly from the hostess herself. Hostesses usually get free or discounted merchandise by hosting a party.

How much they get is based on how much their friends and family shell out on products.

And if one of the guests agrees to host another party with the same sales rep . . . bingo! The hostess has hit the jackpot. That's where the guilt kicks in. It's the dirty little secret of home shopping parties. No one wants to be the only thing standing between her friend and a coveted picnic kit.

There's an odd sort of ritual at the end of these shopping parties. I went to one recently where, after the demonstration, the sales rep set up shop at the kitchen table with her order forms and receipt book. One by one we wandered in from the living room to place our orders in low voices. I didn't want to appear either cheap or extravagant, but I definitely wanted to look as though I was contributing to the cause. It all felt a bit like confession.

Since I work at home and am a known cheapskate, I don't get invited to a lot of these parties. I must admit, I enjoy them—they get me out of the house and force me to actually put on shoes. But some folks are on a veritable home party shopping circuit, it seems, and a bit of giftware fatigue is starting to set in.

"These [parties] are starting to ruin my friendships. The guilt! The obligation! The money wasted on stuff we don't want! We even had two family members in tears last year as they fought over who got to be the Pampered Chef hostess for my sister-in-law's bridal shower," one agonized reader confessed to a reporter for the *Minneapolis Star Tribune.*

A backlash may be coming, but it won't be anytime soon. There are still lots of people like me who like combining a night of shopping with a social occasion. According to the Direct Selling Association, direct sales (including both home parties and one-on-one transactions, such as Avon sales) tote up to $25 billion annually—twice what they were a decade ago—and $82 billion worldwide. More than half of all Americans have, at some point, bought something from a direct sales agent. That's a lot of lemon zesters, lipsticks, and lettuce bowls.

Somewhere, I suspect, Saint Godric is smiling.

# 7 Please Mr. Postman: Catalogs, TV Shopping, and the Internet

*[Mrs. Lynde] had strong views on the subject of octopus-like depart-ment stores, and never lost an opportunity of airing them. "And as for those catalogues of theirs, they're the Avonlea girls' Bible now, that's what. They pore over them on Sundays instead of studying the Holy Scriptures."*
                    —L.M. Montgomery, *Anne's House of Dreams*, 1922

In the early 1990s, before the Canadian dollar took a serious nosedive and made purchases from U.S. mail-order catalogs prohibitively expen-sive, one of my great treats was ordering casual wear from a company called Clifford & Wills. I loved the all-cotton long-sleeved T-shirts and the durable leggings. I adored the fact that if I found something I liked, I could order it in just about every color of the rainbow. But above all, I delighted in phoning my order in to the Clifford & Wills call center.

"Good afternoon, Clifford & Wills, may I help you?" the operator would answer, her voice honeyed with Southern charm. I don't know where, exactly, the Clifford & Wills call center was located, but it certainly appeared to be somewhere south of the Mason-Dixon Line. Their operators sounded like seashores and sunshine. We'd often chat as I was placing my order, and they were invariably pleasant. I'm sure they were probably trained not to waste time shooting the breeze with snow-bound, cabin-crazy Canadians, but they almost always would, for a minute or two at least. Because the whole transaction was so pleasant—and the merchandise was great—I shopped Clifford & Wills for years.

For any company that brings the goods to you, rather than making you go out and get them yourself, the personal touch is crucial. Whether it's QVC hiring cheery hostesses to assure us that the products are genuine, or an on-line retailer sending out a personal message with a real person's name on it to confirm an order, we somehow need to know that there's an actual human being at the other end of the transaction.

### When "remote" was really, really remote

Remote shopping is far from a new phenomenon. "Carriers" took goods throughout medieval England. They provided a vital service, since the country boasted few roads outside the major cities. Noble families living on country estates paid high fees to have goods brought in on horseback or by sea; the nearest town with a shop or market might be 20 miles away, and a major river or small mountain might make access to it particularly difficult.

As late as the 1700s, fashionable families were still equipping their country houses this way. But by then, they had more elaborate shopping tools at their disposal. Rather than relying on an agent or carrier to pick out items based on their descriptions or shopping lists, the country nobles and gentry could also choose merchandise from printed materials. Furniture makers Hepplewhite and Chippendale, for instance, both published catalogs in the eighteenth century.

Many booksellers also published catalogs listing the fare they had in stock, and these publications could even be customized to the tastes of each customer. A man selling books from a London stall in the 1850s described a colleague who distributed a catalog with two pages of "facetiae" at the end. "They're titles and prices of queer old books in all languages—indecent books, indeed," the bookseller told journalist Henry Mayhew. "He sends his catalogues to a [sic] many clergymen and learned people; and to any that he thinks wouldn't much admire seeing his 'Facetiae,' he pulls the last leaf out, and sends his catalogue, looking finished without it."

The custom of mail order spread across the Atlantic, at least among the well-to-do. Before the American Revolution, plantation owners in the colonies routinely ordered the latest fashionable goods by writing to their agents in England. Many other people simply asked relatives "back home" to buy and ship articles for them.

With the coming of the railroads, though, a whole new era in remote shopping began: the age of the big mail-order catalog.

## Chicago: City of the big shoulders and big catalogs

The modern mail-order catalog business really began in 1872, when Chicago-based Aaron Montgomery Ward printed a catalog of 163 items aimed largely at farmers. The idea appealed to rival R.W. Sears, who launched a mail-order watch catalog in 1886. The following year, Sears went into partnership with Alvah C. Roebuck in Chicago and started to produce a more substantial publication. By the time the century was out, the Sears catalog would swell to more than 700 pages, tempting consumers with some 6,000 items, and Sears, Roebuck would have set up shop as a bricks-and-mortar department store.

Chicago became something of a catalog company mecca, due to its central location between the settled East and the pioneer West, and the vast web of railway lines running through the city from just about everywhere in the United States. Another cataloger, Spiegel, would soon emerge in Chicago, too. Meanwhile, north of the border, homegrown catalogs were also becoming big business in Canada.

The effect of these and other North American catalogs, particularly in rural areas, was sweeping. They didn't just sell clothing and gift items, as many mail-order catalogs do today. Many sold just about everything a householder might require, including bird cages, salt boxes, rat traps, milk cans, bridles, bicycle suits, washstands, and butter churns.

## Shopping from sea to sea

Many catalogs became prized sources of consumer goodies for isolated settlers. It's unlikely, however, that many other mail-order publications have claimed such a major place in any country's national psyche as Canada's Eaton's catalog. Americans talk about baseball, hot dogs, and apple pie. The British have queen and country. Here in the Great White North, for almost a century, it was snow, hockey, and the Eaton's catalog.

Unfortunately, we still have the snow and the hockey.

Irish immigrant Timothy Eaton founded his Toronto department store in 1869. Like all of the department store magnates who built their businesses to magnificent heights in the Victorian era, he worked on the principles of fixed prices, cash sales, and guaranteed quality. "Goods Satisfactory or Money Refunded," the slogan the store first used in 1870, was as well known in Canada then as Nike's "Just Do It" catchphrase is today.

Eaton's started a small mail-order business sometime around 1874, when it distributed handbills around Toronto. In 1884, it published its first catalog, a 32-page publication given out to fairgoers at the Industrial Exhibition (which would become the Canadian National Exhibition I remembered so fondly in chapter 2). Those early catalogs focused largely on dry goods, just as the Eaton's store itself did. Soon, however, the store and its catalog expanded into almost every type of merchandise that could be shipped by rail or displayed in a store.

The Eaton's catalog would find its way into just about every Canadian home in the next few decades. If ever a country was tailor made for mail-order shopping, it was Canada in the late 1800s and early 1900s. The Last Spike was hammered into the Canadian Pacific Railway at Craigellachie, B.C., on November 7, 1885, connecting the Pacific and Atlantic coasts. The national census taken four years earlier showed a country with a population of just 4.3 million souls. Three-quarters of those people lived in rural areas, hemmed in by an often-harsh climate and far from all but the most rudimentary stores. A vast swath of land from Ontario's western border to the Pacific Coast was home to fewer than 170,000 people, most of them settlers clearing land who needed everything from fabric to farm implements. And now, the railroad could get those goods to them quickly and securely.

Eaton's quickly built a reputation and an infrastructure to serve the West. So when more than one million people flooded into the Prairies between 1896 and 1914, the company was ready. In many cases, no sooner had a rural family built their first rude shack then the long tentacles of Eaton's would reach them. The company issued a special "Settlers' Catalogue" in 1903, which breathlessly informed these weary folks that Eaton's

... provides every possible need for furnishing the home from cellar to attic; its stocks embrace every Household Help and also include wearing apparel of every reliable kind for man, woman and child. The distance need be no barrier for the Eaton Mail Order System extends to every Town, Village and Post Office in the Dominion of Canada from the Yukon to Nova Scotia.

You half expect Mr. Eaton to claim that his catalog is faster than a speeding bullet and can leap tall buildings in a single bound.

By 1910, the good folks at T. Eaton and Company weren't satisfied with simply furnishing your home: they started selling entire prefabricated houses. And if you didn't trust prefab, a 1917–18 catalog offered house plans and building supplies. For C$1,122.09, you could get everything you needed to build a basic six-room, two-story house, including hardware and paint. Luxuries such as a "hot air heating plant" (C$136) and plumbing (C$200) were extra.

Soon, the Eaton's catalog was part of the national folklore. In *The Hockey Sweater*, a children's story by Roch Carrier, a Quebec mother orders a hockey jersey for her son from the catalog. Instead of using the printed order form, she writes a personal letter to "Cher Monsieur Eaton." Of course, the transaction is not perfect. Mr. Eaton—well, one of his thousands of employees—sends the family a *Toronto Maple Leafs* hockey sweater, and the young boy can't convince his mother to send the hated article back. No self-respecting Quebec boy would be caught *dead* in anything but the red, white, and blue of the Montreal Canadiens. After a lecture on patience and forgiveness from the local curate, the boy prays, as the priest advised him to do. He asks God to send a flock of moths to devour the sweater.

### The taller they are, the harder they fall

But like all good things, the golden age of the mass-market catalog eventually came to an end, in both Canada and the United States. In the 1960s and 1970s, smaller, specialty catalogs that didn't try to be all things to all people began gaining market share, aided and abetted by two developments: bank credit cards (so the cataloger didn't have to provide its own credit service) and toll-free phone technology. As urban populations grew, people had less need to buy general merchandise by mail.

On January 14, 1976, Eaton's pulled the plug on its 92-year-old catalog. Nine thousand Eaton's employees were suddenly unemployed, and the country was stunned. In a self-mocking jibe, the *Winnipeg Free Press* published a cartoon of a country outhouse, with the following comment emanating from inside: "Better renew that *Free Press* subscription, Ma. We ain't gonna get Eaton's catalogues no more."

Even J.C. Barrow, chairman of Eaton's archrival, Simpson-Sears, conceded the magnitude of the announcement. "I'm as surprised as anyone. I suppose if you're Canadian, the Eaton's catalogue is just like the Anglican Church," he told that other bastion of the establishment, the *Globe and Mail*.

American catalogers also fell, one by one, to the wrecker's ball. The mighty Montgomery Ward catalog folded. Spiegel repositioned itself as a fashion and housewares catalog. J.C. Penney was the only company brave enough to enter the general-merchandise catalog fray. And in what has become a classic business school case study of economic hara-kiri, Sears had begun to diversify, and its focus drifted from retailing at the very moment catalog sales were dropping and low-priced competitors were eating its lunch. It even ended up moving out of its own building, the Sears Tower in Chicago. In 1993, Sears discontinued its famous mass-market catalog, only to buy up Land's End in 2002.

### Making magazines thicker: Mail order goes slick

Even during the heyday of the big mail-order catalogs, shoppers had other options if they wanted to shop by mail. General interest and women's magazines were packed with ads for an astonishing variety of products.

Part of the reason that these mail-order ads were so popular was that manufacturers were still having problems distributing their products widely, particularly in grocery stores. One way to get a new item to catch on was to offer inexpensive samples by mail. If the buyer liked it, she was encouraged to trot down to her local grocer and suggest he stock it. Ads in *The Ladies' Home Journal* in the first decade of the 1900s turned around the fortunes of both Kellogg's Corn Flakes and Jell-O.

In 1900, the range of mail-order goods promoted in the pages of that publication would put even a modern mall to shame. Some products were available for free inspection, and many prices included delivery charges.

Farmers could order egg incubators, fruit trees, and seeds. Homemakers could buy books and the bookshelves to display them on, as well as sheet music and the piano to play it on. Ads touted the virtues of various chairs, tables, beds, carpets, china, silverware, stoves, iceboxes, and water heaters. For children there were baby buggies and bicycles, ice cream makers and Shetland ponies (I would have loved to see one of those sticking out a rural mailbox). Dentifrice, toothbrushes, and face powder kept readers presentable. The woman trapped in the back of beyond could buy jewelry, wigs, "perfumed bath wafers," and wedding invitations that offered the illusion of big-city style.

There was clothing of all styles and shapes, from women's suits to union suits. You could buy corsets, coffee, calling cards, and carriages. You could take a correspondence course to learn electrical engineering or journalism, or buy booklets that would help you stop stuttering or speak French—preferably, one hopes, at the same time. The local preacher could buy a communion tray and matching cups.

There was even a contraption of ropes and pulleys that would make Suzanne Somers proud. "THE WHITELY EXERCISER Expands Chest, Develops Bust, takes stoop out of shoulders, brings physical perfection," the ad modestly promised.

Speaking of Suzanne Somers makes me think, inescapably, of all those other "as seen on TV" products. Order now! Operators are standing by!

## But wait! There's more!

"If you're going to talk about crap sold on TV, you've gotta talk about Ron Popeil," my husband said when I started working on this chapter. Innocent that I am, I had no idea who Ron Popeil was.

Well, that's not entirely true. I didn't know his name. But I sure remembered his TV ads for the Veg-o-Matic and the Pocket Fisherman. I even thought the Smokeless Ashtray was a darned fine idea. You had to be living in a cave in the 1970s not to know the name Ronco.

Ronco was the company Ron Popeil started to sell his creations. He comes from a long line of inventors and salesmen. His great-uncle, Nathan Morris, sold kitchen gizmos on the boardwalks of the New Jersey shore. Ron Popeil's father, S.J. Popeil, invented the Chop-o-Matic and countless other gadgets.

But the Popeil-Morris clan is notorious for its internecine feuds, and no one could accuse Ron Popeil of easily inheriting his success. He and his father were barely on speaking terms for much of his life, and Ron and Nathan once took each other to court in a patent dispute. During that case, Nathan had a spectacular heart attack in the courtroom, only to recover miraculously quickly when his great-nephew settled the case.

The one thing S.J. did for Ron was allow him to sell S.J.'s inventions. By age 13, Ron was working from dawn to dusk at a Chicago flea market, drawing captivated crowds to his demonstrations of the Chop-o-Matic. Always, he adhered to the county fair salesman's primary directive: the product, not the seller, is the star. Demonstrate the product, talk about the product, direct everyone's interest to the product. They're paying for a kitchen gadget. The salesman is just the decoration.

At the flea market, on the fair circuit, and in a stint demonstrating products at a Chicago Woolworth's, he honed other family tricks. There's the "countdown," which encourages bewitched shoppers to think the product is worth much more than the actual asking price. "How much would you expect to pay for such a wonderful device? One hundred dollars? But you're not going to pay $100. You're not going to pay $90. Or $80. Or $70." By the time you hear that this marvelous machine, once associated with the price of $100, can be yours, today, for just $9.95, well, you just have to have it.

Ron was making a pretty good living demonstrating S.J.'s products. In 1956, at the age of 21, he even recorded a brief TV ad for the Chop-o-Matic. But then, in 1960, S.J. invented the Veg-o-Matic, the machine that would change late-night television.

Four years later, Ron and a friend founded Ronco, rustled up $500, and made a two-minute TV ad to flog the Veg-o-Matic. Then they drove all over the Midwest, begging department stores to stock the product and begging TV station managers to run their ad in the wee hours of the morning. It all could have gone horribly wrong, but it didn't. The stores couldn't stock enough Veg-o-Matics, and the rest, as they say, is history.

## When the commercials *are* the show

I thought Ronco and its products had gone the way of eight-track tapes and CB radios, but that's only because I rarely watch shopping channels. It turns out that Ron Popeil is something of a star over at QVC, the shopping channel whose name stands for "Quality, Value, Convenience." We don't get QVC up here in Canada, and I've never felt the need to switch it on when I'm in the States—I'm too busy gorging myself on all-day Audrey Hepburn festivals over on Turner Classic Movies, another channel unavailable in Ottawa.

Anyway, home shopping channels are quite the little moneymakers—not surprisingly, since they don't have to bother making those pesky programs to go around the ads.

The idea was born in 1977 when a guy named Bud Paxson, who managed a Florida talk radio station, got stuck with a load of electric can openers from a delinquent client. What in the world was a radio station to do with a bunch of can openers? What else could he do? He got his announcers to flog them on air for $9.95 apiece. To his amazement, listeners bought them. In droves.

Paxson and the station owner, Roy Speer, expanded the idea to a local cable TV station in 1982, calling it the Home Shopping Club. That, too, was a roaring success and they took the idea national as the Home Shopping Network on July 1, 1985. A whole new chapter in the history of insomnia began. Soon, people all over America were voluntarily plunking themselves down in front of the retail equivalent of a PBS pledge drive.

Of course, success always draws competition. The following year, Pennsylvania-based QVC hit the airwaves. The man behind QVC was Joseph Segel, who in 1964 had founded another household-name company, the Franklin Mint. From the beginning, his approach was much more laid back than HSN's. At QVC, pressure tactics were kept to a minimum. No haranguing hosts, no last-minute discounts.

I could get into a long-winded discussion here about the various battles waged by these two titans of gourmet cheesecake and abdominal exercise machines. (By the way, am I the only person who finds something sinister in the fact that these stations sell you both the cause of obesity and its supposed cure?) But this is a book about shopping, not business management, so I'm going to hit you with the fun stuff instead: mind-boggling QVC trivia!

- QVC is now broadcast in the U.K., Ireland, Germany, and Japan. What World War II put asunder, shopping has joined together.
- In 2002, QVC's sales topped $4.4 billion. That's more than the gross domestic product of Estonia, Nicaragua, or Jamaica.
- QVC shipped its 500 millionth package on October 29, 2001.
- In 1997, QVC sold 30,000 locker room caps in 20 minutes on Super Bowl Sunday.
- Also in 1997, QVC featured a $1.9-million farm belonging to Muhammad Ali on its show "First Friday: Extreme Shopping." The price of the farm isn't as worrisome as the fact that there was actually a show called "Extreme Shopping."

### The inevitable Canadian knockoff

As I've admitted, I'm not a longtime viewer of American shopping channels. So I decided to check out the Canadian equivalent, a network with the scintillatingly imaginative name of The Shopping Channel. (Its Web site says it "has always provided customers with high-quality, exceptional value, and convenience." Hmm. Quality, value, and convenience. Where have I heard that before?) I'd last watched the channel years earlier.

When it hit the Canadian airwaves in 1986, TSC was working under a severe handicap. The federal government had decreed—for Byzantine bureaucratic reasons that I won't bore you with—that TSC would not be allowed to show moving pictures. It was limited to photos and text. So what you had, basically, was Ron Popeil as a slide show. They could have used this station to sedate convicts during a prison riot. Eventually, the government relaxed its restrictions and allowed TSC to use cameras and live people.

When I flipped on the channel recently, I stumbled onto "Today's Showstopper": a collection of Jackie Kennedy jewelry. Caroline Kennedy has apparently licensed a number of her mother's bijoux for replication and sale to the masses.

The first item on the block was the Jackie Kennedy Gold Plate and Crystal Friendship Ring, a copy of a ring Bobby Kennedy gave his bereaved sister-in-law. For about 20 minutes, a balding 50-ish man in a dark suit and his blond, 30-ish cohost told the tale of this C$49.87 ring. They showed pictures of Jackie wearing the original. They told viewers that she wore it on her left hand, and advised potential buyers that "You can also stack it up with other rings, just like Jackie did." That last is a bit of marketing genius. You can look like an icon *and* shop more! Run to your telephone now!

Mercifully, the product eventually changed. Unfortunately, it was another piece of Jackie jewelry: the Jackie Kennedy Gold Plate and Rhodium Plate Set of Four Hoop Earrings, just C$69.99. They show more photos of Jackie wearing the originals.

The whole concept struck me as really creepy. Of course, it didn't help matters that the set consisted of a plaster pillar topped with an enormous Greek vase stuffed with roses. Combined with the male host's dark suit, it gave the whole thing the effect of a Veg-o-Matic demonstration in a funeral parlor. I switched the TV off.

I have to admit, the appeal of TV shopping is lost on me. For me, there are two main types of shopping: the utilitarian run to the grocery store or the pharmacy, where I know what I want and where to find it; and the search-and-compare recreational mission to the local mall, where I hold up, sniff, touch, or try on more exotic purchases.

Neither of these functions is well served by TV shopping, in my opinion. If I know what I want, I'm not going to sit through hours of patter for casserole dishes and rotisserie ovens until it comes up. If I don't know what I want, and I'm willing to be inspired to an impulse purchase, there's none of the thrill of the hunt through the mall, none of that feeling of victory that comes when I find the *perfect* black skirt after trying on 20 or so.

It's passive shopping, and I don't really get it. But I'm obviously in the minority. Remember that figure of $4.4 billion in annual sales for QVC.

So what is it about TV shopping that makes it succeed for so many people? Part of the allure appears to be hypnotic. I'm a fairly antsy viewer—if something doesn't seem immediately relevant, I grab the remote and surf over to an all-news channel. But QVC's statistics show that the average viewer will spend about 50 hours watching the channel before making a first purchase. This extended viewing period makes viewers familiar with the schedule, the products, and the hosts, breaking down shoppers' innate tendency to mistrust merchandise they can't touch.

Second, TV shopping has moved far beyond cubic zirconias, at least on QVC. While many products are exclusive to the channel, many others are also available down the street at your local mall—often, at a higher price, since QVC can negotiate major volume discounts. Switch on QVC and you'll see Hewlett-Packard computers, Nikon cameras, Black & Decker tools, Cuisinart kitchen gizmos, and Harman Kardon stereo equipment. Those kind of brand names establish instant credibility and trust.

Additionally, QVC offers almost instant gratification. Ninety percent of the channel's orders are shipped within 48 hours. In addition, computer systems ensure that no one calls up only to be told that an item is out of stock—as soon as inventory is exhausted, the computers won't let operators take any more orders, and the on-air host informs viewers.

The more I think about it, the more I see that there are definite advantages to TV shopping. I decide to tune in once more to TSC.

It's 11:55 P.M., and two young California types are touting the merits of Tan Towel Self-Tanning Towelettes. "Isn't the name a bit redundant?" I think.

Geez, I really need to get out more.

I settle in to watch the spiel. Tan Towels are "truly a beauty break-through," says the cheerful blond hostess in shorts and a sleeveless flowered shirt. Her companion keeps up the patter as the woman absentmindedly rubs a Tan Towel up and down her arm. At midnight, a voice-over announces that the next half hour will be a presentation on the merits of the Total Gym.

TV shopping works for millions, but my attention is wandering. It's definitely time for bed.

### One last brief note on TV shopping

Remember K-Tel, the source of those cheesy compilation albums of "original hits, all by the original stars" that blanketed the TV airwaves in the 1970s? The company still exists, but its main music business these days involves licensing songs for corporate functions. It has developed an interesting little sideline, though: K-Tel Drug Mart.

My original thought was that any kind of drug associated with '70s record albums probably isn't legal to sell on TV. But it appears that K-Tel's audience has shifted from longhaired teenagers to budget-minded seniors. K-Tel Drug Mart's gimmick is to sell cut-price Canadian drugs to American consumers, through the Internet.

Speaking of the Internet . . .

### The brave new cyberworld

In 2002, Silicon Valley was rocked by the revelation that eBay wasn't really founded to sell Pez after all.

Here's the scoop. Pierre Omidyar was supposed to have created the on-line auction site as a way to trade Pez dispensers, those odd tubes in which candy pops out of the mouths of licensed cartoon characters. But in *The Perfect Store: Inside eBay*, Adam Cohen spoke to eBay PR rep Mary Lou Song, who confessed to inventing the story in 1997 because reporters otherwise weren't interested in the little auction site that could (and would).

Pez mythology aside, eBay has certainly worked its way into our consciousness, and our wallets, quickly enough. In 1999, I was in Turkey with a group of journalists. Unable to sleep one night, I came downstairs to the lobby to make a phone call. There I spotted one of the guys from my group, laptop open, typing frantically.

"Jet lag?" I asked sympathetically.

He shook his head. It turned out he collected antique cigarette cases, and he was checking the progress of some of his bids.

From Turkey.

At 3 A.M.

Shopping author Thomas Hine likens eBay to a giant flea market, explaining its success this way: "Electronically rummaging through eBay is like rooting through the dusty merchandise of a secondhand-seller's booth, and you keep going because the treasure may be just one level deeper." By contrast, too many e-commerce experiences require potential buyers to fight through slow-loading animations and applications, fill out invasive questionnaires, and deal with broken links, confusing checkout procedures, and ambiguous privacy policies.

Today, eBay is rapidly becoming one of America's largest dealers of used cars. More than a dozen states use eBay to get rid of foreclosed assets. Disney has been selling leftovers from its movie sets (junk that would usually clog landfills). Many companies, including IBM, are even selling their own products through eBay.

One big factor affecting all cybershopping sites, though, is the lack of face-to-face contact. Many Web surfers are understandably hesitant to cough up their credit card numbers to a screen, with no idea who may be on the other end. An on-line jewelry retailer called Ice.com has tackled this obstacle by allowing customers to pay in installments, after they receive their merchandise. If the company trusts the customer, the rationale goes, the customer is more likely to trust the company. It seems to be working. Unlike many Web sites, Ice.com actually turned a net profit in 2001; total gross sales in 2002 were in the range of $15 million.

### Food from your computer!

The imagery seems almost too perfect.

In 1997, a small e-commerce grocery company called HomeRuns.com had just recovered from a catastrophe: a late-winter blizzard in its home base of Boston had delayed deliveries for days. Just as the exhausted staffers had cleared the backlog and were sitting around a meeting room table, their building shook and huge chunks of masonry started flying off the walls.

A demolition crew working on the building next door had taken a chunk out of HomeRuns' headquarters by mistake. The company's phone systems were knocked out, the building was condemned, and the firm struggled for months to recover.

An article in *Wired* magazine, that cheerleading squad for the dot-com frenzy of the late 1990s, told the story of HomeRuns in all its frustrating detail. As the subhead to the article explained with more prescience than the editors probably knew, "Find customers, take orders, lug deliveries, eke profits—selling groceries online is a crazy idea that'll make somebody millions."

Well, the millions haven't materialized, yet. So far, on-line grocery retailing still seems like a pretty crazy idea.

The temptation to try it, though, is understandable. Not everyone reads, yet on-line bookstores have made inroads in the marketplace (if not great profits, so far). But everyone has to eat. Every day. It's not surprising that entrepreneurs would get a gleam in their eyes trying to snag a portion of the millions spent on groceries every week.

There are just a few little problems. Unlike the books peddled by Amazon.com, pork chops and cartons of milk aren't easy to mail. They have to be hauled around town in company trucks. And the people who like having their groceries delivered—well-off urbanites—often live in historic old neighborhoods with limited parking and cramped houses. That's precisely *why* they don't want to schlep their own groceries home, but it makes life hellish for deliverymen.

Then there's the sheer amount of labor involved. Every order has to be individually assembled, packed, and hauled out to the truck.

Within a year of its launch in early 1996, HomeRuns was handling several hundred orders a week and was running just to keep up. In the days when most groceries were delivered, that figure would have seemed bush league. The original Sobey's grocery store in Stellarton, Nova Scotia, delivered 400 orders a *day* on a typical Saturday in the 1920s and 1930s. The clerks would be up until midnight the night before packing orders. A driver from the horse and buggy days recalled that *he'd* be out until midnight the next night, trundling though rain and slush with his overloaded cart. "I've seen me leave at ten at night with the wagon so full of groceries I'd have the molasses and oil cans tied to the axles," he recalled years later.

### Why we won't eat off our computers

The problem so far with the dot-com grocery model is that it brings an e-grocer right back to those days of midnight packing and overloaded wagons—the days of labor-intensive retailing—in an era where retailers are doing everything they can to get the customer to do as much of the work as possible.

And, just like the general store customers who were initially suspicious of the contents of sealed tins and boxes, many of us are reluctant to trust someone else to pick out our meat and bananas. Books are one thing—Tom Clancy's latest blockbuster looks and reads exactly the same, whether you buy it a corner bookstore or from Amazon.com. And a bad book will rarely give you a stomachache or ruin a dinner party.

Many of those e-grocers who started with such big ideas in the 1990s are now just vague memories. HomeRuns folded in July 2001, just a few weeks after another cybergrocer called Webvan shut its doors.

Not all e-grocers have turned up their toes. Grocery Gateway, a Toronto-area e-tailer founded in 1999, continues to soldier on even though it has struggled to make a profit. Its recently announced partnership with Sobeys may help the cause.

Online grocery shopping has a somewhat brighter future outside car-crazy North America. In the U.K., Tesco was filling 70,000 orders a week by the time it won an e-commerce award in 2001. The Tesco enterprise has a few significant differences from the Webvan and HomeRuns models, however.

First, it is based around actual grocery stores. Employees simply take a cart around the store and fill the shopper's order, a model that HomeRuns abandoned early in its history. It's a bit less efficient than a warehouse model, but it also requires much less capital outlay. After all, the stores are already there—you don't have to build and stock a warehouse. Second, this strategy spreads the risk around. The online grocery part of the business doesn't have to sink or swim on its own merits right away—the bricks and mortar store can support it for a while. Finally, many British cities are compact enough to make delivery economical.

The dot-com crash that killed many other e-commerce companies is one of the reasons for many North American e-grocers' demise. But there are a few others that relate specifically to the grocery industry.

In his 2002 book *Being the Shopper*, retail analyst Phil Lempert says the mistakes e-grocers made included focusing on high-profit items that people actually enjoy buying in person, such as meat and prepared foods, instead of mundane items they hate shopping for, such as toilet paper and detergent. And even when sites did zero in on the most logical products, the range of those products was often too small, with not enough brands and sizes represented to save the shopper a trip to a physical store.

Lempert has hopes that virtual grocery stores will eventually succeed, when the technology has progressed to the point that a trip to a Web site offers much of the variety and interest that a trip to a real store does. The problem at the minute is that online grocery shopping is too mechanical. The shopper makes a list, clicks on the relevant items, and leaves. There are no impulse buys based on an appetizing display or an in-store tasting. If some retailer can figure out how to make the smell of freshly baked cookies or damp cilantro waft from your monitor, as you "walk" the virtual aisles, the company may just have it made.

If you think that idea's revolutionary, Lempert has other suggestions up his sleeve. What about interconnected household devices that would not only tell you the ingredients of the dish you're watching someone eat in a sitcom or make on a cooking show, but would also check out your fridge, let you know what ingredients you're missing, then place an order with a home delivery grocer who will bring that stuff to your door? Some machine will even alert you when it's time to go into the kitchen and start cooking.

It all sounds fun and very Jetsons, but I can't help but think of the hapless British grocery chain that came up with a cool-sounding technological idea in the late 1990s: sell customers a home version of a grocery checkout scanning device, which they could use at home when ordering food from the Internet. When they ran out of something, all they would need to do would be to scan the product's bar code with the device and—presto!—the details would be sent to the on-line grocery store.

There was only one slight problem. The scanner had to be plugged into a serial port. Most people at the time had only one serial port on their computers, and their dial-up modems were plugged into it. It's hard to transmit sales information to a store's Web site when your modem is unplugged.

# 8 Department Stores: The Original One-Stop Shops

*I could trust my own taste, but—because of Bloomingdale's—I don't have to.*
                          —Liz Smith, "Store, spa or subculture? Trust Bloomie's,"
                                                    *Vogue*, August 1976

There's been a bit of doom and gloom in the last few years about the fate of the department store. No one wants to buy everything under one roof anymore, cry the naysayers. They point to the collapse of venerable stores such as the Canadian Eaton's chain as proof that department stores are passé. The future, according to these pundits, lies in the big-box stores ringing every North American suburb.

It's true that most people no longer think of a department store first when they're looking for an armchair, a stereo, or a garden rake. But anyone who believes that the traditional department store is as doomed as the dinosaur hasn't been to downtown Chicago lately.

Admittedly, North Michigan Avenue—"the Magnificent Mile"—is lined with giant specialty stores devoted to just one commodity, whether it be lingerie (Victoria's Secret), athletic shoes (Niketown), or over-hyped toys (the Disney Store).

But a few miles away on State Street, a department store founded almost 150 years ago still sells a huge variety of goods: leather sofa beds, Waterford crystal, designer suits, British videos, and Frango chocolates are all available in elegant galleries beneath a central Tiffany dome.

Marshall Field and Company, which can trace its roots to 1854, became a retail power almost in spite of itself. The company's cofounder, Marshall Field, had envisioned the firm as a wholesaler with a small retail sideline. However, the store's selection of the latest Paris fashions soon drew the wives of the growing city's movers and shakers. And a store manager named Harry Gordon Selfridge came up with endless tricks for keeping those shoppers happy and entertained.

Selfridge invented the bargain basement, set up shoeshine and optometry services, and devised so many other schemes that his colleagues nicknamed him "mile-a-minute Harry." By 1891, the store's tearoom alone was serving 1,500 diners a day. Whether Field had planned it or not, he had a runaway retail success on his hands.

If he was going to run a shop, Field reasoned, it should be a classy establishment that served his customers' every need. According to company legend, Field once heard a manager arguing with a customer. When he asked the manager what was the matter, he replied, "I am settling a complaint."

"No, you're not," Fields supposedly shot back. "Give the lady what she wants!"

### Pre-history: The world before Macy's

That phrase pretty much sums up the ethos of the founders of most modern department stores. The emporiums were designed to give a largely female clientele access to all the material goods women could ever need or want. In fact William Whiteley, a department store pioneer in Britain, modestly styled himself as the "Universal Provider."

While the idea of shopping for a variety of goods under one huge, permanent roof seems natural to modern shoppers, their medieval counterparts would have found the concept utterly foreign. Many European countries were home to powerful guilds that controlled who made and sold what, keeping most stores small and specialized. The mercers, those stores that sold both groceries and fabrics, were the closest medieval shoppers came to a store with any sort of variety.

Guilds weren't the only factors restraining retailers from opening larger, more diversified stores. Until the 1700s—and, indeed, well beyond—only a relatively small group of wealthy people could afford to buy many manufactured goods. Everyone else made their own items, bartered for inexpensive products, or did without. Even the rich rarely paid cash on the barrel; credit was the order of the day. As a result, merchants charged high markups, and turnover was low. Most shopkeepers couldn't afford to maintain a large stock, since the goods might sit on the shelves for months or even years.

Prices varied depending on the mood and desperation of the vendor and shopper; few goods had marked prices, so everyone bargained. It's likely that most people found shopping in these conditions a trial.

Quaker leader George Fox was one of the first to complain about the absence of set prices in English stores. Bargaining encouraged lying and wasted a lot of time, Fox asserted. In 1653, he urged any of his followers who kept a store to mark one price on each item and to charge that price to all customers. The idea made customers uneasy at first. Why wouldn't these Quaker shopkeepers bargain, like everyone else? Was this a trick? However, some shoppers came to see that fixed prices meant "they might sende any childe & be as well used as yᵐselves att any of these shopps." The idea didn't catch on outside the Quaker community, however, and many Quakers themselves eventually abandoned it.

### Ye olde customer is always right

One of the next consumer advocates to step up to the plate was writer Daniel Defoe, in 1723. In *The Complete English Tradesman*, he reprinted with some sympathy a letter from a fabric merchant complaining about what we would today call browsers or window-shoppers. Here is just part of the aggrieved merchant's lament.

> There are many young ladies, and, what is worse, many old ladies, within the bills of mortality, that every Saturday, while their houses are cleaning, take a fancy to have business with me, for no other reason in the world but because they cannot tell how else to dispose of themselves . . . They swim into my shop by shoals, not with the least intention to buy, but only to hear my silks rustle, and fill up their own leisure by putting me into full employment. So they tumble over my goods, and deafen me with a round of questions; till, having found nothing in my shop to their fancy, as they call it, they toss themselves again into their coaches, and

drive on the persecution, to the terror and disturbance of most of the honest shopkeepers from one end of the town to the other.

Even I feel a bit sorry for the guy, and I'm sure any modern jewelry store clerk would be even more sympathetic. Selling engagement rings during the week before Christmas is probably the job they give sinning merchants in Hell.

Nonetheless, Defoe urged his readers to be patient with everyone who came into their stores. "A tradesman behind his counter must have no flesh and blood about him; no passions, no resentment; he must never be angry; no not so much as seem to be so," Defoe counseled. "The case is plain; it is his business to get money; to sell and please: and if some do give him trouble, and do not buy, others make him amends, and do buy: and even those who do not buy at one time, may at another."

It was sage advice, but English shopkeepers weren't quite ready for this big slice of humble pie. It would be another couple of centuries before most would stop looking down their noses at recreational shoppers.

But other signs of change were abroad in the land. At least one eighteenth-century shopkeeper made an effort to overcome the traditional limits on the stock he could carry and the way he could charge for it. In 1750, a Mr. Palmer opened a haberdashery on London Bridge. Open from 8 A.M. until 10 P.M., it offered a relatively wide selection of products at set prices, conveniently arranged in departments. Customers liked it, but other merchants hated Palmer's efforts to compete with multiple types of stores. The store eventually closed, and merchants would ignore Palmer's idea of selling many types of goods under one roof for the better part of a century. The set price idea, however, continued to percolate through the system. In the late 1700s, china maker Josiah Wedgwood used fixed prices in his London store.

In the early nineteenth century, other cracks began showing in the specialty shop system. And as the Industrial Revolution took hold in Britain and other countries, several trends changed retailing forever.

### The more mobile shopper

As I mentioned in the fairs chapter, factories were producing enormous quantities of everything from hairpins to fabric. It simply wasn't practical for them to sell small quantities to thousands of minuscule shops. The new working class slaving away in those factories—unlike their parents, who were likely farmers or poorly paid laborers—suddenly had a little cash to spend. Just as importantly for retailers, a new middle class of factory owners and other entrepreneurs arose. Not only did they have more money than their employees, they were eager to buy goods that would give them an aura of stability and class.

Department stores flourished in tandem with rising levels of prosperity. In France, for instance, the economy grew faster in the middle decades of the 1800s than in any other period between 1815 and 1914.

Cities were also growing at an incredible rate, bringing more and more people within reach of the quintessentially urban institution of the department store. Between 1800 and 1850, the population of Paris grew from 547,000 people to just over 1 million. In the next two decades, it soared to 1.6 million. The story was much the same in many cities on the other side of the Atlantic. Toronto's population, for instance, doubled between 1860 and 1870.

Another development that dramatically changed retailing was the emergence of new forms of mass urban transport, particularly trains and omnibuses. They allowed stores to draw customers from an entire city or region, rather than just their immediate neighborhood. In nineteenth-century New York City, for example, the Sixth Avenue elevated train ran right by Macy's door, and the transit service added extra trains to serve the store during rush hour. In Paris, several stores boomed after Baron Georges Haussmann redesigned the city's street plan between 1853 and 1870, replacing twisty medieval alleys with wide boulevards. These new streets made it much easier for large vehicles to move between the city's quarters, leading to the development of citywide services such as the Compagnie Générale des Omnibus, formed in 1855.

Intercity railroads were also a boon for department stores. Not only did they make it cheaper for manufacturers to ship large quantities of merchandise, they also made it easier for rural residents to come to the big city for a day of elegant shopping. In Toronto, Timothy Eaton of Eaton's department store tried to entice these retail tourists by placing the following announcement in its 1886–87 catalog:

Ladies, you come off the train, you are covered with dust, be-grimed with smoke, you feel unrefreshed, you don't wish to beg anyone to allow you to make your toilet in their rooms without paying them for it, you possibly have a long day's shopping before you, probably you have a number of parcels, you are getting disgusted. Listen! Get off your train, take a Yonge or a Queen Street car, as it may be, and bring your parcels with you straight to Eaton's. Why? During the early part of September our new store will be opened. In the south west corner of the ground floor will be an office expressly for you.

Timothy Eaton and his employees certainly knew how to appeal to the Victorian traveler. The announcement added that visitors could also check their coats for free, make a phone call, send a telegram, and use the washrooms at the store. The icing on the cake came four years later, when a free bus service connected the train station and the steamer dock to Eaton's front door.

Heck, if a downtown store provided all this *now*, I'd shop there.

Even the availability of electricity contributed to the rise of depart-ment stores. Without electricity, shoppers would have been wandering in half-lit gloom in the middle of these vast establishments, and hauling themselves up multiple staircases instead of letting escalators and eleva-tors do the work.

### Dry goods to whet your whistle

Among the first retailers to capitalize on these facts were "drapers" or "dry goods merchants"—people selling fabrics and other items used to make clothing, curtains, and upholstery. (The term "dry goods" origi-nally referred to items the shopkeeper didn't have to pour or weigh.) Many of the firms that would evolve into major department stores, including Macy's, John Lewis, and Eaton's, began life as dry goods shops.

Pointless arguments have been waged to determine the identity of the world's first department store. Some people point to A.T. Stewart's emporium in New York, while others award the title to a Paris store called the Petit Dunkerque or to one of several British shops. All were founded in major cities in the 1830s or 1840s, charged fixed prices, and sold a variety of goods beyond the usual fabrics and notions. Most of them permitted customers to bring back unsatisfactory goods for a refund. (This idea wasn't entirely new; as far back as 1771, the forward-thinking Josiah Wedgwood had allowed shoppers to return goods "if they do not find them agreeable to their wishes.") And the fact that these stores allowed browsing was vital to their success.

Before browsing was widely permitted, a shopper knew the retailer expected her to buy the moment she crossed the threshold. So the first task was to inspect the merchandise, but that wasn't simple. Just about everything was kept in glass cases or behind the counter. As soon as milady expressed interest in a particular bolt of cloth, the sales patter would begin. She would hear how exceptional this fabric was, how unlike anything else offered for sale anywhere it was, what a good price the merchant had been able to secure. But if she failed to be persuaded, she would have to ask the retailer to bring down another bolt, and another, until the clerk was annoyed and the shopper was frustrated. This sort of escapade was the very thing that spurred cranky merchants to pour out their sorrows to Daniel Defoe.

Comparison shopping in such an atmosphere was all but impossible. If the shopper decided not to buy immediately but to come back later, she was guaranteed a chilly reception on her second visit. If she did decide to buy, a long process began. The merchant would state an outrageous price. The customer would counter with an equally outrageous offer. Back and forth it would go, for half the day if the parties had the stamina. As a result of these customs, a startling number of customers must have returned home with water-damaged fabric, hideous hats, and gloves that didn't fit.

### No credit where credit is due

This type of selling was possible in a small shop with few customers. But in the 1840s and 1850s, many dry goods stores simply became too large to allow such labor-intensive, one-on-one service to continue. Most probably allowed browsing out of sheer necessity, rather than any larger strategy. Luckily for them, the system was a roaring success.

In another crucial development, these newfangled dry goods stores insisted that customers pay cash. This strategy allowed them to keep prices lower than traditional prices in an effort to increase turnover. An 1852 ad for one of R.H. Macy's early stores—a small establishment in Haverhill, Massachusetts, that was just a foretaste of the emporium he would eventually run in New York—emphasizes the advantages of cash sales and fixed prices for both customer and store:

1. We buy exclusively *FOR CASH!!!*
2. We sell exclusively *FOR CASH.*
3. We have but one price, and that is named first! No deviation except for imperfection!

These are the three great principles upon which we base our business. Buying *exclusively* for cash, we keep our stock in constant motion and are having new goods from New York, Philadelphia and Boston *every day*. It also enables us to procure many of our goods under the market price, and our customers have the advantage of these bargains for this reason, viz:—selling exclusively for cash, we have no bad debts on our books, consequently our good customers do not have to pay them in the shape of extra profits.

In *The Department Store: A Social History*, author Bill Lancaster argues that cash sales finally extracted drapers from their medieval roots and brought them into the modern world. Writing about the wonderfully named Emerson Muschamp Bainbridge, a British draper who established a cash-only policy, Lancaster remarked, "This cash nexus at once liberated and democratised his shop . . . Bainbridge had discovered the retailers' philosophers' stone that was to prove to be as profound as steam power to industry."

However, none of these early stores was really a department store yet, in our modern sense of that term. They remained rooted in dry goods and stayed relatively small.

### The Louvre—no, the other one

It wasn't until the 1850s and 1860s that true department stores emerged almost simultaneously on both sides of the Atlantic: Marshall Field's in Chicago, Macy's and Lord & Taylor in New York, Eaton's in Toronto, Whiteley's in London, and a Parisian store called the Louvre.

Interestingly, both Whiteley's and the Louvre were inspired by major expositions. William Whiteley, a draper's apprentice from the north of England, visited the Great Exposition in London in 1851. The glittering displays and eager crowds galvanized him, although it took him more than ten years to save the funds he needed to open his store in the emerging London neighborhood of Westbourne Grove.

The Louvre, meanwhile, was founded in 1855 as a small retail component of a hotel built to serve the crowds flocking to Paris for a major exhibition that year. The shop eventually succeeded to such a degree that it took over the entire space originally allocated to the hotel.

But the granddaddy of nineteenth-century department stores was the Bon Marché of Paris, founded as a small Left Bank shop sometime before 1852. The store developed such a stranglehold on the French imagination that Emile Zola would even use it as the basis for an 1883 novel, *Au bonheur des dames.*

### Shopping as fantasy

Like his competitors, Bon Marché owner Aristide Boucicaut offered fixed prices, focused on rapid turnover, and permitted returns. However, he also understood that retailing was, in large part, theater. To sell to a mass audience, he needed to create an atmosphere that encouraged shoppers to dream. When the store moved into new, custom-built premises in 1870, it became the perfect stage for the fantasies of Paris's middle class.

"Selling consumption was a matter of seduction and showmanship, and in these Boucicaut excelled, enveloping his marketplace in an aura of fascination that turned buying into a special and irresistible occasion," wrote Michael Miller in his 1981 history of the store. "Dazzling and sensuous, the Bon Marché became a permanent fair, an institution, a fantasy world, a spectacle of extraordinary proportions, so that going to the store became an event and an adventure."

The interior of the store was a riot of glass, iron columns, and sweeping staircases. Jewel-toned Oriental rugs were draped over balconies, and ribbons and colorful umbrellas dangled from the ceiling. Shoppers overwhelmed by the sumptuous displays and endless bustle could relax in the reading room, art gallery, or restaurant.

Soon, Boucicaut was promoting the store as a famous attraction in its own right. He produced illustrated cards depicting the Bon Marché as the most famous landmark in Paris, a beehive of activity towering over the lesser buildings surrounding it. In 1872, the store began offering daily tours of the premises.

Boucicaut went even further in his attempts to develop an aura of drama around his massive store. Realizing that his middle-class customers wanted to be seen as respectable and cultured, he launched a series of concerts in 1873. Outdoor performances were held on summer Saturday evenings in a square outside the store, while up to 7,000 people jammed the sales halls inside the store for more formal winter events. Other after-hours activities at the store included fencing classes and English lessons.

The hoopla worked. By the end of the century, the Bon Marché led the pack among Paris's department stores in terms of sales, number of customers, and number of employees.

Retailers in other countries took note of Boucicaut's success but were largely cautious about imitating his innovations. American dry-goods merchants, for instance, imported the showy architectural ideas but were reluctant to expand into new lines of goods, such as toys and stationery. British retailers continued to resist the idea of a store where shoppers could wander aimlessly without buying a thing. They nicknamed such browsers "tabbies" and ejected them without ceremony.

But things were soon to change on both sides of the Atlantic. Stores would mushroom into grand emporia and the customer would become the undisputed queen. And waiting at the queen's feet would be an increasingly large army of clerks.

### May I help you?

Until the rise of the department store, most retail establishments were small enough to be staffed by a shopkeeper, his family, and a couple of apprentices. But department stores eventually needed thousands of people to keep them running. In many cases, these people lived in store dormitories, ate in company cafeterias, and generally let the supposedly benevolent storeowner watch out for their welfare. Since many of these owners were severe and sober conservatives, there were all kinds of rules about nights off, dating, and curfews.

Shoppers might be served by men or women in a nineteenth-century department store, depending which shops they frequented. Some stores showed a marked preference for clerks from one sex or the other. In New York, Macy's had a long-standing preference for female employees, even promoting a number of them to management. Over at rival A.T. Stewart's Marble Palace, however, most of the clerks were men. According to a journalist of the time, Stewart had a policy of hiring handsome young men because shoppers liked to flirt with them.

These clerks were just one part of a vast chain of staff. There were also cashiers who handled the money for the whole store. They were usually squirreled away somewhere relatively inaccessible, like the basement, to reduce the risk of theft.

To shuttle money back and forth between the sales counters and the cashier, stores employed small armies of pages. At Macy's, they were called cash girls, and in the 1870s they made up a third of the store's payroll. "Girls" was no misnomer—many of them started working at Macy's when they were 12 or even younger.

When a customer made a purchase, the sales clerk would write the items in a sales book, add up the amounts, put the customer's money into the book, and yell "Cash! Cash!" Immediately, one of the cash girls assigned to the department would dash over to the desk with a basket. If she sauntered rather than dashed, she'd likely catch the eye of the "floor-walker"—the department manager—and be taken to task for her laziness.

Into the basket went the customer's purchase, along with the sales book and the money. The cash girl would hurry with her basket to that department's cashier. While the cashier checked the sales clerk's math in the sales book, stamped it, and made change, the parcel clerk wrapped the customer's purchase and wrote the contents of the package on the wrapper. This list was the only receipt the customer would get.

If the package was to be delivered, the cash girl would have to make a side trip to the delivery department before hustling back to the sales counter, where the customer was cooling her heels while waiting for her change.

I have a sneaking suspicion that all of these girls were very fit.

When the store closed for the night, the cash girl's work was not quite done. She still needed to dust the counters and sweep the floors of her department. And when it was finally time to go home, she had to submit to a thorough and not particularly polite body search, to make sure she hadn't lifted any cash or merchandise.

For all this work, most cash girls earned $1.50 a week, with a silver dollar and a box of candy at Christmas, and a summer picnic on Staten Island. Being a Macy's page was the original McJob.

Not all stores hired girls for this task. Field and Leiter's in Chicago, which would later become Marshall Field, had cash boys. These young employees earned $2 for a six-day week around the same time that most of their female Macy's counterparts were earning $1.50.

Field and Leiter's was the shop where Chicago's rising moneyed class liked to do business. In 1879, the store opened a new building and began a concerted effort to paint itself as an upscale establishment. A uniformed greeter held the door open as ladies alighted from their carriages, and customers were referred to respectfully as "madam" or "sir." It simply wouldn't do, in such an atmosphere, to have clerks bellowing "Cash!" constantly all day. Instead, the store had all the cash boys sit on a central bench under the watch of a cash boy supervisor. When a clerk wanted a particular cash boy, his number would flash on a board set up near the desk. The boys were instructed to dress and act like "little gentlemen." According to a saying at the time, "When you get a cash boy's job at Field and Leiter's, you start shining your shoes every day."

### Movin' on up to deluxe shopping in the sky

As department stores got larger and larger, gobbling up entire city blocks and rising multiple stories in the air, managers had to come up with some way to keep people and money moving around these vast expanses.

Aside from coliseums, cathedrals, and factories, there weren't many buildings of similar size they could use as models. In sports stadiums and cathedrals, most of the people using the building were relatively stationary while they were there. In factories, people sometimes needed to move around, but the building was usually only one or two stories high. And office managers, for instance, usually didn't care much if their employees had to hike up a whole bunch of stairs to get to work. What did they want for nothing? They had a job, didn't they?

In a department store, on the other hand, frequent, directed movement was crucial. If people couldn't see across a good chunk of the store, they'd never bother wandering over to the other side. And if there wasn't an easy way for them to get up to the fifth or eighth or tenth floor, they wouldn't go there. If it took more time to buy something and get the change than it did to select the item in the first place, they wouldn't bother coming into the store at all. As a result of all these factors, department stores became *the* place to go to see the latest architectural innovations and technological marvels.

A.T. Stewart's Marble Palace in New York opened in 1848 on Broadway at Chambers Street, with a 200-foot frontage on City Hall Park. It was impressive, but Stewart's Cast Iron Palace, which he opened in 1862, would change department store design around the world. The six-story building, bounded by Ninth and Tenth streets, Broadway and Fourth Avenue, was supported inside with a series of iron columns rather than walls. These gave shoppers an uninterrupted view of huge areas of the store.

Now that customers could see across one floor, the next trick was to convince them to go up. Women loaded down with shopping weren't keen about climbing stairs, especially since they were hobbled by their clothes. If it wasn't heavy crinolines, it was cumbersome hoops. And if it wasn't hoops, it was a bustle, a train, a hobble skirt, or some other contrivance that may have looked pretty but wasn't particularly practical. I've climbed stairs in a crinoline—I used to do community theater— and believe me, it isn't fun. If crinolines were still around, women's gyms would go out of business. We'd all have legs like marathon runners without setting foot on a treadmill.

To overcome this inevitable drawback of large, multistory shops, department stores looked for inventions that could make shopping less of an athletic event. As a result, Britain's first elevator and first escalator were both installed in department stores, following the example of their American counterparts.

The elevator, added to Wylie and Lockhead's Glasgow department store in 1855, appealed to "[p]arties who are old, fat, feeble, short winded, or simply lazy, or who desire a bit of fun," according to a contemporary report in the *Glasgow Herald*.

Forty-three years later, Harrods in London installed the country's first escalator. There weren't any stairs on it. It was just a conveyor belt, so thrill-seeking passengers who dared to get on the thing had to hang onto the handrails for dear life.

Since a new escalator had attracted fascinated crowds when it was unveiled at Bloomingdale's in New York earlier that year, Harrods' management took precautions: clerks had complimentary cognac and smelling salts on hand to revive overwhelmed passengers. But by all reports, most visitors came through the experience with the fabled British stiff upper lip.

It would be a while, however, before shoppers on both sides of the Atlantic totally overcame their fear of "sky carriages" (Bloomingdale's term for elevators) and moving staircases. A 1901 ad for the New York branch of the Siegel Cooper department store made a point of reassuring readers that its escalator provided "an easy and perfectly safe method of ascension to the Second Floor."

### Extra amenities for the shopping palace

As the idea of shopping for pleasure caught on, department store owners began to realize that they needed more than good prices, varied stock, and spacious, well-equipped stores to attract increasingly sophisticated and choosy shoppers in a competitive market. This realization ushered in a golden age of store services—golden for the customer, that is. For the retailer, these increasingly imaginative offerings were a strain on the budget.

Retailers' amenities were modest at first. In their ads, stores promoted such things as good lighting, wide staircases, and efficient ventilation. But by the 1880s, the race was on to develop unique perks. Soon, shoppers could avail themselves of writing rooms equipped with stationery and pens, and reading rooms with the day's newspapers; telegraph offices, post offices, and public telephones; lost and found departments; and package and coat checks. Department stores were no longer simply places to buy things. They had become luxuriously appointed, all-purpose service centers.

Of course, the more freebies the merchants added, the more the public demanded. Darned customers, always wanting stuff.

Free delivery was a popular service, and it could be surprisingly extensive; by the 1890s, several Manhattan stores prepaid the postage on all deliveries within a 100-mile radius of their establishments, provided the value of the purchase was at least $5. Most also had their own delivery fleets. By the late 1890s, Macy's was delivering 2.5 million packages a year.

Astonishingly, Macy's also guaranteed that any purchase made in its store on December 24 would be delivered *that day* to any Manhattan location. There will be many a Christmas Eve when I'll think fondly of the Macy's of yesteryear.

At the height of the competitive rivalry among New York department stores, customers of some stores received gifts ranging from spools of thread to theater tickets. Inevitably, prices rose to cover these "free" perks (just as they would in American grocery stores in the 1950s, when competitive retailers tried the same kinds of tricks).

The mania for new products and services continued unabated into the early years of the twentieth century. Macy's opened a Japanese tea room in 1904 and began selling "merchandise bonds" (gift certificates) for harried Christmas shoppers around the same time. In 1908, the store launched its first fashion shows, for the spring and fall collections, using the relatively new gimmick of live models for the first time.

However, not all the ideas flew. People were constantly approaching Macy's to set up services such as a manicure parlor, a hairdressing shop, or a dentist's office. One enterprising fellow, Professor Astro, approached the store in 1910 to propose an in-store astrology service. (Sadly, he too was rejected, although you'd think he could have predicted that.) And Macy's attempts to set up "pick-up booths" in railway stations, where commuters could place orders in the morning and pick them up that evening, were unprofitable and eventually discontinued.

In general, American stores were much more aggressive about setting up these perks than were their counterparts in Britain. But in 1909, the complacent merchants of Knightsbridge got a very sudden awakening, when Harry Selfridge decided to start his own store far from his mentor in Chicago.

### Harry spots a window of opportunity

Selfridge had spent more than 20 years with Marshall Field but yearned to run his own show. He left his longtime employer in 1904, and several years later announced plans for an enormous store on Oxford Street in London.

The shop would have all the bells and whistles of Marshall Field's State Street store and more, including a library, a bank, a post office, a first-aid room, several restrooms, an "airiel garden," and a railway ticket office. One of the main things that struck fear into the hearts of London's merchants, however, was Selfridge's fondness for elaborate window displays.

Chicago's stores had long been at the forefront of this new art. L. Frank Baum, who would later write *The Wizard of Oz*, was one of the city's leading window designers. In 1897, he even launched a magazine devoted to window dressing. Selfridge admired Baum's work and hired Baum's equal, Arthur Fraser, to design the windows of Marshall Field.

Like most department store visionaries, Fraser had a sense of theater. Store windows in many cities were customarily curtained on Sundays, to avoid offending churchgoers. Fraser used the opportunity to change his window displays, which he would reveal with a great flourish several days later. Unlike window displays in other cities, including London, Fraser's displays were spare and artful. No jumble of products tagged with huge price stickers here. He often picked a theme or signature color for each series of windows, which looked like stage sets from the street.

Chicago's window dressing techniques were soon the rage across America and in Continental Europe. As Macy's historian Ralph M. Hower points out, New York's store windows became a major cultural touchstone for the torrent of visitors arriving in the city via Ellis Island. Store windows—and the accompanying ads—showed immigrants how Americans dressed and lived. They raised hopes and stoked desires.

Despite their effectiveness in North America, however, elaborate window displays had failed to catch on among British retailers. More than anything else about Selfridge's new London shop, it was the thought of the professionally designed windows that filled shoppers with anticipation and competitors with dread.

When the store threw open its doors in March 1909, Harry marked the event by hiring an army trumpeter to blast a fanfare from the front entrance. Crowds, attracted by a massive newspaper advertising campaign, watched from Oxford Street as a flag in "Selfridge Green" was unfurled. Then they thronged the store to explore the 130 departments. Everyone received a souvenir calendar and notebook to mark the day.

Selfridge brought a number of other ideas to London besides hoopla and elegant store windows. His was the first department store in London to coordinate everything from the carpeting to the delivery vans, giving the place a unified look. He installed a soda fountain and London's first bargain basement.

Of course, he made a few gaffes. When he proudly displayed cosmetics on the ground floor, hoping the pretty colors and fine scents would lure customers through the door, he misread the British shopper badly. Although he would ultimately be proved right—I defy you to name a modern department store that doesn't hit you with a wave of Estée Lauder the moment you walk through the main doors—he hadn't reckoned with the fact that English women of the time were uncomfortable about buying makeup.

But perhaps his most significant contribution to London's retail scene was the fact that he had built a store shamelessly designed to please the middle class. If the aristocracy wanted to come, they were certainly welcome. But Selfridge's was designed specifically to lure the young schoolteacher, the insurance clerk's wife, and the doctor's daughter—the very people who could afford to shop at Harrods but didn't really feel comfortable there. This could have been another miscalculation on Selfridge's part, but it wasn't. He succeeded spectacularly, and the store—along with Harrods—is a London tourist fixture to this day.

### Getting the word out

When Selfridge opened his store, he supported it from the beginning with substantial advertising. Advertising was another key to the rise of the department store. By the 1850s, the large retailers in Paris were already making extensive use of newspaper ads, usually promoting the arrival of a new lot of goods for sale.

During the stock market turmoil of 1873, when many stores collapsed due to insufficient cash flow, R.H. Macy was able to scoop up all kinds of bargains for his New York emporium, because he was able to pay cash on delivery. One of his ads in the *New York Tribune* boldly proclaimed that the store was buying stock ". . . *for a Mere Song*. It will pay you to go to Macy & Co. *Every Day—Twice a Day—Three Times a Day.*"

But there were many more tools an ambitious department store owner could use—and did—to make his store stand out from the crowd.

During the same stock market panic that inspired Macy to buy up stock, Timothy Eaton used a much cheaper but still but successful technique to lure in shoppers to his four-year-old department store: he tipped streetcar conductors to cry cheerily "All out for T. Eaton's store!" at the corner of Queen and Yonge streets.

Publicity stunts at other stores were many and varied. Macy's imported two French "horseless carriages" in 1895, which garnered attention whether they were parked in front of the store or jaunting about town. In another promotion, Macy's built a cycling track on the third floor of its 14th Street store, where experts in the new fad of bicycling performed tricks.

Seasonal sales made their way into the American department store arsenal in the late 1800s as a way of smoothing out cash flow. In 1890, both Macy's and Wanamaker's launched August sales to entice customers into their stores in one of the year's slowest periods.

Retailers duly commemorated anniversaries, news happenings, and special events. In 1892, Macy's hawked a large collection of Italian filigree silver to mark the 400th anniversary of Columbus's discovery of America. During the Spanish-American War at the end of the decade, the store promoted china emblazoned with images of the battleship *Maine* and Admiral Dewey, and unfurled what was billed as the largest American flag in existence.

From London to Chicago, upwardly mobile shoppers knew the place to go to keep up with the latest trends—the department store. In those pre-radio, pre-TV, pre-Internet days, few institutions had a better grip on the middle-class zeitgeist than the big shops did.

### When good promotions go bad: Next on Fox!

After World War I, department stores were no longer the new kids on the block. They'd staked out their markets and built their stores. After the war, they would rarely be the focus of the intense interest and excitement that had marked their early years. But that doesn't mean the stores stayed still, and for the most part it was up to the stores' beleaguered floorwalkers to control the chaos when a marketing stunt worked only too well.

As late as the 1930s, floorwalkers at Eaton's still wore the traditional uniform of morning coats adorned with white boutonnieres. It conveyed a certain air of authority, which they often needed. During the Depression, Eaton's daily clearance sales in January and February attracted crowds of cost-conscious shoppers. Unfortunately, when the doors opened each morning, the shoppers were often trampled by equally desperate owners of small stores, who came to scoop up deep-discount merchandise for resale in their own establishments.

During one of these stampedes, in Winnipeg, a pushy shopkeeper fell and cracked his head against an iron store fixture. James Bryant, who spent four decades in Canada's department store industry, recalled in his 1977 memoir what happened when the man skidded to an unconscious halt at a floorwalker's feet:

> The floorwalker must have descended from a long line of English butlers. Unperturbed by the sudden appearance of an injured man out cold, he casually commandeered the nearest elevator, dragged the injured man by his feet into it, and whisked him up and away.

Also during the Depression, Eaton's came up with a massively successful way to draw children to its store—and, hopefully, inspire them to become lifelong Eaton's customers. What better way to entice young Canadian boys than by selling discount hockey sticks? During the store's "Birthday Sale," any boy under 12 could buy a hockey stick for 10 cents—a 75-cent value. Not surprisingly, the crowds were immense.

Eaton's wanted the boys' custom, but they weren't necessarily thrilled about the idea of hordes of kids running through the store on a busy Saturday afternoon. So in the Winnipeg store, managers roped off the line and herded the kids up a central escalator. "From there children were elevated to the fifth floor, much as wheat is taken up to be poured into prairie elevator bins," wrote Bryant with envious admiration—he was working for a competing department store at the time.

At the top of the escalator, each boy was allowed to buy one stick emblazoned with the slogan "Eaton's the Store for Young Canada" before being shunted back onto another escalator, out another door, and onto the street.

Years later, Bryant tried to repeat the success of this promotion while working at a Simpson's store in Nova Scotia. Eagerly, he launched "Young Halifax Day." In an attempt to appeal to both boys and girls, he decided to sell bags of cut-rate goldfish rather than hockey sticks.

Unfortunately, he hadn't accounted for the fact that fish are harder to control than sports equipment. As soon as the first bag broke and a desperate goldfish began flopping about on the floor, panicked kids tried to help and dropped their own bags. Soon, it was chaos. Children screamed as porters swept up their new pets with mops. Every floor in the building was soon soaked.

In despair, Bryant called a halt to the operation. It took days to locate all the expired fish.

### Bloomingdale's: Good enough for the Queen, good enough to lure you downtown

One of the key aspects of post–World War II society in North America was the flight of the middle class to the suburbs. Levittowns offered veterans and their young families a new house, a big yard, and a driveway for every Studebaker. Suddenly, every urban household was not within easy reach of a streetcar or subway line. Reluctantly, department stores followed their customers out to the far reaches of the city.

The trend had started a couple of decades before the war. In June 1928, Sears, Roebuck opened its first suburban store in the U.S. in Aurora, Illinois, outside Chicago. These early stores were freestanding, but in the 1950s department stores would find their natural suburban homes within another new phenomenon: the enclosed shopping mall.

Early on, mall owners realized that two department stores under one roof would draw many more customers than just one. (It took a few years for them to work out a formula for just how much better they would draw: two department stores would draw four times the customers a single one would attract; three would lure *nine times* the crowd.) The competition to attract these "anchor" stores to these suburban locations was intense.

But the downtown flagship stores retained some of their allure. Sure, you could get just about all the retailer's merchandise in your local, suburban branch. But you couldn't get that downtown buzz. And few stores managed to create as glamorous an aura for themselves as Bloomingdale's flagship store in Manhattan.

Bloomingdale's was a fairly late entrant in the New York department store market. When it opened in 1872, Macy's, Gimbels, and Lord & Taylor were already well established. But the little dry goods store would go on to be more than their match. Due to a combination of strong management and effective merchandising, it would grow to occupy that same hallowed position that Harrods would in the minds of Londoners.

So great was Bloomie's mystique that *Time* did a cover story on the store in December 1975. The following July, the Queen dropped in for a visit during her bicentennial tour of the United States, and the next month, *Vogue* ran two articles about the store's history and allure. The author of one of the stories, Jill Robinson, described her first visit to the store in the early 1960s as something akin to a religious experience.

> The escalator was like the Monorail in Disneyland—it sailed over all these rides. Bloomingdale's is not so much divided into departments as into wish-fulfillment realms where you can pick up the accouterments that transmogrify life into lifestyle.
>
> If you get the right stuff around you, the attitude will catch up. You will feel freewheeling, entertaining, independent, adventurous, and liberated in a kind of stalky, striding-from-the-hip way. In this way, Bloomie's is a triumph of merchandising over matter—for you can often find the same things other places, but it gives a subliminal promise of achievement-oriented, savvy youthfulness that sparks the acquisitive fires.

### Twilight of the true one-stop shop

Not everyone was equally enthralled with Bloomingdale's. Bryant, the Canadian department store executive who had started his career in the 1930s, saw increasingly fashion-oriented department stores like Bloomie's as traitors to their roots.

"Such sacred department store merchandising principles as all departments under one roof, basic stocks, and service based on knowledgeable department store managers have been all but discarded by some historic stores," he wrote with the sadness of someone who is seeing a world he helped create pass away. On a visit to Bloomingdale's in 1973, Bryant was appalled to find that the only type of coat hanger in stock was a fancy, satin-wrapped one designed to be given as a gift.

The 1975 *Time* article did nothing to restore his opinion of the great Bloomie's. Bryant learned that Bloomingdale's had dropped all sorts of lines that were once the cornerstones of the department store business, including cameras, razors, washers, and dryers. Soon, he observed, the store would be nothing but a collection of specialty shops. The days when a department store could claim to be "the Universal Provider" were drawing to a close.

Bryant's memoir is a treat to read. His self-mocking humor and genuine affection for the department store industry shine through on every page. So it seems cruel to point out that the Bloomie's managers were right.

Today, Bloomingdale's soldiers profitably on, despite the fact that it no longer sells many of the goods it did a hundred years ago. It's still such a cultural icon that when the writers of *Friends* wanted to give slim, fashionable Rachel Green her dream job, they made her a buyer for Bloomie's. Meanwhile, the Simpson's chain that Bryant served for most of his career is gone, subsumed under the mantle of its old rival the Bay.

No one ever said the business world was kind.

# 9   Fashion Victims

*The fantastical folly of our nation (even from the courtier to the carter) is such that no form of apparel liketh us longer than the first garment is in the wearing, if it continue so long, and be not laid aside to receive some other trinket newly devised by the fickle-headed tailors . . .*
—William Harrison, *A Description of England*, 1587

*Do not read beauty magazines. They will only make you feel ugly.*
—Mary Schmich, *Chicago Tribune*, June 1, 1997

My friend Stephanie and I join the clot of chatting women milling around in front of the entrance to Holt Renfrew. There's a buzz of anticipation in the air—after all, Holt's has actually *closed early* in order to prepare for tonight's event, called "Girls' Night In." Drawn in by newspaper advertisements promising a fun evening where we can buy the newest perfumes and beauty products, we've shelled out C$25 a ticket for the privilege of being schmoozed.

I'm here completely for research. Really. Ask anyone who knows me and they'll tell you that I'm the least fashion-conscious person they know. I work at home, so my daily ensemble consists of a rotating selection of jeans, shorts, T-shirts, and sweaters. I have precisely three suits, which I wear when I teach or go to conferences. And as for makeup, I refused to wear lipstick even for my wedding pictures, horrifying the photographer who obviously thought I was going to sue her for malpractice once I had recovered from temporary bridal insanity.

But I still love clothes and am intrigued by makeup, although I know next to nothing about either. So I'm here tonight for a baptism into the rites of highbrow consumption.

Holt Renfrew—or Holt's, as it is generally known—is an upscale fashion and cosmetics department store. It's Canada's answer to Barney's and Harvey Nichols. The Ottawa branch, which we're visiting tonight, is home to the city's only Tiffany counter.

At 6 P.M. the doors open and the excited crowd surges toward the entrance. A bevy of clerks, all in black, hands Stephanie and me oversize shopping bags as we struggle into the store. Almost immediately, we're confronted by three choices: a coat check, a long line of manicurists, and a barkeeper installed behind a jewelry counter, doling out free martinis.

We stash the coats quickly and head for the booze.

Trolling the aisles with our pink martinis in hand ("girls," apparently, only drink fruity drinks—the other choices were bottled strawberry daiquiris and vodka coolers), we stumble on a table stacked with pita chips, bread sticks, salmon dip, and olive and sun-dried-tomato antipasto. The drinks and the food have been carefully planned to appeal to an audience of career women, who are digging in enthusiastically, even though it feels somewhat illegal to be noshing in the middle of a store.

Intriguingly, the most enthusiastic nibbler is a man with the tangled gray hair and dusty, threadbare coat that show he spends more time on the street than in the hallowed confines of a luxury department store. An acquaintance of Stephanie's confirms this when we bump into her.

She nods toward him. "He's the Walker," she says, explaining that he walks the streets of her downtown neighborhood every day. But, she adds, she never expected to see him here.

The management of Holt Renfrew probably didn't either. But he apparently paid his fee and thus must be admitted. Those are the rules of the shopping game, and I find them strangely comforting. Because, despite the suit I've dug out of the closet for the occasion, I'm almost as much a fish out of water as the Walker.

I'm astounded by the prices. Gift sets of perfume and lotion for C$150. Nylon Prada handbags, which look to my untrained eye like something I'd wear around my waist on a hike, for upwards of C$400.

I'm just too cheap, I realize, for this sort of indulgence. Or perhaps, to be more precise, I simply have other vices.

It is awfully fun, though, to be fawned over, courted, and spritzed with perfume. The air is thick with the mingled scents of Jean-Paul Gaultier and Coco Chanel. Stephanie mentions that she liked a scent strip for the new Gucci perfume in a recent *Vanity Fair* and wouldn't mind trying a tester.

On our way to the Gucci counter we're waylaid by multiple distractions. First it's a display of Spanx footless panty hose. "I've heard about these!" Stephanie exclaims, filling me in on the basic story of the inventor, who described her product on an American talk show and vaulted to instant success.

We check out the packages, and I learn yet again that I really am cheap. "Thirty-six dollars for a pair of nylons!" I howl. "They'd better not run."

"But they don't have feet, so they wouldn't run as much," Stephanie explains.

We continue to hack our way through crowds of women chattering as they submit to free makeup applications or allow hairstylists to fit them with complex-looking rats. A song by Pink wails over the crowd from enormous speakers in the handbag department: "I'm coming out, so you'd better get this party started . . ."

We pass the Clinique counter and I wax enthusiastic about the benefits of Cool Moisture body lotion. We consider some shampoos and discuss the merits of various manufacturers.

Finally, we wash up on the shores of the Gucci counter, where Stephanie tries out the new scent. It's a bit heavy at first, so she decides to leave it for a few minutes to see how it matures.

The stairs to the second level are open and we meander up there. It's much quieter than the carnival downstairs, and we're happily rooting through racks of clothes—as I exclaim that I would *never* pay C$200 for a pair of *jeans*—when a clerk informs us in a strained voice that the upstairs is closed. She herds us and a few other renegades toward the elevators. Once inside, a 50-ish woman in an elegant pantsuit chuckles and we all join in. Fashion criminals, that's what we are.

Back downstairs, the noise and the crowds (and, perhaps, the pink martinis) start to addle my brain. Sure, C$78 is outrageous for a bottle of perfume. But all these other women are buying. And heck, I deserve it.

Then a sales clerk reminds me that I get the C$25 I spent on the ticket back as a refund if I buy something worth more than C$75. Well, OK then! I'm saving money!

(Discounts are a classic way to tempt shoppers into spending more than they intended. In fact, at least one shopping researcher has floated the notion that we don't shop mainly to get things; we shop for the thrill of spending wisely.)

Stephanie and I fall into the radar of a clerk who wants to tempt us into the world of Jean-Paul Gaultier perfumes. She avidly squirts us with various blends, raising our hands to her nose for a hearty sniff like a wine connoisseur at VinExpo. She pronounces a floral blend delightful on me, while preferring a spicy blend on Stephanie, assuring us that she has a good feel for customers' personalities and what would suit them. Even though we'd just told her that I prefer florals and Stephanie likes spicier scents, we feel absurdly flattered. She *knows* us! She wants to come up with a solution *tailored just for us*!

In the end though, we don't plump for the Jean-Paul Gaultier scents, even though the bottles are hilarious, Barbie-esque glass torsos. Perfume bottles are perhaps the most extreme form of image manufacturing in the retail world—and that's saying something. Stunningly photographed and displayed on six-foot lit billboards throughout the cosmetics department, they are objects of glamour and desire. More than once, I have to remind myself that these elegant little works of art are nothing more than containers for scented water.

It's no surprise that the bottles and marketing are becoming ever more elaborate. In 1983, major manufacturers launched just 38 new "fine perfumes." In 2002, that number had soared to more than 520. The big houses are trying everything they can to make their scents stand out from the pack.

Finally, I bump into another clerk, this one pushing an Alexander McQueen fragrance called Kingdom. She explains that it has just come out this month, and asks if I've bought it yet.

I've been wearing the same perfume—a French brand I first bought on a school trip—since I was 17. I don't exactly keep up on scent trends. I shake my head.

She spritzes a bit onto my wrist. It's unusual and different. And the bottle! A rounded silver wedge, the two straight sides made of ruby-red glass. It's like a post-modern, luxurious apple.

Wow, with a bottle like that on my cluttered dresser, I might almost feel . . . sophisticated.

Besides, the perfume smells really nice.

Then, the clerk explains, everyone who buys a bottle tonight gets a free purse-size bottle as a gift.

Well! Free gifts (the great redundant expression of our time), plus a rebate of my C$25 admission fee. *And* the chance to feel part of this noisy, excited carnival! *And* the chance to pamper myself! I probably work just as hard as all these other shoppers. I've been slaving up to 14 hours a day on the very book you hold in your hands, because my deadline is looming. I deserve a treat. Right?

Now a Bloodhound Gang song is blaring from the speakers: "You and me baby ain't nothin' but mammals, so let's do it like they do on the Discovery Channel . . ." Around us, the chatter and the laughter are rising to a fever pitch.

In a bit of a haze—the martinis and the perfume are really getting to me—I wander over to the perfume counter and plunk down my credit card.

Two hours after we went in, we stumble out onto Queen Street and take a deep breath of damp, unscented spring air.

**Playtime for grown women**

My addled perfume-shopping experience, while heightened by the carnival atmosphere of Girls' Night In, was far from atypical. In a 1992 study, academic researchers studied women at perfume counters, many of whom were buying gifts for themselves. Over one-third of the women they interviewed had not picked a brand before they came into the store—the excitement of trying on different scents was part of the reason for the whole shopping experience. Getting there really is half the fun, it appears, for perfume shoppers.

For that reason, many shoppers viewed the salesperson as a friend or an enemy, depending on whether the salesperson played along and let them enjoy trying on different things, or relentlessly tried to make them focus on one product.

To identify shoppers who are there to play as much as to buy, the researchers advised retailers to train their staff to ask shoppers *why* they came to the store today, rather than *what* they wanted to buy. People who responded that they wanted a little treat for themselves would get more opportunity to sample and experience different scents.

Since all of the eager shoppers who came to Girls' Night In had paid C$25 specifically for the opportunity to sample all the latest brands, Holt Renfrew managers knew we were all there, at least in part, to play. We couldn't possibly have a lot of predetermined notions about scents and makeup shades that had just come on the market. Hence, the herds of happy spritzers—and the parade of dazzled women toting home bags of merchandise.

## When girls shop

Shopping with friends is as much about playing, sharing information, and honing one's hunting-and-gathering skills as it is about buying anything. Just look at the way Stephanie and I wandered through Holt Renfrew. We didn't ask the clerks much, but we traded with each other information gleaned from all sorts of other sources: magazines, talk shows, office gossip. If we'd been allowed up on the clothing floor, in no time we'd have been trying things on and letting each other know that yellow made us look jaundiced and capri pants made our legs look big. (Capri pants make everyone's legs look big, by the way. I don't care what they say in *Vogue*.)

Paco Underhill, the retail analyst, backs me up on my sense that shopping works well as a cooperative endeavor. Women shopping with other women buy more than women shopping alone, he has found in his studies. "Two women in a store can be a shopping machine, and wise retailers do whatever they can to encourage this behavior," he writes in *Why We Buy*. He goes on:

> Women can go into a kind of reverie when they shop—they become absorbed in the ritual of seeking and comparing, of imagining and envisioning merchandise in use. They then coolly tally up the pros and cons of this purchase over that, and once they've found what they want at the proper price, they buy it.

## You really can judge a man by his toga

But when it comes to fashion, what exactly do we buy, and why?

If I knew the complete answer to that, I'd be living in the Cayman Islands for tax reasons. But here's part of the answer: once we've covered the basic needs (warmth and, for all of us except Christina Aguilera and Pamela Anderson, modesty), we buy fashion and cosmetics for four main reasons: to feel good, to show off, to fit in, and to have fun.

It's not exactly a thesis that's going to shake the fashion world to its core, but it does have its basis in history. Much of it starts, as so many things do, with the Romans.

In the Roman Empire, people knew how to decipher a toga the same way some women today can distinguish a real Chanel purse from a clever copy. Only people in the upper classes wore togas in the first place, and different trims meant different things. A white toga with a broad purple border meant the man was a member of the senatorial order; a similar toga with a narrow purple border was the badge of someone in the equestrian order.

A major fashion faux pas among the Romans was excess. Just as women today are advised to get dressed, accessorize, and then remove one piece of jewelry before heading out the door, so the sober young Roman man was advised not to put on too much of a show. A purple *border* was OK. An entirely purple toga was cause to call the fashion police.

Martial, a poet who lived in the first century A.D., once wrote about a young man who felt his former tutor didn't take him seriously. The young man grumbled, "If I put on Tyrian clothes or grease down my hair, you exclaim: 'Your father never did that.'" Tyrian clothes were completely purple silk garments colored with a dye from the rich merchant city of Tyre. (If you'll recall, Tyre was so rich that God threatened to burn it down for its sins.) To Romans, Tyrian clothes were the equivalent of a leather jacket—a sign that the person wearing them was a luxury-loving, thrill-seeking hedonist. This young man even greased back his hair, long before Brylcreem made ducktails fashionable.

Of course, all these complicated style rules fell by the wayside along with the Western Roman Empire. The Visigoths, who crashed into Rome in A.D. 408, were the trailer trash of the ancient world. Soon everyone, male or female, was pretty much making do with one brown tunic, unless he happened to be a king or a bishop. Fashion wasn't a high priority when there wasn't anything to eat.

A few changes in clothing happened anyway, of course. Men realized that trousers, first worn by the conquerors, were more practical than togas. Women's tunics got longer and fuller until they eventually became skirts. Knights on crusade encountered silk in the Middle East and suddenly suspected that rough knitted wool was *so* last year.

As Europe slowly started rebuilding a market economy from the ashes of the Dark Ages, rudimentary markets and fairs sprang up again. But people still weren't much interested in ostentatious clothes. From what few accounts survive, the turning of the millennium was a major restraint on fashion developments, since there was a widespread belief that the world would end on December 31, 999 (or December 31, 1000, for the numerical purists). There's not much sense in investing in a classic black tunic when you don't think you're going to get at least a few good years' wear out of it.

When the millennium turned without major catastrophe, people were in a better frame of mind to think about more frivolous things. As always when humans have extra time and resources, they started looking for ways to differentiate themselves from their neighbors. One way to do this was by making conspicuous use of lots of fabric. Suddenly, sleeves became longer, and skirts and tunics even fuller. When the horizontal loom made it to Europe in the eleventh century, followed by the spinning wheel two centuries later, fabric production and consumption expanded. Fashion was on the rise.

By the fourteenth century, the Italian poet Petrarch was urging his brother to "[r]ecollect the time when we wore white habits, on which the least spot, or a plait ill-placed, would have been a subject of grief, and when our shoes were so tight, that we suffered martyrdom."

### Clothes make the Elizabethan

By the time Queen Elizabeth I ascended to the English throne in 1558, the idea that clothes shaped perceptions was well entrenched in Europe. A character in *Every Man Out of His Humour* by Ben Jonson noted, "To be an accomplished gentleman . . . you must give o'er housekeeping in the country, and live altogether in the city amongst gallants: where, at your first appearance, t'were good you turn'd four or five hundred acres of your best land into two or three trunks of apparel."

Of course, there were those who were suspicious of such ostentatious display. William Harrison, the gent quoted at the beginning of this chapter, was one. Poet John Donne chimed in on the anti-ostentation side, when he wrote in "The Undertaking":

> But he who loveliness within
> Hath found, all outward loathes,
> For he who color loves, and skin,
> Loves but their oldest clothes.

Donne, as any trip to the local mall will tell you, lost this argument in a big way. Part of the problem was that people started moving to cities. In growing cities, where people may not know who your grandfather was, how prosperous you are, or where exactly you fit in the social spectrum, you need to show them. In situations like that, he who has the best hat wins.

### Hear ye, hear ye! I have nice stuff and I'm important, too

Big cities have for centuries been the source of the most fashionable gear. In 1770, a dressmaker in the English resort town of Bath wanted to make sure her upper-crust customers knew she had been keeping up with the trends in the capital, so she published the following ad in the *Bath Chronicle*:

> MRS. WILLIAMS, MANTUA AND SACK-MAKER, in Westgate-Street, Bath, begs Leave to inform those Ladies her Friends, and the Public in general, who may chuse to employ her for the approaching BIRTH-DAY of the QUEEN, that she is returned from London, where she has been (at the Request of her numerous Friends) entirely for the Fashions.

In Mrs. Williams's time, a number of fashionable celebrities emerged in London, partly due to a boom in the English newspaper industry. As literacy and wealth increased, and press censorship was eliminated, newspapers gained new readers avid for details about the latest London happenings. In our own celebrity-obsessed age, we take it for granted the people have always closely followed the doings of the rich and the beautiful, but it wasn't possible to do so easily until literacy rates and road conditions had improved to a point that people could both read newspapers and get them while they were relatively current. And, of course, people had to have the time and energy to spare for such amusement.

One of the style setters who took London by storm in the late 1700s was Georgiana, the Duchess of Devonshire. The vivacious, high-spending duchess was the subject of intense interest from the moment she married the duke on her seventeenth birthday in 1774. Almost immediately, she sparked a craze for ridiculously high coiffeurs. She and her hairdressers created three-foot pinnacles padded with horsehair and festooned with waxed fruit, stuffed birds, miniature ships or, on one memorable occasion, a diminutive rural scene complete with sheep and trees.

Within a decade, a perfumer on Fleet Street was using newspaper ads to promote his monopoly on the duchess's favorite French hair powder. By 1786, fashionable ladies had been reduced to bribing the duchess's seamstress to find out about the design of a particular new gown. Embarrassingly, several thought they each had an exclusive on the pattern— until they all showed up at the same engagement wearing the same dress. Don't you hate when that happens?

### From bespoke to off the rack

In Georgian England, patterns for gowns circulated in a variety of ways other than through bribery. A magazine called *La Belle Assemblée*, launched in 1806, published fashion plates that women throughout Britain brought to their dressmakers with eager hopes. French dressmakers shipped dolls dressed in their latest designs to various European capitals, where the gowns could be ordered or copied.

Until the middle of the Victorian era, shoppers rarely bought readymade clothes, aside from cloaks, coats, and underwear. Occasionally, a dressmaker might have one or two items on display that had not been accepted by the people who commissioned them, for one reason or another, but these were more like advertising posters than "off the rack" clothes.

Instead of buying clothes in a store, people knitted or wove their own materials, or bought fabrics from dry goods stores or itinerant peddlers. Then they either made their own clothes or hired others to do it for them.

This system had its advantages and its disadvantages. On the plus side, you would end up with a dress exactly tailored to fit you, and you could choose everything from the color and the fabric to the lace and the buttons. On the minus side, you had to track all this stuff down yourself or, again, hire a professional to do it for you. And forget about waking up the morning of some major social event and deciding to go out that afternoon to buy your outfit on a whim. Anything but the simplest clothes took a lot of time to make.

The fuss and bother of finding supplies and making decisions didn't always sit well with Jane Austen, who by all accounts usually enjoyed shopping. "I wish such things [as clothes] were to be bought ready-made," Austen once wrote dejectedly in a letter. "I want to have something suggested which will give me no trouble of thought or direction."

The move from do it yourself to off the rack didn't happen overnight. First, around the 1830s, stores began offering partially made dresses—one-size skirts to which a dressmaker could attach a bodice, or pieces of a bodice that could be altered and then attached to a custom-made skirt. Part of the reason for the bodices may have been the increasingly elaborate sleeves of gowns in the 1820s and 1830s, which were much harder to construct than the simple sleeves of the classically inspired Regency dresses that had preceded them.

Completely finished clothes first appeared in stores in the 1850s, their rise coinciding with the growth of department stores. They were a mass product for a mass market, and it would take several generations before they would become truly acceptable at all levels of society.

The idea caught on first among the working and middle classes, who were attracted by the price and the simplicity of "reach me down" clothing. Upper-class customers considered ready-made garments common. After all, what was the use of having money and breeding if one couldn't wear clothes that separated one from the hoi polloi? What if a duchess bought a ready-made dress only to find her children's governess or the curate's wife wearing the same article? Oh, the horrors! Indeed, until the early twentieth century, a woman who considered herself a "lady" wouldn't even wear machine-sewn lingerie, even if it was custom made.

## The prehistoric catwalk

It seems obvious to us today that clothes look better on a human being than they do on a wax dummy or a hanger. However, it wasn't immediately obvious to Victorians.

Like the debate about which establishment can rightfully be called the first department store, the dispute about who was the first person to come up with the bright idea of using live models is an ultimately pointless one. Two or three or ten people may have all hit on it at same time. But the consensus seems to be that the custom started in France, where it was popularized by Worth, and eventually made its way across the channel to England.

There's some evidence that the London drapers Swan & Edgar staged England's first "mannequin parade" (as fashion shows were then known) in 1869, although there is some contention about this. Another London store reputedly used live models in the 1890s. The idea didn't really take off, though, until the models at the Maison Lucile bared all—well, in a Victorian/Edwardian sense.

Until the late 1800s, the few stores that used live models were very careful to avoid any suggestion that they were titillating their customers or exploiting the "mannequins." Many chose the plainest girls they could find, and covered up the bare arms and low necklines of the gowns by requiring the models to wear black bodysuits. Lady Duff Gordon, known to turn-of-the-century London shoppers as the couturier "Lucile," thought the bodysuits were ridiculous. As she later recalled:

> I shall never forget being taken to see the models of a famous house in Paris and the positive shock I felt when I saw lovely evening dresses in pale shades being worn by girls whose arms and necks, in dingy black satin, emerged from the low-cut décolletés. I decided that nothing on earth would induce me to show such atrocities.

Lucile promptly went out and hired a crew of statuesque women—the Edwardians liked their females on the tall side—and let them parade around her salon wearing the dress as the customer herself would. For her fashion shows, she coordinated everything from the carpets to the models' jewelry. Her final coup was to give her designs evocative names. Simple descriptions like "the black velvet" just wouldn't cut it in the hyper-real atmosphere of one of Lucile's mannequin parades. So instead, customers were invited to consider gowns with names like "The Sighing Sounds of Lips Unsatisfied" and "The Meaning of Life is Clear." Yes, they sound over-the-top to our ears today. But the romantic souls of turn-of-the-century England ate this stuff up. Within a couple of years, the concept of mannequin parades had spread throughout Britain and reached America.

And in a footnote that brings to mind the marriages of David Bowie and Iman, and Harry Connick, Jr., and Jill Goodacre, most of Lucile's original models went on to marry millionaires.

**What to wear on death's door**

Fashion shows were one way to publicize style to a select group of people. But soon, mass-market magazines and newspapers brought the latest scoop to everyone. In the late 1800s and early 1900s, articles about the wardrobes of royals, actresses, and opera singers were *de rigueur.*

Women's magazines have long admonished us not to let down our guards for an instant (after all, if there are times when we don't bother trying to look perfect, that represents lost market share for the manufacturers of lipstick and silk shirts).

In the 1930s, *Vogue* featured an embroidered nightgown marketed to convalescents, who of course needed to look their best when well-wishers came to call. The nightgown even had a matching envelope purse designed to hold makeup, which *Vogue* described as a "very convenient little gadget to keep you beautiful in bed."

*Ah,* I can hear the fashion victims of FDR's America murmuring. *I had no idea I had to be on all the time. Oh well, it's off to the store for me, just in case I happen to come down with some debilitating but not contagious disease.* Conveniently, *Vogue* included the addresses of the stores mentioned in every article. They were all in New York, of course. Where else, really, would one go?

Women's magazines of the 1950s took a slightly different tack. By then, the emphasis had moved from glamour to domesticity, and readers were urged to make sure they looked presentable when hubby came home from his hard day selling insurance or designing tail-finned cars. Countless articles advised suburban women to take a few minutes in the late afternoon to change into a nice dress, brush their hair, and slick on some lipstick before mixing a good strong martini for Joe Breadwinner.

Then, of course, women's liberation came along, and domesticity was passé. The trend today is to focus on the latest, the coolest, and the most outrageous, preferably with as much hype as possible. Readers of 2003's "Spring Dictionary of Style" in Canada's *National Post*, for instance, were alerted to the fact that Deanne Cheuk was a name to write down on their to-buy lists. "The New York-based graphic artist is poised to unseat Julie Verhoeven as the fashion world's darling of the moment. She's now completing designs for a denim line for Levi's, in Japan." Other things we were prompted to keep our eyes out for included inspector overcoats, skinny gray jeans, custom perfumes, and anything in Kelly green. Until the next set of do's and don'ts, of course.

## Keeping the mobs away from the good stuff

Of course, with anyone and everyone reading this advice, today's fashionistas face the same problem their Victorian great-grandmothers did when ready-to-wear showed up: how to set themselves apart from the unwashed masses. A shoe you can find at the local mall has no cachet.

Designers realize this and have gone to amazing lengths to ensure that their richest, highest spending customers still feel that they have the inside edge. Like Wanamaker's department store in Philadelphia, which limited its fashion show premieres in the early 1900s to certain socialites, some designers skip stores entirely and sell their wares exclusively through trunk shows. They rent a flashy hotel suite, provide some trendy canapés and wine, and invite the glitterati for a sneak peek. Trunk shows started as a way to bring fashion to glamour girls outside L.A. and New York, but they've become an attraction in their own right. Lately, to keep that important fresh edge, designers have had to add a bit of a twist. So now, in New York, glamorous moms are getting invitations to trunk shows for . . . baby wear. It's never too early to start the little darlings on the road to conspicuous overconsumption, I say.

Stores, most of which are open to any schmo who cares to walk in, have to work even harder to develop that air of exclusivity that's vital to reeling in the big-spending fish. At Bloomingdale's in New York, small items like shoes and scarves are displayed like works of art in a museum in softly lit, glassed-in wall niches (known in the store design trade by the hilariously down-market moniker "cheese holes"). It's a tactic borrowed from the master, Tiffany, which has for years shrunk its large windows on Fifth Avenue into tiny spaces, the better to focus browsers' attention on the pieces within.

Bloomingdale's, like many other high-end department stores, also offers customers the services of a "personal shopper." These elegant women will trot around the store before you arrive, assembling custom outfits for your perusal. Even though store-based personal shoppers rarely charge the client a fee, the whole concept has a "Queen for a Day" feeling to it.

Some stores have managed to put themselves above the fray by simply limiting their customer list. The Parisian jewelry shop run by Joel Arthur Rosenthal, near the Ritz (but of course!), offers just a blank wall to passersby. Most people wouldn't know that the shop behind that wall makes baubles that have found their way, supposedly, into the jewel boxes of folks like the Rothschilds and Barbara Walters. To enter the hallowed precincts, you need a *lot* of dough or a personal introduction. Otherwise, it's off to Van Cleef & Arpels for you, poor soul.

The *sine qua non* of rarity, though, is probably the designer waiting list. Designers are wise enough not to flood the market with their latest gewgaw. It's all about supply and demand. Decrease the supply and you'll increase demand—particularly if you've stoked the fires first by getting fashion editors interested in your latest boot or suit.

And so long before the latest goody from Prada or Hermes or Chanel hits the street, those in the know have already rushed to the store to reserve one. In some cases, the reserving is more the point of the whole exercise than the having. As a fashion stylist who routinely puts her name on the waiting list at Prada once told the *Globe and Mail*, "You wouldn't believe how many people come up to me and say that they've seen my name down. Part of the thrill is voyeurism, seeing who is going to get what."

And the item in question doesn't even have to be new. Probably the best example is the classic Kelly bag, an ordinary looking (to me) little purse that has had a particular luster since Grace Kelly was shown with one on the cover of *Life* magazine in 1956. It was even a focal point of the plot of a recent novel-turned-movie, *Le Divorce*. Want to capture some of that ice princess glamour for yourself? Just step right up, put your name on a list, wait a year, and then cough up something like C$16,000.

Some people really will spend the price of a small car on a purse. Designers are marketing geniuses.

Then again, while marketers can lead us to water, only we can make ourselves drink. When it comes to fashion, most of us, to some degree at least, want to be seduced. We want to believe that that dress, that shoe, that bag will make us a better person. So did the people of Gilded Age New York in the 1870s, as James McCabe, Jr., observed:

> In no other city of the land is there to be seen such magnificent dressing on the part of the ladies as in New York. The amount of money and time expended here on dress is amazing. There are two objects in view in all this—the best dressed woman at a ball or party is not only sure to outshine her sisters there present, but is certain to have the satisfaction next day of seeing her magnificence celebrated in some of the city journals. Her vanity and love of distinction are both gratified in this way, and such a triumph is held to be worth any expense.

Or as Mark Twain is reputed to have put it more bluntly: "Clothes make the man. Naked people have little or no influence in society."

### Embarrassing old clothes and dowager scents

I once asked my friend Brenda, a clothing designer, what fashion was *for*. "Why can't we all just wear whatever flatters us?" I muttered.

It's all about fun, she explained patiently. (We've known each other since we were 14, so she's used to me asking questions whose answers seem patently obvious to the rest of the world.) *Fun* is the reason that designers come up with insane creations of feathers and chain mail to parade down the catwalks of Milan and New York. And *fun* must be the reason that the actresses of *Sex and the City* often sport outfits that I'm sure will make them howl, "Did I actually *wear that*?" a decade or two from now. (Catch an old rerun of the *Mary Tyler Moore Show* and you'll see what I mean.)

The problem with fashion shopping, of course, is that beauty really is in the eye of the beholder. And if you're more worried about what other beholders have to say about your choices than you are about your own satisfaction, you're bound to spend the next 50 years or so watching *What Not to Wear* and scanning *Glamour*'s "Fashion Don'ts" pages. I learned this to my chagrin about a month after my foray to the Girls' Night In event at Holt Renfrew.

I was sitting over Saturday breakfast, reading the Style section of the *Ottawa Citizen*, when a little column called "Counter Intelligence" caught my eye. "Back to the drawing board, Alex," the headline read.

Uneasily, I scanned the short article. It seems four unnamed women had tested Kingdom, the Alexander McQueen perfume I'd so happily purchased at Holt's and had been enjoying ever since. In fact, I was wearing some that very morning. However, the testers had "judged it 'dowagerish,' 'old-lady,' 'fusty' and 'like something Mary Kay would wear.'" The unbylined author of the column concluded that the fragrance was "a little too over the top."

"Old lady? Fusty!" I wailed to my husband, who seemed unperturbed by these revelations about my new perfume.

"But don't you like it?" Paul asked, utterly puzzled.

"Yeah." My voice was a bit mutinous.

"So what does it matter what the *Citizen* thinks?"

He was partly right, of course. In a logical, black-and-white, hermetically sealed world, he would have been absolutely right. I was wearing the perfume, I liked it, and it made me feel pretty. By all accounts, that made it a successful purchase . . . in the private realm. But in just about all shopping decisions, particularly anything to do with fashion, the buyer is not the only person in the change room or at the cash desk. The phantoms of coworkers, neighbors, family members, and friends are all there with us. (That must be why the cubicles always feel so small.) Yes, we're buying things for ourselves. But we're also buying them to impress others. If we weren't, we'd be more likely to wander around in shapeless sack dresses and sensible shoes.

So even though I loved the perfume, and still do, a little of its allure evaporated for me that day. That's what fashion retailers, in the end, depend on—the endless cycle of infatuation, disenchantment, and renewed hope that we will eventually find the one product everyone will love that will make us feel absolutely fabulous. Like Mr. McQueen, we all keep going back to the drawing board.

# 10 Born to Shop: From Bridal Showers to Christmas Stockings

*I write down all the numbers and look around with a sigh of satisfaction. Why on earth have I never registered before? Shopping without spending any money!*

*You know, I should have got married a long time ago.*

—Heroine Becky Bloomwood fills out a bridal registry form at Crate and Barrel, *Shopaholic Ties the Knot*, 2003

Years ago, my husband and I were invited to a large wedding for a buddy of his he hadn't seen since high school. We were pleased and flattered to be included, but we didn't have a clue what to buy. We wanted to avoid looking either stingy or extravagant, and we didn't know what they already owned. In the end, we settled on a nice crystal vase, which we brought to the wedding itself because we were coming from out of town.

At the reception, our position in the gift hierarchy became vividly clear, because the master of ceremonies announced each gift and its giver over a loudspeaker system. As we blushed with embarrassment, our vase was announced . . . smack dab between two much more extravagant gifts (a television and a dishwasher, if I remember correctly).

At first, I was mortified. I felt as though we had huge flashing signs above our heads, blinking "Cheapskate! Cheapskate!"

But in the car on the way home, we reviewed the situation. First, the gifts had ranged all over the economic spectrum, from vases and blenders to major appliances. Second, many of the larger gifts had come from close family members, while the smaller presents had come from work colleagues and more distant friends. In the end, we swallowed our initial mortification and reassured ourselves that, even if our gift had not been as expensive as some, it was suitable to our place on the gift-giver continuum. It was all right, and we hadn't failed.

Academic David Cheal points out that there must be some reason, aside from the merchandise itself, that we persist in giving wedding gifts. After all, these days, many brides and grooms have already lived on their own (or with each other) for a number of years, so they no longer need the traditional blankets and toasters.

And if money alone was the issue, Cheal argues, wouldn't it make sense to do away with both the lavish wedding ceremony and the ritual of giving gifts (two expenditures that, in many cases, virtually cancel each other out), and instead pool resources so that the couple could put a down payment on a house and furnish it the way they want? The deluge of gifts provided to a couple getting married is about much more than simply obligation and greed.

## The gift that keeps getting given

Before exploring how and why we give wedding gifts, it's worth asking how and why we give other kinds of gifts. In ancient and traditional societies, gifts are given as a way of reinforcing social relationships and redistributing wealth.

Gift giving in Western societies can trace part of its roots back to Renaissance courts, where exchanges of luxurious clothing and other gifts were common. Once a middle class developed, it looked to the aristocracy for models of how to act, and began trading presents on its own.

Since we now interact in other ways—through companies and schools, for instance—and since we have more formal systems for exchanging money and value, why do we still give gifts?

When FTD urges us to "Say it with flowers," it isn't just an empty invitation. Gifts are also a form of nonverbal communication—a way to tell someone how you feel about them without coming out and saying it. And because gifts are nonverbal, they expose the giver to less risk, because they're not explicit. For dating couples who aren't sure how each partner feels about the other, a silk tie or a gold necklace is a much less stressful way to say "I care" than actually saying, "I love you."

But because they're nonverbal, we get anxious because we're afraid the gift won't say what we mean. In a 1995 study, one gift giver told researchers, "I felt that I hadn't given him enough to express my love for him." That ambiguity leads to the popularity of greeting cards, which express emotions more explicitly but still don't make the gift giver say them out loud.

And the emotion you want to communicate may not be the one your recipient wants to receive. Think about graduation gifts. Let's say Jennifer, the graduate in question, is a devil-may-care type who doesn't have a domestic bone in her body. Her dream gifts are things like camping equipment and inline skates.

But her conservative Great-Aunt Flossie thinks: "Ah, my flighty niece has her degree. She must finally be ready to settle down." To express her excitement at this thought, and her support for what she thinks Jennifer plans to do with her life, Flossie buys Jennifer a briefcase. She's genuinely glad for her niece, but Jennifer may misinterpret her gift as a not-so-subtle push to live a life she has no intention of living. Both Great-Aunt Flossie and Jennifer will be disappointed, even though both are happy about the graduation and wanted to share their joy with each other.

British academic Daniel Miller takes this idea one step further. As I mentioned in the introduction, he has written or coauthored several books riffing on the idea that even ordinary purchases are stand-ins for love. According to Miller, when we go to the grocery store and pick skim milk over whole milk, we're thinking about our family's health. When we save a few cents on hamburger, we're working carefully to preserve the family wealth. And when we actually pull out our wallet, we're sacrificing our family's hard-earned cash to the greater good—reinforcing the ties that bind.

No wonder, then, that for at least the last 150 years, gift shopping has been strongly associated with women. Gifts are seen as a way of expressing love and emotion, something that women have more leeway to do in Western cultures. Furthermore, during Victorian times, women were enlisted to "domesticate" various rowdy public holidays such as Christmas, replacing street parties and parades with family dinners and sing-alongs around the Christmas tree.

As the wife was supposed to be the heart of the home, she also became the heart of the gift-buying process. One 1990 study showed that women give more Christmas presents, start shopping earlier, and spend more time picking out each gift than men do. I also picked out that infamous crystal vase, which brings us back to weddings.

## Wedding wish lists

If you've ever been invited to a wedding, you can probably sympathize with the nervousness, embarrassment, and ultimate resolution of our gift-buying experience. Because gifts are more than objects—because we use them as ways to build and maintain relationships—there are always going to be a fair share of neurosis built into them. "There is social risk associated with gift giving," point out gift-giving researchers Mary Ann McGrath and Basil Englis. "Giving inappropriate gifts can damage, or even sever, our social ties."

There's a scene in the movie *My Big Fat Greek Wedding* where the parents of the bride and groom meet for the first time, at a party at the home of the bride's exuberant Greek family. The groom's WASP parents bring a Bundt cake, that stalwart symbol of 1950s suburban respectability. The bride's mother feigns delight, yet comments to a family member that the groom's family must be misers—they brought a cake with a hole in it.

The process of picking wedding gifts, if not pre-wedding cakes, has been made much easier by wedding registries. Christophle's, a silver shop in France, claims credit for inventing the wedding registry. Like most such claims, it's a hard one to substantiate. But it's fairly simple to see why wedding registries are popular. At least with a list, you have less chance of bumbling into an etiquette disaster.

Wherever it came from, the concept has certainly taken off. One 1992 study showed that the combined registry run by Dayton's, Hudson's, and Marshall Field had 62,000 registrants and generated $110 million in annual sales.

Feeding our neuroses is big business.

But the idea of telling people what you want to receive still makes some folks very, very uncomfortable. If you ask for it, is it still a gift, wonder the requesters? If you buy something mechanically from a list, wonder the givers, are you still being imaginative and showing your love for and knowledge of the couple?

In one recent U.S. study, between 11 and 16 percent of respondents from across the age spectrum disliked wedding registries, found them useless, or thought they were improper. "The appropriateness of a particular gift is socially constructed and emerges from the intersubjective or shared understanding between giver and recipient," concluded the researchers who conducted the study.

Here, in normal English, is what they meant: if you're going to a wedding, you'd better make sure you know the customs and expectations of the bride and groom before you head off to the store.

The researchers went on to study a group of college students who discussed their own feelings about buying presents. They also interviewed a parent and a grandparent (or someone from a parent or grandparent's generation). Roughly a third of the students and parents found the process "an arduous task." Interestingly, only 18 percent of the grandparents did, a result the researchers partly attribute to grandparents' preference for giving money.

When gifts are given rather than money, they often carry a lot of emotional baggage. Many look ahead to the hoped-for domestic bliss of the couple. That's where all those espresso makers and fondue sets come in. But others look back, trying to bind the couple to tradition and the past—think of linens from the family's traditional homeland or silver dishes for religious celebrations.

Similarly, our angst at buying a gift is tied up in our angst about the event in general. We want the gift to be perfect in the same way we want the marriage to last forever—even though we know that many marriages end in divorce.

Once you start thinking about all this stuff, buying china suddenly seems like a much more complicated experience than debating the merits of a sugar bowl over a soup tureen.

## A world of weddings

A 2001 newspaper story highlighted the problem and added a cross-cultural twist. The father of a Korean-Canadian bride was appalled that his daughter had registered at The Bay. He thought she was trolling for

gifts, which particularly offended him because money is a more traditional gift than objects at a Korean wedding. In the end, it was a tempest
in a teapot, as 95 percent of the guests brought money anyway.

Customs and traditions vary between cultures and change over time,
presenting fertile ground for etiquette advisors. Another 2001 article in a
Canadian newspaper is a case in point. Written for readers in increasingly
multicultural Montreal, it tried to guide shoppers through a potential
minefield of gift-giving faux pas.

In dizzying detail, the article described what to bring—and what not
to bring—to various weddings, complete with price figures. Gold jewelry
or money won't go astray at an East Indian wedding (count on C$100 to
C$150; if it's cash, bring an uneven amount as even numbers may be
considered unlucky). Household items in the same price range will get
an enthusiastic reception at a West Indian affair. Don't even think about
bringing gifts to a Portuguese wedding unless you're a close family
member; bring about C$300 in cash. But if the couple has a British Isles
background, they may be offended by something as "crass" as a check.
And on and on the article went.

No wonder we're putty in the hands of gift shop clerks.

### Sharing the swag

Sometimes, the bride and groom might feel a little abashed about receiving all this largesse. Many compensate, if only slightly, by buying exquisite
gifts for their attendants. In May 1933, *Vogue* advised its readers that
gold sports bracelets and money clips—"all for less than sixty dollars"—
were "knock-out" gifts for ushers and bridesmaids.

I hope the attendants were suitably impressed. In that year, in the
depths of the Depression, the average wage in the U.S. was 43.5 cents an
hour. Someone working a 45-hour week would need to work three
weeks, before taxes, to afford just one of those knock-out presents.

It could be worse. In premodern Europe and in many other societies,
marriages were one of the major ways to transfer money and property
between families.

Both members of the couple might give each other gifts while court-
ing. These tokens showed the partners' commitment to each other, but
they could also be used as proof of a betrothal; in sixteenth-century

France, a Lyon washerwoman cited a young man for breach of promise because he had given her a silver ring and some cloth, "promising marriage," but failed to follow through.

Once a couple was engaged, the partners and their families would often exchange gifts ranging from foodstuffs and small animals to expensive jewels and land. When they married, friends and associates sometimes gave gifts. Monarchs might give jewels or large sums of money; peasants might provide pewter pots, flowers, or gloves.

### The wedding planner—or, more precisely, the consumption consultant

I had always thought wedding planners were an invention of the high-spending 1980s, but in New York City at least, they've been around since at least the 1930s. The same issue of *Vogue* that advised readers to buy $60 attendants' gifts also extolled the virtues of one Manhattan bridal consultant in a paragraph that's a masterpiece of manipulation:

> It's a pretty smart idea for the prospective bride to put herself in the hands of a trustworthy shopping expert. The Wedding Embassy, on East Fifty-Seventh Street, will help her plan the entire performance—censure her more musical-comedy ideas, but not spoil her fun. Tell this establishment (strictly confidentially) just how far Father is willing to go financially, and an elaborate budget which includes every known detail will be worked out. The Embassy will be a welcome buffer between the bride and the bridesmaids, in case the bride wants to go pictorial and the bridesmaids resent the costumes involved. In fact, the Embassy takes all the bumps out of the path to the altar.

Just about all the neuroses surrounding the modern bride's shopping decisions are encapsulated in this paragraph. There's the fear that her tastes aren't rarefied enough—too "musical-comedy" or "pictorial"—for such a momentous event. There's the fear that the wedding won't be splashy enough to impress her friends—or, worse, that the family will look cheap. That's why Father's budget is strictly confidential. Then there's the fear that by the time she's finished her mad orgy of consumption, none of her close friends will speak to her again—that's why she needs a "buffer" to protect them from her flights of fancy. The Wedding Embassy gives the happy bride *carte blanche* to spend to her heart's delight, knowing that she won't offend anyone's sensibilities or wallet.

But before the wedding even happens, happy couples and their friends and relatives have to pick their way through another shopping minefield: the shower.

### Showers without rain

A folk tale currently in vogue on a number of gift-related Web sites says the wedding shower tradition originated in the Netherlands in the early 1800s, when a young woman wanted to marry a poor miller. He was poor largely because he frequently helped other people in the community, extending them credit or giving them flour.

But the girl's father refused to support her choice with a dowry. The townspeople, wanting to see the young couple happy and to reward the miller for past kindnesses, held a party and gave them all they needed to set up a household.

Like most great stories about the origins of things, this one is probably about as truthful as a political press conference—especially since there are competing theories. Some sources trace the origin of the shower to the United States in the 1890s, where newspaper articles advised people holding parties for engaged women to fill an umbrella with gifts and then open it as a surprise, literally showering the bride-to-be. (This also strikes me as a bit dubious—how would you get the umbrella to stay closed if it was stuffed with gifts, and wouldn't there be a risk of concussing the young woman with a kettle or vase?)

Nevertheless, the story of the poor Dutch couple has likely spread because it feeds into so many of our deep convictions about gift giving on major occasions. It involves the community literally having a stake in the marital success of the couple, by "investing" in them at the point when they are in the most financial need.

The same applies to that other shower of gifts: the baby shower. Many cultures have long marked the arrival of a baby with gifts and celebration. In sixteenth-century France, for instance, a new mother would immediately receive gifts of food: things like cider and honey if she was poor, and more exotic treats such as wine and oranges if she was noble. Later, godparents might buy candles for the baptism or pay the midwife. Parents even gave gifts of gratitude to the larger community; a king might issue pardons, for instance, on the birth of his heir.

In a bizarre twist on the tradition, though, I recently read about the latest entry in the "celebrate the baby" pantheon: grandparent showers. It seems that today's hip, upscale grandma needs everything from a top-notch high chair to a designer-label receiving blanket for the times Junior comes over to visit. Retirees who thought their days of buying baby gifts for their friends were over are trooping back to the store once more.

But now it's time to move on to a more common gift orgy: Christmas.

### Gifts for Christmas? How gauche!

In the early 1800s, Christmas wasn't closely associated with presents. If people exchanged gifts at all, they were more likely to do so at New Year's. That tradition can be traced all the way back to *strenae*, Roman gifts that were originally nothing more than green tree boughs—supposedly plucked from a garden devoted to the goddess Strenia—exchanged between family and friends in deference to the goddess.

By the time the Roman Empire had spread across Europe, people had begun tying small presents to the tree boughs, such as sweets, jewelry, and lamps, designed to encourage the gods to bestow sweetness, wealth, or light on the recipient. Since people had been exchanging these gifts long before the Christian Christmas festival came to be tied to the end of the year, the presents were more closely associated with good wishes for the coming year than with any Christian significance.

The tradition long outlasted the Roman Empire. In Elizabethan England, for example, it was customary for lords to shower the queen with baubles such as jeweled fans on New Year's Day. By the 1700s, if not before, the custom had spread across the social scale, although humble people were more likely to give their loved ones cakes or fruit than excessive jewelry.

Christmas presents, if they were given at all, were most likely to be Christmas "boxes" given to servants, apprentices, and others further down the social ladder than oneself. (This is believed to be the origin of Boxing Day, celebrated in Britain and its former colonies; in Canada,

Boxing Day is marked by massive sales.) This English custom had spread to the U.S. by the 1700s—newsboys, in particular, were quite open about requesting the traditional Christmas tip from their customers. On both sides of the Atlantic, the holiday was associated more with roving bands of rowdies than with hearth and home.

The New Year's gift tradition also spread to North America, where growing industrial production and a burgeoning middle class meant that people could increasingly move beyond food gifts: one advertisement in a New York newspaper in 1770 exhorted readers to buy their loved ones gifts ranging from pocket pistols and dress swords to jewelry, silk stockings, and chess sets. From being simple exchanges of useful goods with a simple wish for good fortune, New Year's gifts were becoming an opportunity for ostentatious display of wealth and taste among nonaristocrats who could afford them.

The tradition of giving gifts at the end of the year was also becoming more closely associated with children. By 1784, a Philadelphia bookseller was already promoting children's books as suitable presents.

The New Year's Day custom continued in full force throughout the nineteenth century, with American women's magazines providing accounts of the lavish, refined presents exchanged among rich Parisians in the 1850s, for example. But by that date, Christmas had largely sucked all these competing traditions into its all-encompassing maw.

### Christmas *always* seemed better in the old days

Every year the questions start, sometime around late November. How did Christmas become so commercialized? Why can't Christmas be simple, the way it was when I was a kid? Why do we get so stressed out about gifts? When did it become all about the presents?

The short answer is that special holidays and rites of passage have always been at least partly about the presents. Along with the need to know why we're here, what makes the sky blue, and why the Toronto Maple Leafs haven't won the Stanley Cup since 1967, we all seem to be born—or bred—with an innate desire to give and receive gifts. It's how we show love, demonstrate power, and display our good taste. And it always has been.

It's just that, in the last 150 years or so, retailers have taken that desire and custom-tailored it to their own ends. When you think about some of our treasured Christmas customs, it's amazing how many of them can be traced back to retailers.

The Montgomery Ward department store created the story of Rudolph the Red-Nosed Reindeer for a store souvenir in 1939, and Macy's will forever be identified with Thanksgiving due to its massive New York parade, which serves as the starting gun for the whole Christmas season. Until its demise, Eaton's was linked inextricably in many Canadian children's minds with Toronto's Santa Claus Parade.

But it wasn't always this way. Until the mid-1800s, retailers actually wanted Christmas to be *shorter*. In the U.S., the Puritans and Quakers squelched a lot of holidays on the grounds that all that frivolity wasn't quite holy. And then their descendants, the advocates of the Protestant work ethic, argued that festivals were hindrances to profit, because they took people away from their work.

It was many years before this suspicion of holidays would truly disappear. Until the 1840s, many merchants worked at least a half-day on Christmas. Macy's considered New Year's Day a regular business day until 1882.

### Christmas season magically expands

The extension of the Christmas season started slowly. According to one contemporary account, New York confectionery and toy stores were gaily decorated for the holiday in 1832, drawing crowds of excited families, but most people did the bulk of their shopping on Christmas Eve. Bookstores, museums, and coffeehouses had horned in on the act by the late 1830s. Within a generation, the selection of merchandise elegantly displayed would become so wide and overwhelming that newspapers in New York and other large American cities started publishing gift shopping guides for their readers.

Until the eve of the Civil War, though, Christmas shopping in the U.S. seems to have lasted a week or so at best, but that meant that *everyone* was running out to the shops on Christmas Eve. By 1867, Macy's was staying open until midnight on December 24, doing its best day of business to that date. "Such a crowd as I never before saw in a store," marveled Abiel T. La Forge, who would become R.H. Macy's business partner several years later. From the 1860s through the later years of the Victorian era, it was common for Macy's to stay open until 10 P.M. or later during the two weeks before Christmas. When the doors finally closed for the night, some male clerks slept on the counters, still in their bluish-gray uniforms, resting their weary heads on bolts of cloth. Deliverymen slept in the stables.

Macy's was by no means alone in these late hours. In the 1870s, other New York stores such as Tiffany's also stayed open late into the evenings to accommodate the holiday crowds.

By the end of the century, the search for the perfect present was beginning in early December. On December 1, 1901, a large newspaper ad for the Hearn department store in New York City tried to whip shoppers into a consumptive frenzy that wouldn't seem out of place in the early twenty-first century: "To-day ushers in the month of Santa Claus! BUT THREE SHORT WEEKS to the greatest holiday of the year, when Everybody thinks of Somebody Else, and one's Good Will and Generosity are only bounded by the purse with which Fortune has endowed one." The following year, one retailers' trade publication advised retailers to launch their holiday promotions by November 1.

### Come see Christmas at the store!

Like the gradual lengthening of the Christmas season, store decorations became more elaborate in stages.

By the 1840s, a few enterprising American retailers were decorating their stores with pictures of a largely fabricated Christmas hero called by various names, including Kris Kringle and Saint Nicholas, as well as the more familiar Santa Claus. At least one merchant actually set up a live "Kriss Kringle" to draw mothers and children into his Philadelphia women's store in 1845, although the department store Santa wouldn't become a widespread seasonal fixture until the 1880s.

And, like the illustrated cards of the Bon Marché that Parisians loved to collect, nineteenth-century American shops began producing Christmas trade cards depicting Santa and other seasonal icons. Many consumers loved these cards and made them into Christmas ornaments—a custom that would baffle many a modern shopper, who couldn't imagine hanging a Wal-Mart flyer on their traditional tree. But in these early days, the excitement and abundance of stores at Christmas was a widely accepted part of the seasonal experience.

By the turn of the century, shops and shopping had become almost synonyms for the season itself. A New Yorker named Clara Pardee recalled taking her children "to see 'Christmas'" at Macy's department store in 1894. In that year, the store's elaborate window displays featured 13 tableaux, including scenes from Jack and the Beanstalk, Sinbad the Sailor, and Gulliver's Travels.

By the time Clara and her kids went to Macy's, the store had been famous for its holiday windows for at least 20 years, particularly its complicated scenes populated by a variety of dolls. The 1874 windows, which were apparently the first to feature the dolls in a tableau rather than just a random display, were the talk of the town; the following year, Leslie's *Illustrated Newspaper* ran a picture of crowds gathering outside the store to see the display. Less than a decade later, Macy's upped the ante by mechanizing a window of toys and dolls with steam power, so the goods magically moved. Eventually, the windows would include hundreds of mechanical figures, be on display for a month, and reportedly cost the equivalent of several days' receipts for the entire store.

(Macy's fame for its Christmas displays was all the more remarkable when you consider that the store's windows were notoriously plain and dull the rest of the year. R.H. Macy thought costly window displays just added to the price of the merchandise without notably improving business. His 14th Street store also didn't have windows as large as some nearby rivals in newer buildings.)

Many merchants used ads to intensify the excitement of the holiday, and to make it sound as though the only place to truly experience the season was their store. "The Spirit of Christmas is all over the store. Everywhere you note the resistless, onsweeping animation of intensifying activity," a turn-of-the-century ad for the Siegel Cooper department store informed readers of the *New York Times*.

The Christmas amusements in early department stores weren't confined to shopping or gazing passively at window displays. Many merchants worked hard to make shoppers feel part of the store, and feel that the store was an essential aspect of the Christmas experience. One of the leaders in this regard was John Wanamaker, whose emporiums in

Philadelphia and New York offered a range of "uplifting" entertainments for shoppers.

Wanamaker, a devout Presbyterian, decorated the Grand Court of his store in Philadelphia to resemble a massive cathedral. Up to 14,000 people at a time would jam themselves into this space to sing carols and hymns on Christmas Eve. Both before and after the store founder's death in 1922, store executives would rig up elaborate displays of banners, candlesticks, tapestries, carvings, stained glass windows, and Nativity scenes.

I find photographs of these displays weirdly disturbing. One 1928 photo shows the Grand Court kitted up with pseudo-Gothic choir stalls and dangling red stars, all leading the eye toward the store's massive pipe organ. But instead of pews between the choir stalls, visitors saw display cases of merchandise.

Thank-you letters sent to the store, however, reveal that many shoppers found these displays uplifting rather than sacrilegious. "You have taken a big step in dispelling the fear that so many of us have these days—that of a completely commercialized Christmas," one grateful shopper wrote. Men often took their hats off, as if they were entering church, when they entered the Grand Court.

Holiday sing-alongs and other events in this ersatz church drew herds of people and became a popular holiday tradition in Philadelphia. By the time the 1950s rolled around, the store could take as its holiday slogan, without irony, "Christmas Isn't Christmas without a Day at Wanamaker's."

### Bah, humbug: Anti-Christmas protests

Festivals, from day one, have always been about profligacy, conspicuous consumption, and excess. After all, we're celebrating something good: a big harvest, a new baby, the return of sunlight after a long winter. From the Puritans back to the critics of ancient Roman bacchanalia and beyond, critics have tried to control the periodic outbreaks of misrule that coincide with celebrations. They have also tried to cajole revelers back into the sober, serious world of hard work.

In our day, people decry shopping mall decorations and Santa Claus. In the Middle Ages, Maypoles and mummers drew the wrath of bishops.

Back in Rome, it was Petronius poking fun (and not-so-veiled criticism) at nouveau-riche partiers in *The Satyricon.*

People have been sighing in exhaustion about Christmas shopping for at least 150 years. In 1848, an American named William Mercer noted in relation to Christmas that "I rejoice that it comes but once in a twelvemonth!" In 1907, a New Yorker named Marguerite Du Bois who had spent days shopping and preparing for the festivities grumbled that "this silly Christmas trash makes me tired."

Even the protests about commercialization end up being commercialized themselves, a nice ironic twist that author Leigh Eric Schmidt points out in his book *Consumer Rites: The Buying and Selling of American Holidays.* Slogans such as "Jesus Is the Reason for the Season" and "Put Christ Back into Christmas," emblazoned on coffee mugs and sweatshirts, are hot sellers in Christian bookstores, and the Knights of Columbus buys billboards—another aspect of commercial culture—to promote the same messages.

These days, however, the gift-giving elements of Christmas *are* Christmas for many people. The holiday, stripped of its religious elements, is now celebrated in Hindu India, Communist China, and Shinto Japan. The gift giving is the fun, and around the world, Christmas increasingly has as much to do with Christ as St. Valentine's Day has to do with a martyred third-century saint.

### Trading junk

But gifts, more than any other Christmas tradition, have drawn the wrath of Christmas critics—particularly the ridiculous things so many of us like to buy for each other. Between 1910 and 1940, when Western societies were rapidly becoming more urban and mass culture was evolving, there was an intellectual backlash against the growing popularity of "gimcracks"—cheap novelty items such as figurines and bangles designed expressly as Christmas gifts.

Critics founded groups such as the Society for the Prevention of Useless Giving, and people—particularly those hit hard by the Depression—responded. Many stopped giving fribbles to acquaintances and business associates, sending Christmas cards instead. To family and close friends, they started giving useful items such as carpet sweepers. But, as any survey of a modern gift shop will attest, the will to give useful things didn't last long past the austerity of the Depression and war years. Pet Rocks, mood rings, Chia Pets, and Big Mouth Billy Bass singing fish plaques are all testaments to our continuing fascination with goofy gifts.

### Sending it back

If gift giving was a totally rational exercise, devoid of emotional links, then we wouldn't feel so guilty about taking gifts back to the store. Well, some people do manage to return gifts without shame. In the family of a friend of mine, the annual post-Boxing Day excursion to the courtesy counter is an open and shared event, with everyone from grandma to the grandkids eagerly heading back to the mall to get what they *really* wanted. Wow.

The rest of us feel that returning a gift is somehow an insult to the giver. It's as if we're saying, "You don't know me well enough, value me enough, or love me enough." If we were logical about the enterprise, it would seem completely sane to trade in a set of wineglasses we don't like for another set we've been ogling at the mall for months. But we just can't do it.

In an attempt to capitalize on our usually hidden desires to give ourselves the gifts we really wanted, retailers have tried various tacks. I can still hear an old Sears jingle, rattling around in the recesses of my brain, for which I really wish there was a delete key: "Almost everything you wanted, but didn't get for Christmas, is on sale now at Sears!" A Canadian electronics chain, Future Shop, appeals even more blatantly to consumer greed in its post-Christmas television ads, whose slogan is simply "I Want More!"

But one of the cleverest ads in this vein is one described by academic John F. Sherry, Jr., in a 1996 essay on gift giving. A Chicago chain called Triangle Electronics was running a Father's Day gift exchange promotion that encouraged dads to bring in their unwanted neckties and other gifts and trade them for a cell phone. "All traded gifts will be donated to the Salvation Army," the ad noted.

Pure genius! You get rid of something you don't want, get something you do want, and get to be generous to the less fortunate, all at the same time! You don't have to feel guilty about "rejecting" the gift because it will continue to be a gift . . . for someone else. (Poor people, apparently, don't hate ugly ties as much as everyone else does.)

## The real meaning of Christmas (and weddings)

In O. Henry's famous story "The Gift of the Magi," Jim and Della are desperately eager to buy each other a wonderful Christmas gift. The gift—in this case, as in many cases of gifts among close family and friends—is meant to represent their love for each other. That's why it has to be perfect.

In the end, ironically, their love for each other renders each gift meaningless, at least in terms of the item's function: since Della has sold her hair to buy Jim's watch chain, she has no use for the tortoiseshell combs he gives her; and since Jim has sold his watch to buy the combs, there's no longer a use for the chain.

The young marrieds are happy anyway. They've seen past the function of the gift to its meaning. Readers breathe a happy sigh as the story ends. Shopping is all right, really, because it's not about *stuff*. It's about *love*.

## Giving to the one you truly love

When you get right down to it, wouldn't it be great if you had some reason to splurge on a gift for yourself? And we don't mean "giving" your wife a bowling ball with your initials on it, either. You don't have to be Homer Simpson to shower yourself with little treats. Australian novelist and columnist Maggie Alderson has a fun theory on how we buy for ourselves.

> Isn't it funny how some dollars are worth more than others? It works like dog years. Dollars spent on shoes are worth about twenty cents, whereas in household-appliance money, $1 is equal to $50. We'll call it Shoe Money.
>
> This is why I think nothing of spitting out $150 for a pair of sandals, but resent every cent of the $40 a new toaster is going to cost me. . . . Toasters are boring. They should be free.

One of the first academic studies on "self-gifting," conducted in 1989, concluded that people buying things for themselves feel a mixture of pleasure in and guilt about their purchases, sometimes rationalizing their purchases of frivolous items such as jewelry and dolls by saying that they deserve them. "Or, you say that you're '*collecting*.' That way, you're not *really* indulging yourself," one shopper told the researchers.

In a later study, shoppers said they felt conflicted about buying treats for themselves—many would do so only after they'd met their families' needs. The researchers explained this tension by noting that consumer culture urges us to buy, buy, buy (think of slogans ranging from McDonald's "You deserve a break today" to The Bay's blatant "Shopping is good"), while the Protestant work ethic to which many North Americans still nominally subscribe promotes thrift and delayed gratification.

In 1990, a pair of researchers surveyed 54 college students to find out why they bought gifts for themselves. Some were rewarding themselves for achieving a goal, while others used the gift as motivation to achieve a goal. (Think about that pair of jeans in an "ideal" size. Some people buy them to celebrate reaching their desired weight, while others buy them and hang them in a prominent place to spur them to, one day, fit into them.) Other motivations the students mentioned included cheering themselves up, maintaining an existing good mood, celebrating a special occasion, and simply making use of surplus cash. In many of these contexts, clothing was the most popular self-gift.

Sometimes the act of shopping itself can be seen as a self-gift. In a 1994 study, researchers interviewed a woman who said that the ability to find products she liked at a good price was satisfying in and of itself, regardless of the objects she bought.

So next time Christmas comes around, put a gift for yourself under the tree, too.

# 11 Don't Miss Our Gift Shop on the Way Out

*How to overcome tourism's liability as a status good, the fact that it's an activity performed out of view? Acquire a marker of having been there: a piece of art, a T-shirt, a poster for the wall, pictures, or a video documentary.*

—Juliet B. Schor, *The Overspent American*, 1998

It happened more than a decade ago, but I remember my indignant shock as though it were yesterday. I was munching on a sandwich in the boardroom/lunchroom of the small magazine publishing company where I worked, when one of the ad sales reps joined me. We chatted about inconsequential things, until for some reason the talk turned to travel. I mentioned I had been to Ireland twice, and I was thrilled to learn that she'd been there too.

Ireland is one of my favorite places on the planet: I love the unstintingly friendly people, the electric green landscape, the noisy pubs, the long literary history. When I shared some of my enthusiasm with my colleague, however, her response was swift and withering. "I hated Ireland," she said bluntly. "There was nowhere to shop."

*"Shop!"* I wanted to bellow with all the haughty disdain that only a 23-year-old public radio listener with intellectual pretensions could muster. "You don't go to Ireland to shop!" But I refrained, and in retrospect it's probably a good thing I did.

First of all, Ireland has become just as much of a shopper's paradise as any other Western country, thanks to the combined forces of the

Celtic Tiger tech boom and a vast infusion of European Union investment. On my last visit, in 2001, I found Dublin's Grafton Street lined with trendy fashion shops. My husband and I spent more than was probably wise on Aran sweaters in Dingle. And the largest grocery store I've ever clapped eyes on—a Sainsbury's in Newry, in Northern Ireland— was more than up to the challenge of amply supplying everything that an extended family of 12 could need for a week-long stay in two self-catering cottages.

The second reason I'm glad that I didn't turn sanctimonious in the lunch room is that my former colleague isn't alone in her desire to shop on vacation. Many people base their travel decisions, to some degree at least, on the opportunity to shop. And, a little shamefacedly, I must confess that I'm one of them.

No, I haven't succumbed to the lure of the shopping-oriented bus tour. And I doubt I'd ever spend a week in a hotel at the Mall of America or the West Edmonton Mall. But it's rare that my husband and I return from any trip without at least one small item for our house. His taste, fortunately, runs to light, portable items like coasters. Mine, unfortunately, runs to the unwieldy.

I have a particular weakness for ceramics, and once carted a blue and white Turkish plate through five airports in three countries, cursing all the way. Whenever I catch sight of it hanging on my wall, though, I feel a pride akin to that a Victorian sahib must have felt when he gazed upon the stuffed head of a tiger on the wall of the library in his country estate.

I like to think that my plate hasn't led to the same sort of environmental disaster that the sahib's tiger's head did. As far as I know, ceramic isn't about to go extinct. And the woman who ran the shop made all the plates herself, or at least she told me she did, so I'm hoping no small children were kept out of school so that I could have a wall ornament. And yet, the diesel fuel those airplanes burned to get me from Ottawa to Antalya and back isn't doing the atmosphere any favors. Once you start mixing shopping and tourism, the politics of consumption get much, much trickier.

But for good or for ill, shopping and tourism are becoming more and more entwined.

## Taking more of a bath than they knew

The link between travel and shopping is a long-standing one. Wherever people have flocked to swim, or rest, or gamble, shopkeepers have followed. What better time to convince people to buy a treat than when they're on vacation?

In the 1700s, the spa town of Bath was England's equivalent of Las Vegas, with the major advantage that Céline Dion hadn't been born yet. Built on the site of ancient Roman baths, it drew a crowd of moneyed gamblers, convalescents, and holidaymakers.

This rich, leisured, captive market inevitably attracted tailors and dressmakers, hatters and shoemakers, chandlers and milliners and china retailers. And they were quick to ensure a steady stream of rich customers by working out kickback deals with servants, a tidy arrangement known as "poundage."

The shopkeeper would give the servant a shilling for every pound the master spent in his shop. If the hapless master was careless with his bills, and didn't check anything aside from the total, the servant would receive "double poundage"—two shillings per pound spent—all without the master's knowledge, of course.

By 1725, a contemporary observer noted that Bath's narrow streets were lined with shops doing a thriving trade among the upper classes. One particularly popular thoroughfare was lined with lime trees on one side and fancy gift shops on the other.

Retail development continued to flourish in Bath throughout the century; by the 1770s, Josiah Wedgwood himself feared he wouldn't be able to set up a china shop grand enough to compete with the establishments already there. In 1772, while looking for possible locations for a showroom, he implored a business associate to send stock, and fast: "I hope you will send us some enamelled Tea ware, and in short everything to make a complete shew of it, or we had better do nothing, for I think the Toy [gift] and China shops are richer and more extravagant in their shew here than in London."

## The joy of victory—and the agony of defeat

By the 1890s, the link between tourism and shopping was well entrenched, if an 1895 article in *The Atlantic Monthly* is any indication. Author Agnes

Repplier describes a shopping trip to an Egyptian bazaar in affectionate detail.

"Now, shopping on the Nile is a very different matter from shopping on Chestnut Street or Broadway," she tells her readers, priming them for that key shopping-and-travel experience: exotic difference. She explains the etiquette of bargaining, something her readers' parents and grand-parents would have understood but that late-nineteenth-century shop-pers had little experience of.

She then outlines the range of goods available, making sure to tell the readers which are good deals and why, and which are scams designed to dupe unsuspecting tourists into thinking they're getting something old, or culturally authentic, or both. But it's when she starts describing her love for "the famous red and black pottery of Assiut" that I start to realize that Agnes is a kindred spirit.

"How can we resist this beautiful and brittle ware, though we know by sad experience the difficulty of carrying it unbroken?" she asks. "The most charming pieces, too, are invariably the most fragile." I nod my head in agreement. A hundred years later, Agnes would have been right beside me in that Turkish ceramics shop, running her fingers over the blue and white plates.

She knows, in her head, that a dish or a paperweight would be rela-tively easy to carry. But the dish doesn't take her fancy, and she dismisses the idea of a paperweight with typical *Atlantic* decisiveness. "[A]n Assiut paper-weight is a violent accommodation of native pottery to the needs of a saddened civilization which fills me with abhorrence." So there. It's quite all right to shop on vacation, my dear, as long as you're not tacky about it.

What really catches her eye is an oval incense box with a delicate stand. She ponders the purchase.

> My companions look askance upon this exquisite and useless toy, the price of which is a paltry shilling, and remind me unkindly of somewhat similar pieces I bought at Assiut, and the fragments of which now lie buried at the bottom of the Nile. But the most wonderful thing about my incense-box is that it unscrews, actually unscrews into five parts, and may be packed and put together again whenever and wherever I please. This discovery makes it

irresistible. I point out triumphantly how safely it can be carried, pay my shilling, and walk proudly away. Five minutes later, a small Arab boy, darting through the bazaars, jolts violently against me. My box shivers, unscrews itself with extraordinary facility, and, before I realize what has happened, the stem lies shattered on the ground, while a murmured chorus of "I told you so" rises distinctly, and, I think, joyously, around me.

As Bill Clinton might have said, "I feel your pain, Agnes."

### Who put commercials in my culture?

Cultured, discriminating people like Agnes are just the sorts of folks who go to museums while they're on vacation. And these days, more and more museums are trying to get her twenty-first-century equivalent to purchase today's version of Egyptian incense burners.

But just like the friends who, later in the article, urged Agnes to forget the bazaar and come with them to see some ruins, there are people in the arts community who think museum visitors are spending too much time shopping and not enough time learning, to the detriment of both the visitors and the museums.

In many countries, both state support for the arts and private philanthropic donations have fallen in recent years. Museum managers, however, still have expensive collections, expert staff, and expansive buildings to maintain. Increasingly, following the early example of the Metropolitan Museum of Art in New York, museums are turning to gift shops and other forms of merchandising to improve their bottom line.

The boutique at the Museum of Fine Arts in Boston is a typical example of a museum gift shop. High-quality clothing embellished with reproductions of famous artworks lines the shelves. Coffee mugs, stationery, books, and jewelry vie for patrons' souvenir dollars. Nonchallenging jazz patters quietly from hidden speakers. (Can someone please tell me when jazz became the official Muzak of the chattering classes? Just wondering.)

A substantial proportion of museums' gross income comes from stores such as this one. A recent study of the relationship between museums and merchandising, published by the National Center on Non-Profit

Enterprise (NCNE), revealed that shops accounted for between 17 and 20 percent of the gross income of nine American museums every year between 1989 and 1999.

Statistics in other countries tell a similar tale. In 1999, museums surveyed by Statistics Canada earned 2.6 times as much from "sales counters, giftshops, and other" activities as they did from memberships and admission fees combined.

The blockbuster exhibitions that provide so much of many museums' revenue often rate their own purpose-built emporiums, usually strategically located at the exit to the exhibition itself. The items for sale run a predictable gamut, from "educational" toys and puzzles to coffee table books and posters. The juxtapositions can be somewhat jarring, however.

## Come for the dead people, stay for the scented candles

In early 2003, I went to an exhibition called *The Mysterious Bog People* at the Canadian Museum of Civilization in Gatineau, Quebec. The exhibition itself was rather unnerving, based as it was on a number of exhumed corpses of people who had been tossed into European bogs. But the attached gift shop was even weirder. What, exactly, scented candles and luxury bath bombs have to do with the resurrected bog folks is a question best left to greater minds than mine.

I'm not alone in my unease with the policy of placing unavoidable gift shops at the exit to major exhibitions—a technique, incidentally, that museum managers borrowed from theme parks. A few years ago, the Metropolitan Museum hosted a Van Gogh exhibition. After an emotionally stirring selection of paintings in the last room of the show, visitors emerged, blinking, into a souvenir store. As museum director Philippe de Montebello explained in the *New York Times*:

> We had a flurry of letters saying, "We walked out of the exhibition in tears, a great experience ruined by the shops." And I had to say: "Look, I'm sorry we had to have the shops. Would you have preferred not to have an exhibition at all?" Because without the shops, I couldn't have afforded to do the show.

The authors of the NCNE study, however, argued that this widely held perception on the part of many museum managers isn't entirely true.

According to the NCNE's figures, even though gift shops brought in roughly a fifth of the studied museums' *gross* revenues, the highest percentage of *net* revenues they contributed in any one year was two percent. In 1994, according to the study, the net revenues from gift shops were zero. In other words, the cost of running these stores could severely undercut the benefits they brought to the museums studied. (I say *could* because these statistics are averages. So in some years, some museums might have profited quite well from their shops, while others lost money.)

So why are modern museums honeycombed with stalls, kiosks, and shops? The NCNE study put forth some intriguing theories. One of them was a variation on the "If Johnny jumped off a bridge, would you jump off too?" question our mothers tossed at us when we were little. According to the study's statistics, small museums race to set up gift shops and other "auxiliary" services (such as restaurants and parking garages) when they see larger institutions increasing their gross incomes by doing so. They may even feel they *have* to provide stores because visitors have come to expect them and will be grumpy if they don't have a chance to shop.

Another theory was that museums see shops as a way to both draw visitors to the museum in the first place and to educate them further when they finally do get them through the museum doors. In a 1998 interview with National Public Radio, which the NCNE study quotes, a museum executive argued that a visit to a museum shop broadens the experience for many visitors: "For some people, it's the best part of their experience, because it's a way to actually put their hands on something."

This makes sense to me. In the nineteenth century, stores evolved from places where the clerk kept everything behind the counter into vast emporiums where the shopper was encouraged to touch, smell, and try on the merchandise. We're used to being able to cart home anything that catches our eye, if our credit limits allow it. Even public libraries, another institution where materials are shared for the good of all, allow us to actually take most of the books home. So a museum, where we are allowed to look but not to have, is an increasingly alien experience for the western consumer. As one museum's 1991 annual report put it, "the

Museum Store, with a greater range of merchandise, clearly responded to many visitors' long-expressed desires."

### When dollars visit euros

A good museum, of course, is there to attract tourist dollars. Visitors who snap up Van Gogh posters and Picasso T-shirts bring money to the places they visit.

Museum stores are not alone in their quest to combine a holiday with shopping, if a 2001 study conducted by the Travel Industry Association of America (TIA) is any indication. The study looked at the shopping habits of domestic business and leisure travelers in 1999, and it found that 63 percent of them—or 91 million Americans—shopped on at least one trip they took that year. Of those "shopping travelers," as the study calls them, about 40 percent said a trip wouldn't feel complete if they couldn't go shopping.

So where do these shopping travelers shop, what do they buy, and how much do they spend?

Malls are the most popular destination, followed by outdoor "main street" shopping districts and outlet malls. Shoppers like to visit stores they can't find at home—an increasingly difficult ambition to fulfill, given the ubiquity of national chain stores, particularly in malls.

They want to buy things that represent the place they're visiting, but not necessarily ashtrays made of seashells. Clothes and shoes are the most popular purchases, but it's unclear whether those items are $500 jackets made by local artisans or $10 T-shirts printed offshore. Souvenirs are still a popular choice, along with books, music, toys, jewelry, and furniture. Low on the priority list are home electronics, cameras, artwork, luggage, and sports equipment. Interestingly, people under 35 were more likely than people in other demographic groups to buy electronics; baby boomers were more likely to buy luggage; and "matures" (shoppers over 55) didn't outscore the other groups in any category, but showed a strong preference for clothing.

Shopping travelers represent big business for local merchants. Nearly half of these roaming consumers will spend at least $250 in stores during their vacation; one in ten will spend more than $1,000.

## Preparing for the big binge

The high-spending shoppers (those in the $250 and up category) do their homework. They tend to poll family, friends, and coworkers for advice on good shops before they leave on their trip. Other sources of shopping advice include guidebooks, magazines in hotel rooms, and information desks.

The shopping information business has become an industry of its own in the last couple of decades. The *Born to Shop* series of guidebooks, for instance, first hit the stands in the mid-1980s. The idea was born when coauthor Judith Thomas was out for a birthday dinner with friends. When they started talking about her upcoming trip to Europe, the recommendations for don't-miss shops started flying thick and fast, until the tablecloth was covered with scribbled notes.

Reading one of these books is like getting advice from a cool, trusted friend. Just about everyone likes getting the inside scoop on something; that's why the books have been phenomenally successful. What savvy shopper wouldn't want to be included in the sales at this upscale fashion boutique, described in the 1988 version of *Born to Shop Los Angeles*?

> The sales begin as private events. You actually get a handwritten letter from your saleswoman, or a postcard, that invites you to come in. Only after the private customers have been notified do the mere mortals learn about the sale.

As I mentioned in the fashion chapter, exclusivity is a powerful draw when it comes to shopping. And if you buy something at an off-the-beaten-track store while *traveling*, even better. There's even less chance someone you know will walk into the store and come out with the same dress, or, even worse, a better deal.

## From buttons to Bond

The *Where* chain of visitor magazines is another example of a business built on the premise of helping travelers shop. As of late 2002, the magazine published editions in 46 cities and regions, from Baltimore to Budapest, and from San Diego to Singapore.

Sure, the magazines talk about other things: museums, festivals, and similar tourist stuff. But the twin pillars of advertising revenue are restaurants and shops. Restaurants I'll leave for someone else to dissect, but let's look for a minute at the retail-related advertising in the November 2002 issue of *Where New York*. (The largest cover headline blared, "Let Us Shop," as though anyone, anywhere, was preventing people from hitting the stores.)

Most shopping ads in the magazine fell into a few definite categories, such as high fashion, jewelry, art, and department stores. Then there were ads for the specialty stores that probably rely substantially on tourists seeking things they can't find at home: the NBC Experience Store (where you can buy products related to the network's shows), the NBA store (for basketball paraphernalia), Tender Buttons (which sells nothing but buttons), and Quark Spy (for all your James Bond needs), as well as shops specializing in Broadway soundtracks, tennis gear, and other niches.

Since the magazine came out just before the Christmas season kicked into high gear, there were also several ads for holiday parades, each more bombastic than the last. Macy's full-page ad boasted that the store's Thanksgiving Day Parade was "the nation's most beloved holiday tradition," while the Toys "R" Us Holiday Parade ended at the eponymous store, which humbly billed itself as "The Center of the Toy Universe."

The tone of the editorial in *Where New York*, like all the other magazines in the chain, has the sort of "insider" tone that makes the *Born to Shop* books so appealing. "Move over, Chelsea. Could Greenwich Village be New York's next hot art district?" asks one writer.

There's also the interest in the new and unusual that characterizes the high-spending shopping traveler. One article alerts readers to the fact that the *USS Target*—an outlet of the Target department store on a ship—is pulling into Chelsea Piers for some pre-holiday shopping. (I'm glad to hear the *USS Target* is affiliated with the store; it'd be a singularly unfortunate name for a navy vessel.)

### Five-figure souvenirs

Another constant in *Where*'s shopping coverage is a strong focus on high-end products. The chain's slogan, after all, is "The Magazine For

The Affluent Traveler." Back about a million years ago, when I worked for the company that published *Where Ottawa*, I remember the staff's amazement when a company-wide memo urged editors to focus on furs, diamonds, and other chichi items.

People may come to New York or London, or even Montreal or Toronto, to buy haute couture and high-end jewelry. But, trust me, they don't come to Ottawa to buy the latest trendy duds. Many of them come here to (a) attend conventions (b) lobby government officials (c) visit relatives or (d) show the kids the Parliament Buildings, whether the offspring like it or not. That's why there was a fair bit of bafflement in our office about the edict from headquarters to focus on ritzy stuff.

I'm not sure how many $50,000 furs make it into the pages of *Where Ottawa* to this day, but it's clear that in New York—a city where some visitors and locals have lots of disposable income—the *Where* staffers have embraced the upscale concept with open arms. Products profiled in the "Holiday Gift Guide" in *Where New York*'s November 2002 issue included a $28,700 Cellini rose gold watch studded with more than 100 rose sapphires, a $2,200 Lalique crystal decanter, and an $85,000 brooch (with $56,000 matching earrings) from Ellagem.

Interestingly, not all the recommendations would burn a hole in the reader's wallet; there were also $9.50 chocolates, a $38 running jacket, and a deck of playing cards for $5. The assumption seems to have been that even though many readers would have budgets that stretched only as far as the running jacket, they liked having that jacket placed in the context of $56,000 earrings. They might not be able to afford the earrings, but they could afford the jacket, so at least they were *in the ballpark*.

### Going on a mall-iday

Fact: shopping travelers put a high value on unique stores and unusual goods. Another fact: the mall is their preferred destination. Given these two facts, it only stands to reason that, eventually, unusual malls would evolve to cater to tourists. These traveler-oriented malls include mega-malls, upscale specialty malls, and outlet malls (the latter is in a category of its own in the TIA survey, ranking just behind traditional malls in popularity with travelers).

As I mentioned in the mall chapter, the 4.3-million-square-foot Mall of America in Bloomington, Minnesota, draws more than a third of its shoppers from more than 150 miles away. There are airfare deals and hotel packages to encourage visitors to come and stay, and the deals must work—the mall is the state's top tourist attraction. Eerily, the logo of the city of Bloomington isn't a lake or a state animal or some kind of flower. It's a shopping bag.

## From Vegas to Newfoundland: Tourists will shop anywhere

Cities and regions looking for something new to attract jaded tourists who may think they've "been there, done that" are increasingly seeing shopping as the new Holy Grail. Orlando, for one, is starting to offer more than just theme parks. The new Mall at Millennia is home to retailers that most certainly wouldn't feel at home with Mickey and Minnie, including Gucci and Tiffany.

Meanwhile, Las Vegas has tried restyling itself as a family-focused destination, and part of that marketing effort involves shopping. No longer do people go to Caesar's Palace just to throw money away on slot machines, roulette, and cheap steak dinners; now they can throw it away at the Forum Shops at Caesar's. That 283,000-square-foot complex, opened in 1992, has been so successful that it's now in the middle of a 200,000-square-foot expansion.

Less tourist-focused destinations are also getting in on the act. In a connection that's almost surreal in its weirdness, Icelanders are swooping down on St. John's, Newfoundland, to go shopping. Some 1,000 Icelanders come each year, plunking down an average of more than $1,200 during a four-day stay, according to estimates from the local tourism department. It all started when a Reykjavik tourism operator began bringing in Christmas shopping groups in 1998.

It's only possible to appreciate how weird this is when you know that the unemployment rate in Newfoundland hovers around 17 percent, *and* the provincial and federal sales taxes on retail goods total 19 percent, *and* that St. John's is a 1,600-mile plane trip from Reykjavik. By most conventional definitions, St. John's shouldn't be anyone's shopping mecca. And yet it's new, it's different, and prices on many brand name goods are half what they are in Iceland.

In Winnipeg, Manitoba, a former downtown railway yard has been redeveloped as The Forks National Historic Site and Market. In the years since the first phase of the complex opened in 1989—boosted with lots of federal, provincial, and municipal cash—The Forks has become the province's top tourist destination, with more than 3.5 million visits a year. The businesses are a mix of food stores, restaurants, craft shops, and gift emporiums. A line from *Tourism*, a promotional magazine published by the Canadian Tourism Commission, is telling: "The market can't be thought of as a typical mall: shops and stores are independently owned and unique to The Forks Market, with authentic food outlets that reflect the cultural diversity of Winnipeg."

Notice the words that hit all those buttons that the TIA pegged in its shopping tourist survey: *independently owned, unique, authentic, cultural diversity*. These are the things that matter to tourists and leisure shoppers. They're not particularly relevant to the busy mom or dad popping the kids into the van to run errands on weekends.

### You'll shop—even if you don't want to!

Some destination marketers believe that if they can just get visitors to come to the place, they'll shop even if they don't intend to. In 2001, researchers surveyed tourists shopping in downtown Montreal and found that only 18.8 percent of them said they had come downtown to shop— the most common reasons for visiting were to people-watch or visit a tourist attraction, such as a museum.

However, even though less than 20 percent of visitors intended to shop, 27 percent of them ended up spending $100 or more during their visit to the shopping neighborhood. While some of that money undoubtedly went to tourist attractions and restaurants, some of it at least must have gone to stores. (And, for what it's worth, the shopping in Montreal *is* pretty awesome.)

Some destinations have even tried to promote their shopping holidays to people who are sick and tired of shopping. With not a trace of irony, the Prince William County-Manassas, Virginia Convention and Visitors Bureau distributed a news release in November 2002 headlined "Holiday

Shopping Got You Down . . . It's Time for a Shopping Holiday!" Apparently, the remedy for shopping fatigue is not to stop spending—it's to start spending in more congenial surroundings.

"Browse quaint streets in historic small towns for unique crafts . . . navigate your way through antique corridors filled with untold collectibles and perfect gifts just waiting to be discovered . . . or fill bags with bargains at an outlet mall unmatched in value. Doesn't this sound like a better way to finish that seemingly never-ending holiday shopping?" the release began.

Again, note the key words designed to appeal to the shopping traveler: *quaint, historic, unique, perfect, bargains, value.*

### Now boarding at gate 6: Sunglass Hut

These days, even the harried traveler who doesn't have time to do any shopping during his or her trip doesn't need to despair. Just like cruise ships, casinos, and museums, airports have been bitten by the retail bug.

Shannon Airport in Ireland and Schiphol Airport in Amsterdam have long been famous for their excellent shopping. But now, it seems, everyone's getting in on the act, creating terminals that look more like malls than transit points. Sometimes, it's easy to forget the planes sitting right outside the windows.

It used to be that no one shopped at the airport. Rightly or wrongly (usually rightly), most people suspected they were being gouged by retailers who knew they had a bored and captive audience.

Then the British Airports Authority started ensuring that shops in its facilities charged the same prices as their High Street counterparts, and promoting this policy. People caught on, and sales increased. Other airports followed suit.

With the rise in day and weekend trips throughout the European Union, due to the emergence of a spate of discount carriers, the BAA has even launched a personal shopper service for travelers passing through Heathrow and several other British airports. Just call ahead, tell them what you're looking for (a Paddington Bear? a Burberry umbrella?), and a charming shopper will be waiting with your purchase when you get off the plane.

Perks at other airports throughout the world vary. You can relax in rocking chairs in the AirMall in Pittsburgh, or get a hit of concentrated oxygen at a spa in Calgary.

The new security restrictions put in place after September 11, 2001, have had both positive and negative effects on airport retailers. The sight of soldiers strolling around with guns and metal detectors doesn't exactly put potential customers in a happy shopping mood. And the fact that security barriers have been moved closer to the entrances of some airports means that shops that were normally open to the general public, including people dropping off travelers at the airport, are now open only to passengers with boarding passes.

On the other hand, people are spending more time at the airport than ever, since airlines are advising travelers to arrive early to avoid delays. Once passengers have checked in and run the security gauntlet, why not shop?

### Just in case we're not shopping enough . . .

So intense and important is the modern connection between travel and shopping that a whole organization has been invented to encourage it. In my mind, this is a bit like founding an organization to encourage teenage boys to think about sex, but what do I know?

Shop America was founded in the late 1990s to encourage cooperation between major tourist-draw malls and the hospitality industry—hotels, airlines, and tour operators. "They're two totally different industries," says Rosemary McCormick, the association's president. "Our mission is awareness of shopping as the number one important tourist activity."

When Shop America was formed, she notes, few malls aside from the Mall of America were marketing themselves as tourist attractions. Then they realized that the average tourist spends four to ten times as much during a mall visit as a local does—and rarely returns things. Even if visitors get buyer's remorse a few days later, they're probably already several states away.

"One of the advantages that we have in this country, that we don't promote properly, is that we have the best shopping in the world," McCormick says. Woodbury Common, an outlet mall near New York City, recently compared the price of a basket of branded products at its stores to the same basket of products in the U.K. Even with the exchange, the American goods were 52 percent cheaper. So now Shop America has been promoting the States as a destination for high-spending Britons. If they spend enough, the argument goes, they'll "save" enough to cover the cost of their airfare and hotel.

So why do people shop when they travel? "The number one reason," says McCormick, "is because they have the time and the money."

### Everybody's waiting for the weekend

For years, urban hotels catering to business travelers have been promoting weekend package deals to leisure travelers in an attempt to keep rooms full when the suits aren't in town. In the last decade, though, the focus of these mini-breaks has changed. In 1997, an article in *The Wall Street Journal* billed the weekend shopping trip as "a '90s-style vacation for today's time-starved couples." The article noted that the popularity of store-prowling weekends had surpassed romantic-getaway larks at some hotels.

So what do you get as part of a weekend shopping package? Goodies vary by hotel, but common perks include discount coupons and cards, gift certificates, the services of a personal shopper, foot massages (for mall-battered tootsies), gift wrapping, package delivery, and shuttles to stores. Advertising promotes touches that make guests feel special; in the *Wall Street Journal* story, a guest said she felt "very much pampered" when she received a free tote bag and rose. In the winter of 2002–03, the Fairmont Chicago's "Shop in Style" package included free valet parking or breakfast in bed for two.

Hotels aren't the only ones trying to lure tourist shoppers' dollars into their coffers. Malls, individual retailers, and tourism bureaus are all getting in on the act. In the summer of 2002, for instance, the "Shop Toronto" program shuttled tourists from 23 hotels to three downtown shopping neighborhoods, on a continuous loop. Participants received a discount-shopping pass as well.

Later that year, just west of the city, the Southern Ontario Tourism Organization (SOTO) promoted 24 one-day and weekend holiday shopping packages designed to appeal to harried urban dwellers. "No big box stores or frantic line-ups," promised SOTO's Shopping Getaways booklet. "Only traditional quality and service—wrapped in warm hospitality." Despite the cozy introduction, the packages were designed to appeal to just about every type of shopper, from folks who wanted to stroll along a refurbished Main Street in a rural village to big spenders who wanted to spend a weekend trolling the casino and outlet stores of Windsor.

Around the same time, a group of businesses in West Hollywood, California, launched a holiday shopping promotion with a news release that promised visitors a "celebrity-style shopping experience during the Holidays." The Christmas shopping package included the usual discounts on hotels and stores, but the news release was designed to hit a number of other leisure shopping buttons. It noted that the Beverly Center mall, one of the partners in the promotion, boasted "neon escalators that wrap the sides of this eight level complex, reminiscent of the Centre Pompidou in Paris."

And if the notion of Parisian glamour wasn't enough to lure visitors, there was the added hope of spotting "regulars like Madonna, Cameron Diaz, Jennifer Anniston [sic] and Brad Pitt, who frequent this premier shopping destination." European style, possible celebrities, and retail discounts? What better way could there be to celebrate Christmas in the new millennium?

### French cooking, Indian curry, and Bermuda onions

If Parisian élan, California style, wasn't good enough for you, you could go for the real thing courtesy of four hotels in the Paris fashion district. In the winter of 2002–03, visitors could sign up for a "Luxury Shopping Package" that included deluxe hotel rooms, a welcoming bottle of champagne, and "VIP treatment at select stores"—upscale emporiums that included Cartier, Christian Dior, Baccarat, Burberry, and Van Cleef & Arpels.

Of course, there are travelers—*not* tourists, please—who search for something less commercialized and more "authentic." They've long been drawn to less-developed areas of the world. But even those places aren't immune to the twin sirens of tourism and shopping.

Kochi, a city in the scenic state of Kerala in India, held a month-long "shopping and tourism" festival in December 2001 designed expressly to attract well-heeled international tourists. "Our focus is to attract class tourists, and not mass tourists," the local tourism minister, T. Balakrishnan, told an Indian on-line magazine. "The state gains from the former, while there will be a net outgo from the latter."

Kerala isn't alone in its focus on wealthy tourists. Destinations that have been overrun by planeloads, shiploads, and busloads of bargain hunters are starting to repeat that old saw, "Be careful what you wish for . . . you might get it." Others have watched the paving of South Florida and the infestation of fish-and-chip shops in ports on the Balearic islands and taken note.

Tourism planners in Bermuda, never an inexpensive destination, have made a conscious decision to appeal mainly to rich visitors, specifically so that the island can avoid being overwhelmed by tourist volume. Since the island is one of the most geographically isolated settled places on earth—600 miles from the nearest landfall—retail prices are always going to be high. With international banking and other high-paying industries forming the foundation of the economy, there's a lot of local money to support chichi restaurants and five-star hotels. As a result, there aren't many dollar stores or T-shirt shops in Hamilton, but you'll have no problem finding diamond earrings or Waterford crystal.

### Extremely exclusive tourism

Other potential tourist destinations have taken a more radical tack. Instead of focusing on moneyed tourists, they've decided to discourage *all* mass tourism. The village of Tenakee Springs, Alaska, made headlines in 1998 when it gave passengers on a ship called the *World Discoverer* a distinctly chilly reception.

The previous year, when the 120-passenger ship had made a stop in the village of 114 people, residents complained that the visitors picked berries from private gardens, wandered into at least one home uninvited, and generally didn't endear themselves to anyone. When the ship came back, locals passed out flyers informing the startled passengers that mass tourism was unwelcome in Tenakee Springs, although the village would be glad to see smaller groups. The few local businesses, including the only gift shop, closed their doors.

Tellingly, an official from the cruise ship company, Society Expeditions, expressed his bafflement at Tenakee Springs' hostility by emphasizing the difference between his ship and crasser tourist ventures. He told the *Juneau Empire* that his tours are "expeditions" and participants aren't "tourists" who like "knickknack shops and shuffleboard."

## Cruising for values

But whether tourists—or travelers, or explorers, or seekers—are looking for authentic local crafts or mass-produced ashtrays, they can't help changing the character and the economy of the places they visit. One hundred and twenty doesn't sound like a major influx, but the visitors outnumbered the permanent residents of Tenakee Springs.

Cruise ships are also attracting increasingly negative publicity, in Alaska and elsewhere, for their environmental and social policies. The people of Tenakee Springs may have been just as fearful of water pollution as rabid shoppers.

But the sheer volume of cruise ship traffic can overwhelm even the most eager tourist town. In 2000, my husband and I took a Caribbean cruise. The reaction of islanders to the herds of people shuffling along the harborside shopping streets varied from port to port, as did the reaction of the passengers. It was like the meeting of Rainer Maria Rilke's two solitudes, and there was little of love about it. But first, a little background.

Our shopping experience began the moment we walked up the gangplank and a cheerful photographer snapped our picture. Later in the cruise, of course, we had the opportunity to buy this lovely picture of ourselves, jet-lagged and bewildered, from a public display of similar mug shots.

The orientation materials included a full description of the ship's shops. Like passengers on many other cruise ships, we were also subjected to daily pleas to check out the art auctions—an increasingly popular way for cruise lines to make money. Each cruise line gets a percentage of every sale, and those sales figures are substantial. In 2000, Michigan-based Park West Gallery sold some 200,000 pieces of art through auctions on more than half a dozen cruise lines.

I must admit, we did check out the shops on the ship and we weren't averse to buying a few things. Apparently, we're not alone in that urge; in 1999, the average cruise ship passenger (on all lines) dropped between $220 and $232 *a day* on things that weren't included in the "all-inclusive" price of the trip. Our onboard spending included more than shops, of course; those $100 shore excursions and $10 martinis can add up pretty quickly, trust me.

But Paul and I like to tell ourselves that we are *travelers*, not *tourists*. We truly wanted to learn at least a bit about the places we were visiting—the history, the music, the culture, the food. So when we saw that there would be presentations about each port we would visit, we eagerly hustled off to the first one.

It wasn't exactly Harvard at sea. Rather than the slide show and music we'd been expecting, it was an earnest presentation by a cruise-line employee about the "approved" shops in the next port of call. These stores, she assured us, would provide quality merchandise at good value. The subtext was that these were "safe" places to shop. (What no one mentions is that, in almost all cases, the only thing "approved" about a retailer is the fact that it has paid a cruise line a hefty fee for that designation.)

The great irony is that the harborside streets in just about every Caribbean port of call have been converted into what amounts to tourist shopping theme parks. Squeezed into picturesque old buildings or custom-built mini-malls is a numbingly familiar parade of pricey shops such as Little Switzerland and Diamonds International.

Occasionally, of course, a local craft shop or gallery would make it onto the approved list. But most of the time, the list covered the usual jewelry stores, liquor outlets, and perfume shops. At one time, when many islands levied low or no duties, these luxury goods were a real bargain in the Caribbean.

That's no longer the case, but the idea that good deals abound in the region remains. One of the passengers assigned to our dinner table announced that the whole reason he had come on the cruise was to buy a tanzanite ring in Saint Thomas. It seemed to me that the price of the cruise was a hefty surcharge on the jewelry, negating any savings he might have made, but I politely kept my mouth shut.

We ended up skipping most of the seminars, but this isn't to say that we didn't lay down our share of dollars. In San Juan, Puerto Rico, we bought bags of Christmas presents in an admittedly touristy gift shop that was a bit—just a little—off the cruise ship passenger beaten path. Then we had one of the best meals of our lives at a small restaurant we'd discovered by accident. We were looking for another place on the same street, recommended in a guidebook, when we stumbled on this one. It looked charming, so we went in. Largely deserted, it served up magnificent fried plantain and hearty, spicy meat dishes. Even the orange-flavored butter was homemade and superb.

Feeling eminently satisfied with ourselves, we waddled home with our purchases, eager to share our exciting day with our dinner-table companions the following night. We thought they'd be impressed with our explorations.

They were horrified.

"How did you know where to go?" they asked, knowing that we hadn't gone to the port-of-call seminar.

"We had a guidebook, and we just wandered around."

"But that restaurant—how did you know it was safe?"

*Puerto Rico isn't exactly Chechnya*, I wanted to shout. *And the extensive wine list and white linen tablecloths were a pretty good indication that the place wasn't dishing up horsemeat.*

"It looked nice," I replied lamely.

"But weren't you afraid to drink the water?" one of the women persisted.

At that point, I had to remind myself that underlying much of the communication on cruise ships is the implication that every port you're going to visit is a hotbed of drugs, muggings, and people hoping to rip you off. No one comes right out and says that, of course, but the insinuation is there. The solution to the largely manufactured problem, of course, is to shop only in cruise-line approved shops, and to travel only on cruise-line arranged tours. More money for the cruise line, more safety for the passengers—everyone wins, or so the rationale goes.

And, to be honest, port cities—like any cities, anywhere—aren't completely problem free. When you mix a bunch of comparatively wealthy, obviously leisured visitors into a place where people work long hours for low pay, there's bound to be resentment and suspicion. And resentment and suspicion will sometimes lead to crime. At the very least, they're likely to lead to bad feelings.

### Charlotte Amalie isn't the cute girl
### you had a crush on in high school

Consider the case of Charlotte Amalie in Saint Thomas. Cruise ships are big business for Charlotte Amalie. The port can handle half a dozen cruise ships at a time, which can translate into more than 10,000 people a day flooding into town. According to figures from the local chamber of commerce, each of those day visitors drops an average of $243 on the island. Saint Thomas, with a population of just 50,000 people, gets more than one million cruise ship visitors annually. Do the math—cruise ships are a *major* part of the local economy.

The downtown shops, within striking distance of the cruise ship terminal, are the predictable mix found in most cruise ship ports. It's the kind of place tailor made to keep visitors content. But the day I happened to visit Saint Thomas, I didn't find it the happiest place to shop. This isn't to pick on Saint Thomas, particularly—I suspect the same thing happens, depending on the day and prevailing mood, in just about every cruise ship port.

On the afternoon in question, it was raining. Passengers from the six ships in port were cranky about the weather. Many who might have spent the day lying on a beach or going on an outdoorsy expedition if the weather had cooperated opted instead to prowl the narrow streets of the town. It was about ten days before Christmas, so I probably wasn't the only one feeling a bit of pressure to finish my gift shopping.

Whatever the reason, there was a distinctly inhospitable feeling in the air in Charlotte Amalie that day. Panhandlers on the streets were cursing at passersby who refused to give them money, and salesclerks were harried as they rushed around crowded shops.

Eventually, I made my way back to Havensight, a small outdoor shopping mall near the cruise ship docks. I'd nipped into a gift store to buy some stocking stuffers when the heavens opened. The rain, which had been merely steady, was now lashing down in sheets. I resigned myself to being trapped in the store until the storm let up a bit.

As I was browsing through a display of decorated golf balls, a couple next to me launched into a heated discussion with a salesclerk. They wanted her to give them a refund on a gold chain they'd bought at the store on a previous trip. Due to some store policy that I didn't hear, she couldn't do that. The husband became more aggressive, demanding to see the manager so that he could return "this piece of crap you sold us." The manager hurried over, alerted by the raised voices before the clerk could summon her, and tried to smooth things over.

By this point, however, the couple could not be appeased. Their voices grew louder, their insults to the store and its staff harsher. Finally, the manager agreed to replace the necklace, and the still seething customers departed.

Tentatively, I approached the manager to pay for my golf balls. She was muttering under her breath, seemingly not even seeing me as she rang up my purchase. I made a sympathetic comment, and she looked up.

"These tourists, they have all this money, and they come in my store and make a fuss over a six-dollar necklace," she said.

I didn't know what was sadder—the fact that the shoppers had expected a six-dollar necklace to be more than a "piece of crap" or the fact that the only way the manager could hang onto her dignity in the face of their tirade was to quote store policy.

Meekly, I paid for my golf balls and fled into the storm, which was still raging. It was more comfortable outside than in.

### Politically correct tourism

And yet, and yet. Even with all the reasons to hate the cruise industry, cruising is powerfully attractive. Like chocolate cake and reality TV, I *know* it's bad for me, bad for the countries visited, bad for the environment. But when I'm trapped in my home office in a winter blizzard, the thought of a carefree week in a floating hotel stuffed with waiters bearing mai tais suddenly seems awfully appealing. What difference can I make by being righteous, I think? All that will happen is that I'll be frowning and pasty skinned when friends and clients come back from their own sun-splashed holidays.

Are the cruise ships, and the mass shopping they engender, a benefit or a blow to port cities and towns? Would it be better if we all went home, taking our tourist dollars with us, leaving the towns to depend on the largesse of the World Bank for their development needs? Or do so few of our tourist dollars even make it into local pockets that the question is merely moot?

A whole movement, the socially responsible tourism industry (of which eco-tourism is a large part), has sprung up in answer to this question, which really lies outside the scope of this book. But the guilt many people besides me feel about their holiday shopping habits is just part of a larger ambivalence about shopping itself. I'll get into that in more detail in chapter 14.

# 12 Extreme Retail Therapy:
## Shopaholics and Kleptomaniacs

*Years ago a person, if he was unhappy, didn't know what to do with himself—he'd go to church, start a revolution—something. Today you're unhappy? Can't figure it out? What is the salvation? Go shopping.*

—*The Price*, Arthur Miller, 1968

In the last few years, a British novelist who goes by the pen name Sophie Kinsella has gained fame and prime bookstore placements with her *Shopaholic* books. They chronicle the career of fictitious Becky Bloomwood, a London twentysomething with champagne tastes and a beer budget. As the series begins, Becky is stuck in a job she hates: writing personal finance articles for a middling magazine. Perhaps to compensate for that dissatisfaction, she just can't stop spending. Over the course of several books, she ends up on the run from her bank's credit manager, has to auction off her collection of designer clothes to pay her bills, and spends an inordinate amount of mental energy hiding her indebtedness from her parents, her friends, her boyfriend, and herself. It's all done for laughs and the books are a hoot. But for many people, shopping to excess is no laughing matter.

The opportunities to exceed our credit card limit are legion. In fact, the success of modern retail is largely based on tempting us to buy things we had no intention of buying when we walked into the store. That's one of the reasons stores succeed.

Impulse buying vaulted department stores and supermarkets over their counter-service competitors. When people can handle the merchandise freely, rather than having to ask the permission of a supercilious clerk, they have more opportunity to "sample" products in a low-risk environment. With no one hovering around them, they can take as long as they need to deliberate the merits of the product. If they decide they like it, they'll usually buy it. Right then. Right there.

Paco Underhill, the shopping analyst, wrote that spur-of-the-moment shopping decisions are vital to the success of any store. "In such moments the very heart of retailing lies, and if shoppers suddenly ceased to buy on impulse, believe me, our entire economy would collapse. For many stores, add-on and impulse sales mean the difference between black ink and red."

So stores have a strong motivation to tempt us—but they're not totally to blame. We like to be tempted. And ever since credit was invented, we've been succumbing to temptation.

## A short history of credit

In the late Middle Ages, when many people still bartered for goods rather than paying cash, it was nevertheless possible to run up substantial cash debts. Sir William Stonor, an English member of Parliament and landowner, had his steward begging him to settle various debts with the ale brewer and bread baker, who were hounding the steward daily to get their money.

As money came into slightly more widespread use in England in the 1500s, people were perplexed as to what to do with it. No banks existed, so one solution immediately became apparent: buy things! But even when they didn't have a purse full of coins, Britons were finding shops increasingly entrancing.

Credit was widely available. By the 1700s, many stores were letting customers run tabs for up to a year. This policy, not surprisingly, led to a lot of disputes and unpaid bills. After receiving the merchandise, a customer might arbitrarily decide it wasn't worth the price the merchant had charged and haggle over the bill. But shopkeepers denied credit at their peril. If shoppers couldn't put purchases on account in one store, they could usually find a retailer in the next street or the next town who would be only too happy to let them do so.

As I mentioned in the department stores chapter, department stores boomed when they insisted that customers pay in cash—the policy increased cash flow and wiped out the problem of bad debts. But in the early 1900s, department stores slowly started allowing customers to set up credit accounts, when they realized that some people would buy more with imaginary money than with cold, hard currency. Even grocery stores have started allowing shoppers to charge their purchases.

Credit cards have been around longer than you might think. You could use them to buy gasoline in the 1920s. In the 1920s and 1930s they were introduced in department stores. Diner's Club, the first credit card accepted in a wide range of stores, was introduced in 1950; Mastercharge (now MasterCard) and Chargex (now Visa) followed.

Credit gives shoppers the opportunity to walk out of a store with a product for "free." Oh, sure, the bill will come due eventually. But at the moment you're buying, there's no penalty. There's no pain. There's no spouse angrily waving a statement in your face. There's just the sheer joy of acquisition.

For some of us, that rush is just too compelling.

### Doctor, I just couldn't help myself

The idea of a mental condition that makes people shop uncontrollably isn't precisely new. Around 1915, a German psychiatrist named Emil Kraepelin described it in a textbook, christening it *oniomania* (from the Greek word for price, *onos*). Neither the name nor the idea caught on for almost a century.

Of course, there have always been people who have shopped to spectacular extremes. In 1861, Mary Todd Lincoln was flambéed in the press for spending over her $20,000 budget to redecorate the White House. At one point, it also came to light that she had bought 400 pairs of gloves over a four-month period. She loved buying clothes and considered her contemporary, Empress Eugénie of France—who could rack up apparel bills equivalent to $250,000 in today's dollars—a role model in that regard.

Another first lady, Jackie Kennedy, probably set some kind of record for political spouse spending. In JFK's first year in the White House, she accumulated clothing bills of over $100,000. The following year, the tab topped $120,000. One department store bill alone totaled more than half of JFK's trust fund income of $75,000.

After the tragedy of JFK's assassination, Jackie's shopping binges became more and more extreme. While married to Aristotle Onassis, she regularly exceeded her $30,000 monthly allowance. She bought three dozen silk shirts or pairs of shoes at a time, and could easily run through $100,000 in a ten-minute visit to an upscale boutique. In the seven years she was married to Onassis, she would spend $42 million. After his death in 1975, when she began working at the Doubleday publishing company in New York, she sometimes spent the equivalent of her $10,000 annual salary during one lunchtime shopping trip.

Such high spending among celebrities is sometimes considered atypical. These are rich people leading glamorous lives, we tell ourselves. Maybe $10,000 to someone like Jackie Kennedy is like $50 spent on a pair of buyer's remorse shoes to the rest of us.

But by the end of the twentieth century, unusual addictions were big news. Everyone had them—not just the rich and famous. The media were full of stories of compulsive gamblers and sexaholics. And then two high profile court cases and a Stanford study brought oniomania—now known by the more pronounceable name "compulsive shopping disorder"—into the spotlight.

In one case, management consultant Elizabeth Randolph Roach was accused of siphoning $241,061 from her employer, Andersen Consulting (now Accenture), to pay for her unstoppable shopping. In binges on Chicago's Magnificent Mile and elsewhere, Roach bought luxurious goods like a $7,000 belt buckle from Neiman Marcus. But the allure of the products wore off as soon as she got them home; most of her purchases ended up stashed in closets unused, their price tags still dangling from them.

Roach could afford a fairly upscale lifestyle: she earned $150,000 a year at Andersen, and her husband earned an equivalent amount as a corporate lawyer. So the question naturally arose—what would make someone in such comfortable circumstances buy so much that she had to steal to pay off her American Express card?

The other case that hit the headlines around the same time was even more spectacular and baffling. Over just six months in 1999, Rosemary Heinen of suburban Seattle embezzled over $3.7 million from *her* employer, Starbucks. Like Roach, Heinen used the money to finance shopping sprees that were almost incomprehensible to most people who heard about the case. Heinen and her husband had a collection of 32 cars worth a total of more than $1 million. Their house was so crammed with goods—including three grand pianos and more than 600 Barbie dolls—that they hadn't been able to have visitors over for years. There was no question of Heinen enjoying most of this stuff; she could barely move around it.

While these two cases were making their way through the news, a research team at Stanford University was working on a study to determine whether an antidepressant called Celexa could be used to control compulsive shopping disorder.

The media went wild.

On one side were reports trumpeting the arrival of the "shopaholic pill"—an inherently ridiculous-sounding concept that nonetheless had a magic-potion appeal to everyone with an overdue credit card balance and a closet full of unworn clothes. On the other side were the scathing skeptics, who thought the concept of compulsive shopping was just the latest manifestation of the Western world's fascination with addiction and treatment. This latter group took particular glee in pointing out that the Stanford study was funded by Forest Laboratories, the pharmaceutical firm that makes Celexa. Ironic coincidence? The reader was asked to be the judge.

As the old joke goes, I'm not a doctor. I don't even play one on TV. But I suspect that the answer to the riddle of why someone would go out and shop until their life falls apart lies somewhere between the two camps: part nature, part nurture. Excessive shopping is an accepted symptom of a range of other mental illnesses that appear to have genetic and brain-chemical origins. It isn't that much of a leap of faith to see excessive shopping as a disease in itself.

Or is this just another case of society trying to turn something women do naturally into some kind of disease? According to the rudimentary statistics available, up to eight percent of the American population may suffer from some degree of shopping disorder, and nine out of ten of these people are female.

If it does turn out that compulsive shopping disorder is just medical mumbo jumbo, or if it transpires that the disorder is much rarer than we currently think it is, the story will sound awfully familiar. Because in the days when the first department stores were attracting crowds, folks muttered darkly about a new disease sweeping the ranks of respectable middle-class women: kleptomania.

### Victorian ladies out of control

The word *kleptomania* was coined around 1830 to describe an irresistible urge to steal things one can easily afford. No one could explain such a bizarre urge except in terms of a mental disorder. And, since shopping was already closely identified with women, kleptomania quickly became a "feminine malady," right up there with hysteria.

Middle-class women in the 1800s were considered too delicate to work or vote, and many doctors believed that the menstrual cycle made women mentally unstable. The increasing commercialization of society, and the rapidly mounting opulence of department stores in particular, were deemed to have created an impossibly tempting environment for female shoppers. It seemed reasonable to society that these poor souls just couldn't help themselves. Bloomingdale's made them do it.

Flash forward into the mid-twentieth century and skepticism about the theory starts appearing. As James Bryant put it wryly, "True kleptomania must be extremely rare. Moreover, it is an ailment that never seems to afflict the poor." In his four decades in the Canadian department store business, from the 1930s to the 1970s, he could recall only two substantiated cases of kleptomania: a doctor's wife and a minister's wife.

It's easy to understand the appeal of the kleptomania theory, though. We can all understand, if not condone, kids stealing candy bars on a dare. We're even more sympathetic to poor people who steal food and clothes for their families. Even the rubbie who steals things he can trade for booze has an understandable, plausible motivation, and will likely be sent to counseling rather than to jail.

But what about the rich person who steals?

### When movie stars act out

The firestorm of media attention and late-night standup routines that erupted when actress Winona Ryder was arrested for shoplifting attest to our endless fascination with the subject. According to the tale that has attained the status of myth among readers of *People* and viewers of *Entertainment Tonight*, Ryder walked into a Saks Fifth Avenue store in Beverly Hills, clipped the security tags from about $5,000 worth of women's clothes, and strolled out of the store without stopping by the cashier's desk first. On November 7, 2002, after less than a day's deliberation, a jury convicted her of grand theft.

The *Little Women* star is far from alone on the celebrity shoplifting circuit. Film critic Rex Reed and 1940s glamour girl Hedy Lamarr have both been accused of lifting small items; in both cases, charges were dropped.

### Garden-variety theft

Bryant may have been joking when he said he thought kleptomania was extremely rare, but that indeed is the conclusion psychiatrists have reached. They're not willing to take kleptomania off the books entirely, but they're arguing that it's nowhere near as prevalent as the Victorians thought.

So now, we're left with plain old shoplifting, just a slightly fancier name for theft.

Psychologists offer a variety of explanations for shoplifting, which apply as much to the rich and famous as they do to the rest of us. Sometimes the crime is linked to depression, anger, guilt, or trauma, which a thief wants to take out on something inanimate, like a store. Some shoplifters are addicted to the thrill of evading detection, or to the feeling of power they get when they realize they can acquire anything they want.

Attitudes toward shoplifting and other forms of retail theft have wavered over the decades. Department stores used to be wary about prosecuting employees who shoplifted, because they considered their employees to be part of the family and thought that such matters were better handled privately.

But they were also reluctant to prosecute shoppers for the same crime, for a variety of reasons. Some thought it might result in unwelcome publicity for the store, attracting other shoplifters to the premises. Children who were first-time offenders would be sent home with a warning; managers considered it cruel to subject them to anything sterner.

Even now, stores are very reluctant to charge a customer with theft unless they have incontrovertible proof. Otherwise, the shopper may sue for false arrest, and those cases can be costly. In the 1970s, a woman named Laureen Bernstein won $1.1 million from a Korvettes in Brooklyn in a false arrest suit, throwing a severe chill over stores' interest in prosecuting shoplifters.

As long as there have been goods to trade, it seems, people have been trying to get them for free, whether out of necessity or just for kicks. Literature and music are rife with stories of desperate people stealing food because they're starving. The impulse remains the same; it's just the punishments that have changed. Jean Valjean of *Les Misérables* was in jail for stealing a loaf of bread. And an Irish folk song, "The Fields of Athenry," spells out the Van Diemen's Land fate that awaited one light-fingered dad:

> By a lonely prison wall, I heard a young girl calling,
> "Michael, they are taking you away
> "For you stole Trevelyan's corn, so the young might see the morn,
> "Now a prison ship lies waiting in the bay."

# 13 The Politics of Shopping

*Do you hate consumer culture? Angry about all that packaging?*
*Irritated by all those commercials? Worried about the quality of the*
*"mental environment"? Well, join the club. Anti-consumerism has*
*become one of the most important cultural forces in millennial*
*North American life, across every social class and demographic.*
—Joseph Heath and Andrew Potter, "The Rebel Sell,"
*This Magazine*, November–December 2002

Poor old Charles C. Boycott. There he was, happily installed as the estate agent for the Earl of Erne in County Mayo, Ireland. He probably made a decent living collecting the outrageous rents the earl charged his tenants. Who would have guessed that he'd pay so heavily for his sins that his name would live in infamy?

In 1880, Irish freedom fighter Charles Parnell decided that any landlord who refused to lower rents, or who evicted a tenant, was going to be cut off: no mail, no farmhands, no service in the stores, completely *persona non grata*. The Earl of Erne refused to cooperate, and the brunt of Parnell's wrath fell on Boycott. Eventually, Boycott fled the country, and in 1881 a new law protected Irish farmers.

We all boycott nowadays. Who among us hasn't left a particularly bad restaurant vowing never to go back? In 2002, when the *Ottawa Citizen* fired its popular publisher, hundreds of readers canceled their subscriptions in protest. So did we, but it wasn't that much of a sacrifice. I don't have time to read the paper half the time, and my husband often reads it free at a local coffee shop.

Speaking of the coffee shop, as Paul sits there with his paper, he sometimes wonders whether he should buy coffee that is "Fair Trade Certified," meaning that the Third World growers who produce the beans get a better deal for their hard work. Until 1989, the International Coffee Agreement regulated coffee prices. However, according to Global Exchange's Coffee Campaign, the U.S. undermined the agreement in favor of market forces, leading to a global coffee surplus that has depressed prices and hurt farmers.

Paul likes this particular coffee shop. The coffee's good, the price is right, and the shop is convenient to our house. But the beans aren't Fair Trade Certified. It's sometimes tricky to be both politically correct and economically caffeinated at the same time.

Sadly, when there's only one daily in town that we like, it's even hard to be principled about newspapers. Sheepishly, we renewed our *Citizen* subscription a few months after we dropped it.

### The real power shopping

If the politics of shopping seems to be something new, think again. Today, anyone with a credit card can buy the dresses worn by the fashion elites at the Oscars. But it wasn't so long ago that elites kept a firm grip on who wore what. In *Monty Python and the Holy Grail*, the peasants are able to identify their king because he's the only one who isn't covered in excrement.

In societies where goods are extremely scarce, you show your power by flaunting your stuff. That's why even today, rappers from the 'hood, like 50 Cent and Snoop Dogg, make sure to showcase the bling-bling (in other words, the jingly jewelry).

It's also why, in those old epic tales—*The Iliad, The Odyssey,* and all that—the heroes are never looking for a place that can make a good martini. They don't want experiences or ephemeral joys. Instead, they're looking for loot that symbolizes power: the Holy Grail, the Golden Fleece, Helen of Troy (the original trophy wife), the Land of Milk and Honey, and so on. (One of the notable exceptions is Gilgamesh, who quested for the secret to immortality, but we can take that to be a reversal of the old bumper sticker that says whoever dies with the most toys wins.)

The flip side of living in a world in which objects represent power is that it can lead to have-nots envying the haves. Envy leads to angry mobs with pitchforks, and nobody—even folks in gated communities—wants that.

## Don't get ideas, young peasant!

Centuries ago, just on the off chance that the lower orders might manage to get their grubby little mitts on the finer things in life, the elites passed sumptuary laws that forbade poor people to wear anything above their station. Although hard to enforce and widely ignored, these laws were common in Europe, but also in such class-conscious societies as Japan. In 1683, for example, the Tokugawa Shogunate (the same folks who decided to isolate Japan from the rest of the world) enacted six new sumptuary laws, including one that forbade embroidery on women's clothes.

Generally, the targets of sumptuary laws weren't peasants, who could barely afford to keep their sod roofs over their heads. The real threat came from the merchant class. Buying and selling, it turns out, could be even more profitable than watching the serfs till your land for you. Clustered in cities, an increasingly affluent merchant class began to pose a real political threat to the nobility, especially since the merchants were bankrolling all those wars the nobles fought against each other.

By 1800, Europeans, especially the Protestant ones, were looking at luxury in a whole different way than their great-grandfathers did. The rising mercantile middle class didn't see luxury as some sort of indicator of personal corruption, but as a reward from Providence for a job well done.

In 1905, Max Weber made a huge splash in sociology circles with his book *The Protestant Ethic and the Spirit of Capitalism*. He claimed that stiff-upper-lip Protestantism had led pretty much directly to Western capitalism. But sociologists have been picking at Weber ever since, pointing out flaws of logic and fact (including one notable example in which the figures in a table somehow add up to 109 percent).

Even if we want to get cocky and chortle at Weber for his poor mathematical skills, we still need to explain how we jumped from a world where the aristocracy had all the nice goodies to one in which anyone can buy cubic zirconia jewelry from QVC.

### Death and democracy

To avoid a lengthy discourse about the Industrial Revolution and the rise of capitalism, let's just invoke the plague.

In dramatically oversimplified terms, the Black Death killed off so many people that those left behind were in a better negotiating position. Merchants, artisans, and peasants suddenly had clout in this radical environment; books rolled off those newfangled printing presses that challenged the aristocracy with scary ideas about free enterprise and the equality of all men (but not women, naturally). Most hair-raising of all, the notion arose that maybe governments weren't blessed by God after all, but instead got their legitimacy from the people.

Combine this social mobility with a boom in new technologies, and next thing you know, they're dumping tea in Boston Harbor and chopping off well-groomed heads in the Place de la Concorde. As you can imagine, the last thing anybody was worried about at this stage was whether the wrong people were wearing the right dresses.

Besides, restricted access to "the good life" hardly mattered anymore. Instead of craftspeople taking their time to produce treasures, factories could now churn out cheap goods that were often better than anything handmade. And there were mountains of this stuff, just lying around waiting to be bought.

Of course, as Buddha would have predicted, the more stuff we have, the further the line separating luxury from necessity shifts.

### One man's luxury is another man's necessity

In his 1971 book *Rich Man, Poor Man*, Herman P. Miller dug up the 1960 stats for Tunica County, Mississippi, which he described as "the poorest county in our poorest state." Eight families out of ten lived on less than $3,000 a year, well under the official poverty line of the day. Despite that, roughly half owned a TV, a similar number had a car, and more than a third owned a washing machine. This, remember, was in 1960, before

Lyndon Johnson's "War on Poverty." As Miller concluded, "These families might have been deprived of hope and poor in spirit, but their material possessions, though low by American standards, would be the envy of the majority of mankind today."

Of course, at the beginning of the twenty-first century, the rest of the world is starting to catch up. When Mao Zedong came to power in poverty-wracked China in the 1940s, he vowed to provide everyone with the "Four Musts": a bicycle, a radio, a watch, and a sewing machine. His successor, Deng Xiaoping, believed that "to be rich is to be glorious," and so he did Mao one better (actually, four better) and called for all Chinese to have the "Eight Bigs": a color television, a refrigerator, a stereo, a camera, a motorcycle, a suite of furniture, a washing machine, and an electric fan.

Today, of course, the Four Musts and Eight Bigs have been long forgotten at the Sam's Club in Shenzhen, which Wal-Mart opened in 1996. There, they are mostly concerned with following Sam Walton's "Ten Rules for Building a Business."

Mao must be rolling in his grave (or, more exactly, in his crypt in Tiananmen Square, where the Great Helmsman's embalmed corpse has become a tourist attraction, complete with vendors hawking the Mao kitsch now so trendy in the People's Republic).

## It's all about choice

Like any attempt to summarize four centuries of dramatic social, political, economic, and cultural change in about 500 words, the preceding analysis is good enough to repeat quickly at a cocktail party, but try it on a serious historian and she'll eat you for lunch. Nevertheless, the unprecedented upheaval in everything that had ordered human existence for centuries can be traced back to things like annoyed burghers who weren't allowed to embroider their wives' clothes.

As Thomas Hine puts it in his 2001 book, *I Want That*, "In seventeenth-century England, people began to feel they had many choices . . . They could go into a shop and choose fine brocades. They could choose their religion and dress all in black. They executed one king, then deposed and replaced another."

This freedom of choice is the basis of free market ideology. If you don't like what they're selling in Booth A, you mosey along to Booth B and see what they have on offer. When rationality and self-interest govern the marketplace, everybody benefits and everybody is better off, or so the theory goes. In fact, one of the bibles of the libertarian movement is *Reason* magazine, and Ayn Rand called her philosophy/personality cult "objectivism."

### Who said we were logical?

But what if it turns out that our decisions about what brand of peanut butter to toss into our cart aren't all that rational at all? A new field called behavioral economics mixes psychological experimentation with economic theory. Unlike traditional, theory-based economics, behavioral economics tests what people actually do, not what they should do. And the results aren't pretty. We shop for hours to save pennies on cheese but make snap decisions when buying a house. We buy lottery tickets but complain about insurance premiums.

You can tell the field is political dynamite because those crazy kids at the Objectivist Center call it "misbehavioral economics."

Choice itself is starting to look a little frayed around the edges. For many critics of the free market, it is meaningless to say that someone barely making a living has enough economic power to "choose" for whom to work and under what conditions. They insist that real informed choices depend on access to product information that is increasingly locked away as proprietary, not to mention a Solomon-like ability to discern kernels of truth from endlessly repeated spin and marketing.

For example, in 2000, the Canadian Health Food Association released a survey that showed that 95 percent of Canadians wanted labels indicating foods that had been genetically modified. But at the same time, Greenpeace and the Council of Canadians accused Loblaws, the grocery chain, of lobbying the federal government to stop mandatory GM labeling. It seems that choice in the grocery store is only a good thing when it prompts consumers to actually buy things.

In Naomi Klein's *No Logo*, she argues that choice is further diminished when "big box" retailers sweep into town, using nationally advertised brand names and economy-of-scale low pricing to become "category killers"—stores that can decimate legions of smaller, independent com-petitors. And because these stores are usually on the outskirts of town, they can destroy vibrant small downtowns.

Although consumers get a broader selection of goods at lower prices at big box stores, they also rely more on fewer stores. And as any free enterprise devotee can tell you, the less competition there is, the less pressure a business is under to satisfy its customers.

### Censorship, shopping, and Barbie

Moreover, some national chains are susceptible to special interest cam-paigners, who successfully get them to remove "offensive" products from the shelves, even if those products have established markets.

This affects your choices directly. Blockbuster won't rent NC-17 movies, so many studios, if they make NC-17 versions at all, make special bowdlerized versions for Blockbuster. In 2003, Wal-Mart banned *Maxim*, a magazine known for pictures of scantily clad women, and it refuses to carry any "offensive" CDs. It even banned a Sheryl Crow album because one of its songs referred to Wal-Mart's policy of selling guns. Since Blockbuster and Wal-Mart account for a substantial proportion of U.S. video and CD sales, many artists censor themselves rather than risk losing markets for their work.

Conservative squeamishness is becoming an issue at the video store in a surprising way. Software programs designed to allow video produc-ers to retroactively add product placements are instead being used to "censor" movies by changing lines of dialogue and covering up naked actresses.

The Directors Guild of America and a conservative video store in Colorado are, at this writing, suing each other over whether consumers have a right to alter copyrighted material. The court case could also affect whether artists can use other people's intellectual property, from Mickey Mouse to *Gone With The Wind*, to make statements of their own.

Although right-thinking people (or, I suppose, left-thinking people) are horrified by homemade video editing, there is little difference between this kind of "re-contextualizing" and what director Todd Hayes did when he used Barbies to tell the story of anorexic singer Karen Carpenter, or when Danish pop group Aqua released the song "Barbie

Girl," which mocked the doll's not-so-covert sexuality. Mattel lawyers fought both, blocking Hayes but losing to MCA-backed Aqua.

Meanwhile, according to Klein, McDonald's has decided that it owns the Scottish "Mc" prefix and has sued McAllen's sausage stand in Denmark, a Scottish-themed restaurant called McMunchies, and even establishments named for people named McDonald.

Corporations are censoring citizens as well as artists and businesses. Legally, a mall is private property. So, while it is legal for me to wander around downtown handing out pamphlets demanding that chimpanzees be given the vote, if I try that in a mall, the security guards will probably kick me out. In one notorious example, during the run-up to the 2003 invasion of Iraq, the Crossgates Mall in Albany, New York, forcibly ejected a man wearing a "Peace on Earth" T-shirt. Ironically, he had had the shirt custom made in that very mall, that very day.

Appearing on Dennis Miller's talk show, George Carlin once marveled that in America people have plenty of choices about everything that doesn't matter. There are dozens of flavors of ice cream and brands of cereal. But when it comes to political parties, there are only two.

**Now on special: Political ideas!**

The confluence of politics and shopping has now come full circle. Until the early 1950s, U.S. political advertising consisted of buttons and whistle-stop stump speeches. But in 1952, the Republicans hired ad wiz Rosser Reeves to develop an ad slogan to help the GOP displace the Democrats, who'd controlled the White House for 20 years. Rosser had developed M&Ms' famous slogan, "Melts in Your Mouth, Not in Your Hand." Rather than simply do a motto for the Republicans, he developed a whole TV ad campaign called "Eisenhower Answers America."

The spots ran in the three weeks before the election and were heavily concentrated in states with close races, running right alongside, as a key Democrat put it, ads "throbbing with the merits of Follicle shampoo, or some new, improved detergent that takes the drudgery out of your Laundromat."

Unhappy about politicians selling complex policies the way Procter & Gamble sells simple soap? Well, you could always give the perpetrators the Charles Boycott treatment.

# 14  Our Conflicted Attitudes to Shopping

*The world is too much with us; late and soon,*
*Getting and spending, we lay waste our powers:*
*Little we see in Nature that is ours;*
*We have given our hearts away, a sordid boon!*
> —William Wordsworth,
> "The World Is Too Much With Us," 1807

Wordsworth's complaint about our focus on getting and spending sounds eerily familiar today. Many social critics at the dawn of the twenty-first century take us to task for spending too much time in malls and not enough on the activities they deem more worthy—canoeing the Nahanni River, playing with our children, training for a marathon, or reading improving books usually being among them.

But Wordsworth's sentiment would have also been old news to his contemporaries. For at least two millennia, people around the world had been uncomfortable with shopping. Part of that discomfort stemmed from a suspicion of riches themselves.

### Give to Caesar what is Caesar's

Most early religions developed an ambiguous relationship with wealth. In the Koran, for example, we read, "As to those who hoard gold and silver and spend it not in God's path, give them, then, the tidings of a painful agony: on a day when these things shall be heated in hell-fire, and their foreheads, and their sides, and their backs shall be branded therewith." But on the other hand, parents are urged to teach their children diligence, so that their "wealth shall increase."

In Timothy 6:10, Saint Paul wrote, "The love of money is the root of all evil, which while some coveted after, they have erred from the faith, and pierced themselves through with many sorrows." In other words, it is not the coins themselves that lead us astray, but rather the lust for lucre.

A continent away in India, Buddha had already come to the same conclusion. The root of all misery, he realized, is humanity's endless wanting. The more stuff we have, the more we want. Back in the groovy 1960s, we asked, "Do you own your possessions, or do your possessions own you?" Buddha would have given that sentiment an enthusiastic thumbs-up.

It wasn't just stick-in-the-mud religious types, or just plain muddy hippie types, who were suspicious of wealth. Several strains of ancient Greek philosophy condemned acquisitiveness. The original Cynics included people like Diogenes of Sinope, who ate coarse bread and lived in an earthenware tub. When Alexander the Great came stomping through and offered the sunbathing Diogenes anything he wanted, the Cynic is said to have merely asked that the conqueror get out of the way of his rays.

### Having money is bad enough, but for heaven's sake, don't spend it!

Wordsworth's worries about getting and spending didn't relate merely to wealth itself. They related specifically to the point where *spending* met spirituality, and those concerns had existed in England since before the Norman invasion in 1066. As we've seen, fairs and markets sprang up naturally in churchyards, where a large, dependable audience was available regularly. By 1285, the Statute of Winchester outlawed such commercial enterprises, but the law was widely ignored. In 1448, King Henry VI tried again; this attempt, too, seems to have fallen on deaf ears. In some cases, shoppers and sellers just moved their business into the church itself. By the 1500s, deans of Saint Paul's in London were complaining about the motley crew of entrepreneurs who sold souvenirs, drafted letters for illiterate clients, and measured customers for suits in the nave of the hallowed cathedral. By 1554, the Common Council of London had to take action to ban people from walking their horses through the church.

But our conflicted attitudes about shopping can be traced back even further, to another man who expelled commerce from a religious site in a particularly dramatic way. Here's how it's described in the Gospel of John:

> [...] Jesus went up to Jerusalem,
> And found in the Temple those that sold oxen and sheep and doves, and the changers of money sitting:
> And when he had made a scourge of small cords, he drove them all out of the Temple, and the sheep, and the oxen: and poured out the changers' money, and overthrew the tables;
> And said unto them that sold doves, Take these things hence; make not my Father's house an house of merchandise.

Clearly, we had mixed feelings about shopping long before the National Labor Committee urged us to boycott Kathie Lee Gifford's sweatshop-made clothes. And one of the earliest sources of our ambivalence relates to the long hours that often ill-paid workers put in to fulfill our shopping desires.

### They work so we may shop

Before 1100, some European religious authorities didn't approve of shopping in churchyards, but most didn't have much of a problem with Sunday shopping elsewhere. Sunday was a day of rest from work and a day of prayer, but those two ideas didn't preclude a little buying, selling, and general frivolity in the eyes of the lawmakers.

It wasn't until the twelfth century, when the term *Christian Sabbath* made its first appearance, that church leaders began arguing that any work on Sunday was a mortal sin. By the fourteenth century, worried observers were loudly complaining about the unholy mix of religion and shopping on the Sabbath. As one French writer put it, ". . . on those holy days on which God ought to be worshipped above all, the devil is worshipped."

The Reformation increased the pressure to make Sunday a sober, wholly religious day. In England, various laws made it a crime to miss church on Sunday (1551), to work on the Sabbath (1677), or to charge for public entertainment on the Lord's Day (1781).

Puritan settlers exported this idea of strict Sabbath observance to America, and took it a step further: in 1610, a Virginian who had been caught three times skipping church and catechism could be sentenced to death. The expression *blue laws* goes back to New Haven, Connecticut, where a 1781 law restricting Sunday activities had been written on blue paper.

Despite all this, religious holidays and the marketplace continued to mix. In the late 1700s and early 1800s, street sellers converged on Albany, New York, during the celebration of Pinkster (Dutch Whitsuntide), selling food and alcohol. Later in the nineteenth century, hucksters made the most of Carnival in New Orleans and evangelical religious revivals across the Midwest. In the early twentieth century, peddlers descended on New York City's East Side to sell goods to Jewish residents celebrating Sukkot.

Eventually, the debate expanded from shopping on religious holidays to long retail hours in general. In England, Charles Dickens and editors of women's magazines were some of the most outspoken proponents of the Early Closing Society. Unlike the Sabbath advocates, they didn't base their arguments on religious grounds. They simply wanted to ensure that retail clerks had more reasonable working conditions. In some stores, employees were on the job—and on their feet—from 8 A.M. to 10 P.M.

Owners of small shops agitated against the movement, claiming that legislated shorter hours would eliminate a key competitive advantage they had over the monolithic department stores. The debate raged on for decades, but stores' opening hours gradually shrank.

Concerns about shop clerks' mental well-being spread to North America. In the 1890s, the Shop Early movement took root in New York City, sweeping the country by the 1910s. It urged Christmas shoppers to hit the stores early in the day and early in the season, to decrease stress for weary clerks. In this case, it wasn't just a labor issue; it was a moral issue. "For the sake of humanity, shop early," the crusaders urged Americans.

The campaigners won the battle, but they ultimately lost the war. As historian Leigh Eric Schmidt has pointed out, by encouraging people to shop before the Christmas rush, the Shop Early movement had the ironic effect of extending the Christmas season.

### If I can see *Indiana Jones*, why can't I buy a rump roast?

Ambivalence about the mixture of commerce and religious holidays continued into the late decades of the twentieth century. In the 1980s, for example, Canadian legislators and judges began seriously wringing their collective hands over the question of what to do about Sunday shopping.

When elected in 1985, Ontario's provincial government had promised to maintain existing limits on Sunday retailing. Sunday shopping had long been outlawed in many provinces by laws such as Ontario's *Retail Holiday Business Act*, which the Supreme Court of Canada upheld as valid in a landmark ruling in 1986.

"The desirability of enabling parents to have regular days off from work in common with their child's day off from school and with a day off enjoyed by most other family and community members is self evident," wrote then-chief justice Brian Dickson in the majority judgment in that case.

But times were changing. In two-career families, Mom could no longer pick up the family groceries on a quiet Thursday morning and longed for the convenience of an extra day to run errands. People noted that you could go to a movie, a football game, or a play on Sundays. You could even go to *some* stores—the Ontario legislation permitted pharmacies and convenience stores to open on Sundays. So why not fling the retail doors wide open?

The debate on both sides was fierce. Groups such as People Against Sunday Shopping and the People for Sunday Association picketed stores that opened illegally on Sundays. They argued that Sunday shopping would increase prices by forcing retailers to pay more in salaries while spreading six days' of shopping over seven. They maintained that it would increase stresses on families.

One letter to the editor put the contrast between commerce and contemplation succinctly, arguing that instead of shopping on Sundays we should "stop and enjoy the work of our hands, take some time to stand and stare, look about, take a leisurely walk, a bike ride or a drive, visit a few friends, lie on the beach, read a book."

Ironically, some of the fiercest opponents of Sunday shopping were the owners of small stores—the colonial heirs of the shopkeepers who had fought Dickens's efforts to shorten shopping hours more than a hundred years earlier. This time, the retailers' concerns revolved around their desire to have some semblance of a family life.

But advocates of Sunday shopping countered with the argument that Ontario was a multicultural society, and any law that gave special status to Sundays was a religious affront to people who observed their day of rest on other days, or who didn't adhere to any religion.

Others also noted that when one jurisdiction allowed Sunday shopping, nearby jurisdictions would be forced to follow suit or lose business. That was the justification the state of Massachusetts used when it permitted Sunday shopping in 1983—it was trying to compete with neighboring New Hampshire.

In Ontario, the issue came to a climax in February 1989, when the provincial government walked away from any responsibility for legislating store hours, allowing each municipality to set its own rules. Predictably, chaos ensued.

Many cities allowed only shops in "designated tourist areas" to open on Sundays; merchants whose stores lay just outside those areas howled. Sunday-closing associations appealed bylaws and wrote beseeching letters to newspapers. Politicians of all stripes tried to read the wind and support the winning side.

Courts increasingly came down on the side of Sunday-shopping advocates, ruling Sunday-closing laws invalid. By June 1992, the fans of Sunday shopping had won the day. The last remaining provincial restrictions on Ontario shopping hours were lifted, and it was open season.

Within a decade, a pattern had emerged in most cities: large chains and some small stores opened for limited hours on Sundays, usually between 11 A.M. and 5 P.M. Other small stores stayed closed. An uneasy equilibrium had been reached.

But the fight rages on. As I was working on this book, a fiery debate on the pros and cons of Sunday shopping erupted in Nova Scotia, the last Canadian province to widely ban the practice. Aside from a short land border with New Brunswick, Nova Scotia is surrounded by the sea, which may be one of the reasons it had been able to hold out for so long. But when malls in Moncton, New Brunswick, began opening on Sundays, the pressure on merchants in nearby Amherst, Nova Scotia, began to build.

The province's premier, John Hamm, had made no secret of his opposition to Sunday shopping, but it appeared that the tide of public opinion was slowly turning. Voters and newspaper columnists mocked Hamm and his ilk as backward and paternalistic. One editorial bluntly asserted that "this old-fashioned policy is incompatible with the realities of our increasingly secular society" and that busy families had the right to "both weekend days to fulfill their consumer needs."

When this book went to press, it looked as though Hamm would try to sit on the fence by allowing Sunday shopping in the weeks before Christmas, but banning it at other times of year.

When we shop is, clearly, still, a bone of contention. But what we buy can also be a lightning rod for criticism.

### Fashion takes a beating

Fashion and beauty shopping has come in for particular scorn over the centuries. James D. McCabe, Jr., the minister-turned-journalist who observed the excesses of Gilded Age New York, was appalled by the overconspicuous overconsumption he saw all around him in 1872.

"Extravagance is the besetting sin of New York society. Money is absolutely thrown away," he wrote. Not only were the wealthy spending like sailors, but even worse, they were inspiring people of more modest means to follow them down the same path, often into ruin, he argued.

But the sheer waste of money, which McCabe considered criminal in a city with so many wretchedly poor people as New York had in the 1870s, was not the worst aspect of profligate spending. These people weren't merely wasting money. His voice reverberating with tones of the preacher he used to be, McCabe argued that they were wasting their very souls.

Keen observers see every day women whose husbands and fathers are in receipt of limited incomes, dressing as if their means were unlimited. All this magnificence is not purchased out of the lawful income of the husband or father. The excess is made up in other ways—often by the sacrifice of the woman's virtue. She finds a man willing to pay liberally for her favors, and carries on an intrigue with him, keeping her confiding husband in ignorance of it all the while. She may have more than one lover—perhaps a dozen. When a woman sins from motives such as these, she does not stop to count the cost. Her sole object is to get money, *and she gets it.*

While I'm sure there were women who were doing just as McCabe suggests, his arguments have a whiff of hyperbole about them. Surely a woman who was servicing the amorous needs of a dozen Manhattan millionaires wouldn't have any time left to shop for her finery?

But even this wasn't the worst of the fashion victim's sins, thundered McCabe.

Don't seek to analyze her character as a wife or mother. You may find that the marriage vow is broken on her part as well as on her husband's; and you will most probably find that she has sacrificed her soul to the demands of fashion, and "prevented the increase of her family" by staining her hands in the blood of her unborn children. Or if she be guiltless of this crime, she is a mother in but one sense—that of bearing children. Fashion does not allow her to nurse them . . . they grow up without her care, removed from the ennobling effect of a mother's constant watchful presence, and they add to the number of idle, dissolute men and women of fashion, who are a curse to the city.

So let me get this straight. Because she buys too many dresses, a woman is likely to be a prostitute, an abortionist, and a bad mother, unleashing a generation of degenerates onto an unsuspecting world? You know, somehow I doubt it. McCabe's tirade almost makes you feel sorry for these outrageously rich, pampered women.

I agree with McCabe's basic beef, truly. The amount of money squandered in Gilded Age New York was horrifying. It's just too bad he was channeling Oral Roberts when he went after the perpetrators.

## Seller's remorse

Even some retailers, it appears, are ambivalent about shopping.

"I hate the beauty business. It is a monster industry selling unattainable dreams. It lies. It cheats. It exploits women," wrote Anita Roddick, founder of the Body Shop chain, in her 1991 book *Body and Soul.* "In my view the cosmetics industry should be promoting health and well-being; instead it hypes an outdated notion of glamour and sells false hopes and fantasy."

OK, think about this statement for a minute. Roddick has become successful and famous by promoting a vast range of body scrubs, moisturizers, shampoos, eye shadows, and other products. Yes, they are packaged in recyclable containers. Yes, they aren't tested on animals. And, yes, the company has tried to use ingredients from indigenous producers in developing countries. These are all good things. But by any definition of the word, the Body Shop is definitely in the "beauty business." And while Roddick may hope that the customers in her stores embrace her environmental causes, the unfortunate truth is that many of them may, perhaps, possibly, just want to spruce themselves up with a great new lipstick for a hot date on a Saturday night.

## A nation of shopkeepers

Our conflict about shopping even extends, in some cases, to the shopkeepers themselves. Retailers were looked down on in the early Middle Ages, as parasites living off the labor of others and merely extracting a cut as they passed along goods from producer to buyer. Although that stigma eventually faded, the whiff of something unpleasant surrounding the profession would remain for centuries.

Around the time of the American Revolution, there was growing acknowledgment that Britain's factory owners (and, by extension, the shopkeepers who sold manufactured merchandise) were shaping the country's foreign policy. In the 1760s, clergyman Josiah Tucker argued against warring with the colonies by using a retail analogy: "A shopkeeper will never get the more custom by beating his customers, and what is true of a shopkeeper is true of a shopkeeping nation."

Adam Smith tweaked Tucker's expression into the phrase "a nation of shopkeepers," in 1776's *An Inquiry into the Nature and Causes of the Wealth of Nations*, published in 1776, and his opinion of such a nation is favorable:

> To found a great empire for the sole purpose of raising up a people of customers, may at first sight appear a project fit only for a nation of shopkeepers. It is, however, a project altogether unfit for a nation of shopkeepers; but extremely fit for a nation whose government is influenced by shopkeepers.

Other countries, however, thought that a focus on selling and profits was not something to be particularly proud of. In 1794, Bertrand Barère tossed Smith's phrase back at Britain as an epithet ("Let Pitt then boast of his victory to his nation of shopkeepers")—shorthand for a country of small people with petty ideals.

Until they found themselves facing skyrocketing death duties and soaring costs to repair ancient family homes, British aristocrats looked down on just about anyone forced to earn their living from anything but vast tracts of land, but they reserved particular scorn for those "in trade." Artists shared the dukes' disdain for moneygrubbers. In "September 1913," William Butler Yeats equated the rise of commercial culture with the destruction of lofty political ideals. Irishmen were more disposed to "fumble in a greasy till" and "add the half-pence to the pence" than to pursue their dreams of independence, according to the poet. "Romantic Ireland's dead and gone/It's with O'Leary in the grave," he mourned.

As late as the 1980s, there were those who dismissed Margaret Thatcher as a mere grocer's daughter—although Thatcher famously exploited her working-class origins at every opportunity. And even in 1997, when Diana, Princess of Wales, died in a car accident with Dodi Fayed, a hint of snobbery ran through British newspaper accounts of the tragedy. References to the fact that Dodi's father was the owner of Harrods department store were often slyly scathing. The implication was that the mere son of a shopkeeper—granted, the very rich shopkeeper of a very prestigious shop—wasn't good enough for the Queen of Hearts.

**Christmas crisis**

By the time of the Civil War, gifts had become such an inextricable part of the Christmas season that Jo March could sigh in *Little Women*, "Christmas won't be Christmas without any presents." Of course, since author Louisa May Alcott was a sober Yankee, the March girls learn that Christmas is, indeed, about much more than merchandise. They use the money they intended to spend on items for themselves to buy gifts for their hard-working mother—that sort of spending is all right, because it isn't spending on themselves—and spend Christmas Day itself sharing their meal with a poor family.

This tension between the urge to splurge and the guilt splurging entails follows a direct line from Alcott to Dr. Seuss. The Grinch's efforts "to stop Christmas from coming" in *How the Grinch Stole Christmas* are all about stealing the trappings of the day: trees, tinsel, food and, especially, presents. Once he takes every gewgaw in town, he's confident that he's foiled the celebration. Anyone who has witnessed the symbiotic relationship between Christmas and shopping over the last several centuries would think the same. But as we all know, the Grinch is astonished to hear the Whos down in Whoville singing on Christmas morning. How could Christmas be here without loot? "It came without ribbons! It came without tags! It came without packages, boxes or bags!" the Grinch marvels. And we marvel right along with him.

Commentators have also been decrying the excesses of Christmas shopping for well over a century. An 1880 editorial in the *New York Times* railed against what Thorstein Veblen would later term "conspicuous consumption" during the holidays. "Very few Americans have the moral courage to be economical or even sensible at this season of the year," the editorialist wrote in evident disgust.

Perhaps Agnes Repplier was thinking of exhortations such as these when she wrote the article I mentioned in the tourism chapter, about Christmas shopping in Egypt. She was fully aware that shopping was considered a rather lowbrow activity, and yet she gleefully didn't care.

She begins her article by remembering a young English girl and her mother she had once overheard on the steps of a hotel in Paris. The mother was trying to convince her daughter to visit a museum, palace, or other worthy site, but the child replied that she'd really rather go shopping. Repplier faces a similar conflict when she considers cruising the bazaars of the Nile.

> In vain our dragoman suggested a second trip to Philae, and the really intelligent sightseers of the party reminded me severely that I had not examined half the inscriptions on my previous day's visit. In vain the conscientious members urged that we had never been to the island of Elephantine at all, the sacred island where the god of the cataracts dwelt in his hidden shrine. In vain a few adventurous spirits urged us to ride to a Nubian village amid the sandhills and see a sword-dance,—"the real thing this time, and no mistake." It was Christmas Eve. Shopping was the legitimate employment of the day. I thought of the English girl, and her fine rejection of the Louvre, the Luxembourg, and the Salon, gathered a few unintelligent, unconscientious, and unadventurous idlers around me, and started for the bazaars.

Repplier treats the implication that she and her fellow shoppers are "unintelligent, unconscientious, and unadventurous" as a joke, but the fact that she mentions it at all shows that it resonated with her to some degree.

### We love Santa, we love him not . . .

Almost since he emerged as a major Western icon in the mid-1800s, social critics have been suspicious of Santa Claus as the commanding general of an army of shopaholics, exhorting us to spend more and more. Turn-of-the-century churchmen railed against "Santamas" and the prevailing notion that Santa, rather than Jesus, was the source of all Christmas blessings.

Then came the "Put Christ Back into Christmas" campaign, launched by the wonderfully named Milwaukee Archconfraternity of Christian Mothers in 1949. The idea took off across America in the 1950s and continues to have currency to this day. Ironically, many of its biggest early boosters were retailers, who eagerly tried to appeal to the latest customer zeitgeist by setting up Nativity scenes in store windows.

In a similar vein, an organization now called Alternatives for Simple

Living was founded in 1973 by Rev. Milo Thornberry to campaign against Christmas consumerism. It distributes a booklet called *Whose Birthday Is It, Anyway?* to churches across the United States every Christmas season. One recent edition of the booklet included a letter a family had written to their friends and relatives, asking them to give their time to a community organization rather than a present to the letter writers, who promised to do the same in return.

Some deep compulsion in us, though, seems to compel us to celebrate the season with mistletoe and secular songs, rum punch and foolish office parties, and, yes, Santa and shopping. As much as many people protest the secularization and consumerism of Christmas, we get cranky if anyone threatens to truly take them away from us.

Phillip Tengg, a one-time divinity student from Austria, learned this when he started an ill-fated campaign to trump Santa's supremacy. In December 2002, Tengg and his Pro-Christ Child Society were forced by worldwide public ire to issue an apologetic letter to Santa fans for producing stickers featuring Santa's face with a red line through it. Putting Christ back in Christmas is all well and good, it appears, as long as you don't mess with the big guy in the red suit.

### Shopping and the environment

One of the overriding concerns about shopping (and consumption in general) these days relates to its environmental effects. It's a very real worry.

Tetra-Paks from our children's lunchboxes clutter up landfills, while the rusting hulks of our automotive dreams clog scrap yards across the continent. Our lust for cheap home electronics leads manufacturers to set up plants in Mexico, which subsequently spew hazardous chemicals into the water system.

There are so many of us here, so avid for the next big thing, that the speed with which we can alter the planet is mind-boggling. About a decade ago, a few gourmet chefs decided to anoint a South American fish, the Patagonian Toothfish, as the new king of the upscale restaurant dinner table.

First, they gave it a catchier name. Hello Chilean sea bass.

Then they featured it pan seared, topped with mango chutney, served with exotic sounding reductions, or garnished with artistically arranged herbs.

The public went wild. Amateur gourmets started serving Chilean sea bass at home. Prices soared. Fish stocks tumbled. And today, scientists estimate that if we don't stop noshing on Chilean sea bass immediately, the fish will be commercially extinct in about five years.

Fifteen years from unloved to extinct.

More than 700 chefs have signed onto the "Take a Pass on Chilean Sea Bass" campaign. They're urging people to try other kinds of similar tasting fish, like halibut and striped bass. A little while ago, I read a thought-provoking column in the *Ottawa Citizen*—the column that reminded me of the sea bass boycott in the first place. The author, Peter McMartin, is taking a slightly more radical approach to the sea bass question. He's not switching to halibut, or striped bass, or even tuna. Convinced that we don't have a clue what we're doing when it comes to managing fish stocks, he's decided to drop seafood from his diet forever.

I admire that kind of resolve. And I find myself wondering whether, by the time I'm 80, there will be a lot of other creatures we won't be eating, or wearing, or simply watching through binoculars. All it might take is one photograph.

In late 1961, Jackie Kennedy commissioned a custom-made Somali leopard-skin coat, which she wore the following year for a cover shoot for *Life* magazine. As her biographer Marian Fowler points out:

> After Jackie was photographed for *Life*'s cover in her leopard coat, which probably cost about $6000, the price of one jumped to $40,000 and the animal went on the endangered species list where it still remains. This is serious fashion influence. Jacqueline Kennedy almost single-handedly cleared the jungles of these big cats.

Heaven forbid a celebrity should take a liking to teak coffee tables or ivory jewelry anytime soon.

But we can't lay the blame for environmental degradation solely at the feet of celebrities, or at the doors of manufacturers, retailers, and advertising agencies. They don't "make" us do anything. We're all big folks. We all make choices. And they all have effects.

Those effects don't only alter the natural environment. They also affect our urban environment, and the social structures we inhabit.

## Economies of scale blot out human-scale retailing

Remember the chain grocery stores I talked about in chapter 4? Not everyone was happy to see them arrive and grow. And grow they did—by 1930, A&P alone had 15,737 stores.

Unlike the independent grocer or even the public market, these stores had no roots in their communities. They were built cheaply and would be closed in a flash if they didn't perform up to company-wide standards. Unlike the locally owned store, where the grocer might quietly extend credit to a family in need or serve as a conduit for local gossip, the chain store was all about squeezing profit out of customers. Any social function was purely secondary and was usually discouraged by head office.

Another black mark against these stores was the fact that they were driving existing independent grocery stores out of business. Independent grocers were often active in the community, and their associates on the board of trade and the church committee weren't pleased to see them lose their livelihood.

As Senator Hugo L. Black put it in a speech to Congress on January 8, 1930, "The local man and merchant is passing and his community loses his contribution to local affairs as an independent thinker and executive."

The fear of chain grocery stores wasn't limited to the United States. North of the border in Canada, a 1927 article in the *Canadian Grocer* slammed them as a "sinister and anti-social development." Two years later, the Montreal *Daily Star* went even further, claiming that the growth of chain stores was "lowering the standard of Canadian citizenship, because it robs the individual of that sturdy independence of character which is an essential requirement in the building of a virile nation."

Similar concerns would echo through the history of shopping throughout the twentieth century. Communities across North America have fought bitter battles to keep giant stores such as Wal-Mart from setting up shop and killing local businesses. Vermont was the last state in the Union to hold out against the advances of the giant retailer. And although many social activist groups and community planners applauded Vermonters for their determination, their David-and-Goliath fight made them a bit of a laughingstock in some circles. When they finally lost the battle in 1994, the schadenfreude in some of the mainstream media was obvious. Here's the beginning of an article that ran in *Time*:

> You've got to hand it to the resolutely rustic citizens of Vermont: they know how to bend outsiders to their will. Outraged by the thought of Wal-Mart megastores sprouting among their sugar maples and dainty shops (Ye Olde Wal-Marte?), antigrowth protesters have repeatedly fought off America's No. 1 retailer and made their state the only one in the country to remain Wal-Mart free.

If you don't like Wal-Mart, the article implies, you're rustic, stubborn, and manipulative (although, weirdly, your shops are dainty). You're a boob and a rube. Get with the program. Hop on the progress train. Grow up and enter the real world.

I sympathize with the Vermonters—but mostly because I don't shop at Wal-Mart. My weakness is giant bookstores. There's a chain up here called Chapters—like Borders, or Barnes and Noble—and I practically live in the place. I know for a fact how the downtown Ottawa Chapters has devastated the independent bookstores in the area. There used to be a downtown store devoted mainly to cookbooks. Another specialized in Canadiana. Both are gone. Even the smaller chain bookstore in the mall across the road, an outlet of a chain that Chapters absorbed, has closed its doors. (According to Chapters' own statistics, shoppers spend up to five times longer in the giant stores than they do in the smaller outlets, and spend almost twice as much per visit; it's no wonder that the company is closing the little shops.)

The effects have been obvious and brutal. They've narrowed my book buying choices. And yet I continue to go to Chapters. Why? First of all, the store has a wider selection and longer hours than any independent could possibly manage (although the stock, annoyingly, is increasingly dominated by DVDs, yoga gear, and other giftware). And second, I don't have much choice anymore. Chapters' competitors are down to a handful. And yes, I'm partially responsible. Hoist with my own petard.

I suspect that author James William Kunstler would be strongly sympathetic to the anti-Wal Mart folks in Vermont (and a bit less sympathetic to my book-buying rationalizations). He described the sad decline of the upstate New York town of Schuylerville in his 1993 book *The Geography of Nowhere*. First the rail line was ripped out. Then Interstate 87 passed the town by. The final nail in the coffin was the opening of a large mall on the outskirts of nearby Saratoga Springs in 1972. The retail businesses that had kept downtown Schuylerville alive collapsed.

When Kunstler wrote his book, the most prosperous retailers in town were two nationally owned convenience stores serving drivers hurtling down Route 29 on their way to the interstate. The people who worked in the stores didn't make enough money to be pillars of the community, as local storekeepers once were. And the mini-marts' profits were sucked back to head office. The stores' owners couldn't have cared less whether Schuylerville's historic buildings were preserved or its streets were paved. "Their success is measured strictly by the tonnage of Cheez Doodles and Pepsi Cola they manage to move off the shelves," Kunstler wrote despondently.

## We shop, therefore we are?

Apparently, even after several millennia of trading, humans still haven't reached a consensus on what shopping means or what shopping should be.

Like Jesus, we're not keen on having the market clutter up our sacred spaces. Like James I, we worry that our kids are spending too much time hanging out at the electronics store and not enough time studying.

And yet, we join in the very thing we profess to disdain. Like the Duchess of Devonshire, we like to play games with our possessions, using our clothes and our accessories to amuse ourselves and others.

We've even twisted ancient myths and fairy tales to make consumption the star of the show. Ask most people (particularly women) which scene they remember best from the hit movie *Pretty Woman*. I guarantee most of them will mention Julia Roberts's shopping spree on Rodeo Drive. In the original fairy tale, virginal Cinderella got a lovely coach and an invitation to a ball; in our modern retelling, the hooker with a heart of gold gets Richard Gere's charge card.

In the end, I think, we're conflicted about shopping—both fascinated and repelled—because shopping isn't a black-and-white endeavor. It doesn't have a fixed moral value. We all do it. To at least a basic degree, we all need to do it.

In fact, shopping is a lot like eating. It can be a chore or a pleasure, a habit or a hobby. We can do it for fun or we can make it our job. We can do it with friends or we can do it alone. (It's starting to sound a lot like a third basic human drive, but I won't even go there.)

Like eating, it can nurture us or, taken to excess, it can kill us.

Out of all the people I talked to and read about while writing this book, the one who I think came closest to the average human's relationship to shopping was Wordsworth. He worried that we were wasting too much time getting and spending. But when he visited London, he couldn't take his eyes off the shops.

# Sources

Since this isn't an academic book, I've avoided using footnotes, but the following notes should point you in the right direction if you're looking for more detail. I've noted references that were particularly useful for each chapter, followed by citations for specific passages (when the source isn't provided in the main text). For the full citation for the works mentioned in these notes, please see the bibliography.

## Introduction

The classic work on gift giving in different cultures is *The Gift: Forms and Functions of Exchange in Archaic Societies* by Marcel Mauss; I relied on it for information on Haida customs in particular. Other useful sources for this chapter were two excellent books: James Twitchell's *Lead Us Into Temptation* and Kim Humphery's *Shelf Life: Supermarkets and the Changing Cultures of Consumption.*

14    "merchants are princes," Isaiah 23:8.

14    "When thy wares went forth," Ezekiel 27: 33–36.

15    "shopping is an investment in social relationships," Daniel Miller, *Shopping, Place and Identity.*

17    "[M]en who profess to enjoy shopping," Cele Otnes and Mary Ann McGrath, "Perceptions and Realities of Male Shopping Behavior," abstract, *Journal of Retailing*, spring 2001.

20    statistics on young children and brand names, Sarah Schmidt, "Branded babies: Marketing turns tots into logo-conscious consumers," *Ottawa Citizen*, May 6, 2003.

## 1    Around the World in Search of Merchandise

Valuable background on the spice trade came from the American Spice Trade Association and an unbylined article, "The spice trade: A taste of adventure," *The Economist*, December 19, 1998. General histories and encyclopedias were also useful.

26    "In 1759, New England exported," George Louis Beer, *The Commercial Policy of England toward the American Colonies*, 82.

## 2    A Fair is a Veritable Smorgasbord

This chapter draws on several rich sources, including Cornelius Walford's *Fairs Past and Present: A Chapter in the History of Commerce*; Fernand Braudel's *The Wheels of Commerce: Civilization and Capitalism, 15th–18th Century*; and David Alexander's *Retailing in England during the Industrial Revolution*.

31    "for one merchant who comes to the fairs," quoted in Braudel, *The Wheels of Commerce*, 90.

33    Sturbridge Fair proclamation of 1548, quoted in Walford, 79–87.

34    "the younger sort are or may be drawn," quoted in Walford, 115.

34    "an old weather-beaten pulpit," Ned Ward, quoted in Walford, 132.

35    "some very agreeable ladies of Cambridge," quoted in Walford, 129.

35–36 Daniel Defoe's comments, cited in Walford, came from *A Tour Through the Whole Island of Great Britain*, Volume 1, Letter 1 (1724).

37    "[t]hat all unhonest women," quoted in Walford, 155.

38    statistics on Las Vegas trade shows, Las Vegas Convention and Visitors Authority.

38    statistics on more than 13,000 trade and consumer shows, *Exhibition Industry Census*, Center for Exhibition Industry Research.

38    statistics on the CNE came from the fair's management office.

## 3    To Market, To Market

Witold Rybczynski's *Waiting for the Weekend* provided fascinating information on market day schedules. Sources of information on early European markets were "Early Fairs and Markets in England and Scandinavia" by Peter Sawyer and Molly Harrison's *People and Shopping: A Social Background*. *Retailing in England during the Industrial Revolution* by David Alexander offered details on English markets in the early 1800s. Henry Mayhew's *The Street Trader's Lot* provided general information on the atmosphere of Saturday night markets. *Gotham: A History of New York City to 1898* by Edwin G. Burrows and Mike Wallace was a vital source of details on New York markets. I'm indebted to James M. Mayo's *The American Grocery Store: The Business Evolution of an Architectural Space* for background on markets across the country.

40    "trade might attract," Cornelius Walford, *Fairs Past and Present*, 6.

41    "that merchants shall have safety," quoted in Walford, 20.

43    "that one weight shall be kept," quoted in Walford, 25.

45    "great disorder and bad language," quoted in Walford, 49.

45–46 "My heartiest customers," quoted in Mayhew, 46.

50    "The ricketty [sic] old buildings," James D. McCabe, Jr., *Lights and Shadows of New York Life*, 487.

50    "who are too smart to come," McCabe, 489.

## 4    Eat, Drink, and Be Shoppers

James M. Mayo's *The American Grocery Store* was an invaluable reference for this chapter. Other excellent resources included James Twitchell's *Lead Us Into Temptation*, Kim Humphery's *Shelf Life*, and Harry Bruce's *Frank Sobey: The Man and The Empire*. Vince Staten's *Can You Trust a Tomato in January?* was a good source of fun facts on grocery stores and their products, as was the Association of Science-Technology Centers Inc. (the latter provided much of the detail about the history of frozen and canned foods). Most of the statistics on grocery store sales, size, procedures, and stocks, unless otherwise cited, came from the Food Marketing Institute.

55–56 statistics on grocery-buying trips, Staten, *Can You Trust a Tomato in January?*, 30.

55    long weekends, catastrophes, and afternoons, Phil Lempert, <www.supermarketguru.com>.

56–57 fertility rate statistics, United Nations, *World Population Prospects: The 2002 Revision*.

57    "With minimal growth," Food Marketing Institute, *Food Retailing in the 21th Century—Riding a Consumer Revolution*, 5.

57–58 history of European mercers, Fernand Braudel, *The Wheels of Commerce: Civilization and Capitalism, 15th–18th Century*, 64–66.

58    statistics on grocery stores in New York in 1819, Edwin G. Burrows and Mike Wallace, *Gotham: A History of New York City to 1898*, 485.

59    statistics on prices in the Arctic, <www.dougandtheslugs.com/inuvik.html> and <wwwbigbeanbag.net/inuvik/inuvik-page.html>.

63    "[t]he package is an extremely important substitute," W.G. McClelland, quoted in Humphery, *Shelf Life*, 65.

65    *The Grocers' Assistant*, quoted in Humphery, *Shelf Life*, 55–57.

67    "[The Loblaws store] was full of customers," Frank Sobey, quoted in Harry Bruce, *Frank Sobey: The Man and The Empire*, 152.

69    "Depression-weary housewives," *Progressive Grocer*, quoted in Humphery, *Shelf Life*, 69, and Bruce, *Frank Sobey*, 150.

75  statistics on UPC scanning failures, Arizona Department of Weights and Measures, *2001 UPC Pricing Accuracy Report.*

76  "The customers came in a little bewildered," Sainsbury's, *J.S. 100*, 60, quoted in Humphery, *Shelf Life*, 74.

77  "How to Shop" instructions, quoted in Humphery, *Shelf Life*, 134.

78  Robert McMath's collection, Tom Alderman, "The National," CBC Television, January 20, 2000; also Chris Turner, "The Legend of Pepsi A.M.," *This Magazine*, November–December 2002.

80  Jordanian shampoo choices, Rami Khouri, "So much to buy, so little to buy it with," *Globe and Mail*, April 27, 2000.

81  "Will you join me," Kelly Egan, "Shopping areas on a human scale," *Ottawa Citizen*, December 9, 2002.

## 5    From Mesopotamia to Minneapolis: It's a Mall World

Particularly useful references for this chapter included Spiro Kostof's *A History of Architecture: Settings and Rituals*, Margaret MacKeith's *The History and Conservation of Shopping Arcades*, and Mark Girouard's *Cities and People*. The International Council of Shopping Centers provided valuable information on the history of the development of the modern American shopping center, as did the Web page of Steven Schoenherr, a history professor at the University of San Diego, <www.history.sandiego.edu/gen/filmnotes/shoppingcenter.html>.

88  "At the top of the street," Arieh Sharon, *Planning Jerusalem*, London, Weidenfeld & Nicolson, 1973, quoted in MacKeith, *The History and Conservation of Shopping Arcades*, 9.

90  "A stranger . . . appreciates," Carl Philip Moritz, *Journeys of a German in England in 1782.*

92  "Everything that can be found in Paris," N.M. Karamzin, *Letters of a Russian Traveler*, New York and Oxford, 1957, 215, quoted in Mark Girouard, *Cities and People*, 204.

93  "As far as possible convenience," Ralph Redivivus, *Civil Engineer and Architect's Journal*, March 1839, quoted in Margaret MacKeith, *The History and Conservation of Shopping Arcades*, 1.

94  "I don't think there is a shop," Augustus Sala, quoted in Alison Adburgham, *Shopping in Style*, 102.

94  "The Burlington Arcade provides," <http://www.burlington-arcade.co.uk>.

96  "In a region which is often beset," Southdale Shopping Center fact sheet, 1956, <http://www.southdale.com>.

98  "When people yearn for a return," Daniel Miller, et al, *Shopping, Place and Identity*, xi.

100  "We're trying to blur the lines," David Scholl, quoted in Jeanie Straub, "Regional shopping mall's design banks on meshing indoors, outdoors," *Boulder County Business Report*, December 17, 1999.

### 6    On the Road Again: From Peddlers to Avon Ladies

Important references for this section included *History of Pedlars in Europe* by Laurence Fontaine; David Alexander's *Retailing in England during the Industrial Revolution*; *Lights and Shadows of New York Life* by James D. McCabe, Jr.; and, particularly, Henry Mayhew's *The Street Trader's Lot*.

103    statistics about Brazilian Avon ladies, "Pots of Promise," *The Economist*, May 24, 2003.

104    "If we don't include," Andrea Jung, quoted in Byrnes, "Avon's New Calling."

105–6  statistics on Avon's sales in the 1990s, Nanette Byrnes, "Avon's New Calling," *Business Week*, September 18, 2000.

106    "snapper-up" and "silly cheat," William Shakespeare, *The Winter's Tale*, Act IV, scene 2.

106    "I will steal," quoted in Fontaine, *History of Pedlars in Europe*, 2–3.

106    "Thus aspiring," Reginald of Durham, *Life of St. Godric*.

107    "to Denmark and Flanders," Reginald of Durham, *Life of St. Godric*.

108    "The newly urbanized," Alexander, *Retailing in England during the Industrial Revolution*, 75.

112    "I can't tell what first make dem," Mayhew, *The Street Trader's Lot*, 113.

112    "Chestnuts all 'ot," Mayhew, *The Street Trader's Lot*, 4.

113    "Please gentleman, do buy my flowers," Mayhew, *The Street Trader's Lot*, 53.

113    "If we cheats in the streets," Mayhew, *The Street Trader's Lot*, 24.

113–14 "Gentlemen does grumble," Mayhew, *The Street Trader's Lot*, 66.

114    "Gentlemen 'out on the spree'," Mayhew, *The Street Trader's Lot*, 74.

114    "Watches, jewelry, newspapers," McCabe, *Lights and Shadows of New York Life*, 831.

114    "The dealers in these articles," McCabe, *Lights and Shadows of New York Life*, 833.

115    "When the day is wet and gloomy," McCabe, *Lights and Shadows of New York Life*, 834.

116    $15.7 billion in drinks, *Vending Times, Census of the Industry 2002*.

116    information and statistics on *jihanki*, Calvin Campbell, "Convenience, Japanese-style," *Globe and Mail*, February 22, 2003, and Vanessa Asell, "Food & Drink: Vending machine," *Metropolis Tokyo*.

118    "When two women shop together," Paco Underhill, *Why We Buy*, 102.

120    "These [parties] are starting to ruin my friendships," quoted in Kim Ode, "Living room, salesroom: It's big bucks and strained friendships," *Minneapolis Star Tribune*, April 23, 2003.

### 7 Please, Mr. Postman: Catalogs, TV Shopping, and the Internet

Useful resources for this chapter included Molly Harrison's *People and Shopping*, and several articles in the June 1, 2001, issue of *Catalog Age*.

122 "They're titles and prices," Henry Mayhew, *The Street Trader's Lot*, 81.

125 "provides every possible need," Eaton's Settlers' Catalogue, 1903, quoted in G. de T. Glazenbrook, Katharine B. Brett, and Judith McErvel, *A Shopper's View of Canada's Past*, vii.

126 "Better renew that *Free Press* subscription," *Winnipeg Free Press* editorial cartoon, quoted in James Bryant, *Department Store Disease*, 119.

126 "I'm as surprised as anyone," J.C. Barrow, quoted in *Globe and Mail*, January 14, 1976.

127 "THE WHITELY EXERCISER," *Ladies' Home Journal*, March 1900.

130 QVC trivia came from QVC.

133 "Electronically rummaging through eBay," Thomas Hine, *I Want That! How We All Became Shoppers*, 106–7.

134 statistics about Ice.com, Zena Olijnyk, "Dot-com wonder boys," *Canadian Business*, April 14, 2003, and Bob Tedeschi, "Online Jewelry Sales Increase," *New York Times*, December 9, 2002.

134 "Find customers, take orders," Scott Kirsner, "Express Lane," *Wired*, May 1999.

135 "I've seen me leave," quoted in Harry Bruce, *Frank Sobey*, 82.


### 8 Department Stores: The Original One-Stop Shops

Essential references for this chapter were Ralph M. Hower's *History of Macy's of New York 1858–1919: Chapters in the Evolution of the Department Store*; Michael B. Miller's *The Bon Marché: Bourgeois Culture and the Department Store, 1869–1920*; James Bryant's *Department Store Disease*; and Bill Lancaster's *The Department Store: A Social History*. William Stephenson's *The Store that Timothy Built* provided useful details about Eaton's.

140 "I am settling a complaint . . . no you're not," Lloyd Wendt and Herman Kogan, *Give the Lady What She Wants! The Story of Marshall Field & Company*, 223.

141 "they might sende any childe," quoted in Hower, *History of Macy's*, 89.

141 "There are many young ladies," quoted in Daniel Defoe, *The Complete English Tradesman*, 64.

142 "A tradesman behind his counter," Defoe, *The Complete English Tradesman*, 60–61.

144 "Ladies, you come off the train," quoted in G. de T. Glazenbrook, Katharine B. Brett, and Judith McErvel, *A Shopper's View of Canada's Past*, v.

145    "if they do not find them," Josiah Wedgwood, quoted in Hower, *History of Macy's*, 90.

146    "We buy exclusively *FOR CASH!!!*," ad reproduced in Hower, *History of Macy's*, 21.

146    "This cash nexus," Bill Lancaster, *The Department Store*, 9.

147    "Selling consumption was a matter," Miller, *The Bon Marché*, 28.

150    "When you get a cash boy's job," Wendt and Kogan, *Give the Lady What She Wants!*, 153–54.

151    "[p]arties who are old," *Glasgow Herald*, quoted in Lancaster, *The Department Store: A Social History*, 48.

152    "an easy and perfectly safe," Siegel Cooper ad, *New York Times*, December 1, 1901.

155    "*for a Mere Song*," ad in *New York Tribune*, November 10, 1873, quoted in Hower, *History of Macy's*, 118.

157    "The floorwalker must have descended," Bryant, *Department Store Disease*, 103.

157    "From there children were elevated," Bryant, *Department Store Disease*, 104.

159    "The escalator was like the Monorail," Jill Robinson, "Store, spa, or subculture? Go to Bloomie's," *Vogue*, August 1976.

159    "Such sacred," Bryant, *Department Store Disease*, 130.


**9    Fashion Victims**

164    Statistics on perfume launches, Mireille Silcoff, "Getting up our noses," *National Post*, December 7, 2002.

165    1992 study of women buying perfume, David Glen Mick, Michelle DeMoss, and Ronald J. Faber, "A Projective Study of Motivations and Meanings of Self-Gifts: Implications for Retail Management," *Journal of Retailing*, volume 68, number 2, quoted by David Glen Mick in Cele Otnes and Richard F. Beltramini, editors, *Gift Giving: A Research Anthology*, 109.

166    "Two women in a store," Paco Underhill, *Why We Buy*, 115–116.

167    "If I put on Tyrian clothes," Martial, *Epigrams*, 11:39, excerpted in Jo-Ann Shelton, editor, *As the Romans Did*, 33.

168    "[r]ecollect the time," Petrarch, quoted in Captain W. Jesse, *The Life of Beau Brummell*, 9.

168–69    "To be an accomplished," Ben Jonson, *Every Man Out of His Humor*, 1599, Act I, Scene 1.

169    "MRS. WILLIAMS," ad, *Bath Chronicle*, January 11, 1770, excerpted in Trevor Fawcett, compiler, *Voices of Eighteenth-Century Bath: An Anthology*, 31.

171 "I wish such things," Jane Austen in a letter to her sister Cassandra, excerpted in Penelope Hughes-Hallet, editor, *My Dear Cassandra*, 34.

172 "I shall never forget being taken," Lucile (Lady Duff Gordon), quoted in Alison Adburgham, *Shops and Shopping*, 247.

173 "very convenient little gadget," Shop-Hound, "Tips on the shop market," *Vogue*, May 1, 1933.

174 "The New York-based graphic artist," "Spring Dictionary of Style," *National Post*, March 8, 2003.

175–76 "You wouldn't believe how many," Susie Sheffman, quoted in Leanne Delap, "Waiting a year for a purse that costs $16,000: trendy," *Globe and Mail*, July 8, 1999.

176 "In no other city of the land," James D. McCabe, Jr., *Lights and Shadows of New York Life*, 141.

177 "judged it 'dowagerish,'" "Counter Intelligence," *Ottawa Citizen*, May 17, 2003.

## 10  Born to Shop: From Bridal Showers to Christmas Stockings

For this chapter, I found two books invaluable: *Gift Giving: A Research Anthology*, edited by Cele Otnes and Richard F. Beltramini, and Leigh Eric Schmidt's *Consumer Rites: The Buying and Selling of American Holidays*.

180 David Cheal, "Gifts in Contemporary North America," in Otnes and Beltramini, *Gift Giving: A Research Anthology*, 85–97.

181 "I felt that I hadn't given him enough," quoted by Julie A. Ruth, "It's the Feeling that Counts: Toward an Understanding of Emotion and Its Influence on Gift-Exchange Processes," in Otnes and Beltramini, *Gift Giving*, 199.

182 1990 study of female Christmas shoppers, by Fischer and Arnold, cited by Cheal, in Otnes and Beltramini, *Gift Giving*, 88–89.

182 "There is social risk associated with gift giving," Mary Ann McGrath and Basil Englis, "Intergenerational Gift Giving in Subcultural Wedding Celebrations: The Ritual Audience as Cash Cow," in Otnes and Beltramini, *Gift Giving*, 123.

183 study that found up to 16 percent of respondents disliked wedding registries, McGrath and Englis, "Intergenerational Gift Giving," in Otnes and Beltramini, *Gift Giving*, 131.

183–84 Korean-Canadian bride, Carolyn Pritchard, "Brides and grooms will always take your cash," *National Post*, May 12, 2001.

184 multicultural wedding customs, Susan Semenak, "Marrying the gift to the wedding: Picking present is no walk down aisle," *Gazette* (Montreal), June 9, 2001.

184 "all for less than sixty dollars," Shop-Hound, "Tips on the shop market," *Vogue*, May 1, 1933.

184 statistics on 1933 wages, *Monthly Labor Review*, September 1933, 728, quoted in *Why the Minimum Wage Law Causes Unemployment*, National Center for Policy Analysis, note 44, 1996.

185 "promising marriage," Natalie Zemon Davis, *The Gift in Sixteenth-Century France*, 27–29.

185 "It's a pretty smart idea," Shop-Hound, "Tips on the shop market," *Vogue*, May 1, 1933.

188 New York newspaper ad from 1770, Schmidt, *Consumer Rites: The Buying and Selling of American Holidays*, 113–14.

189 "Such a crowd as I never before saw," Abiel T. La Forge, quoted in Ralph M. Hower, *History of Macy's of New York 1858–1919*, 125.

190 "To-day ushers in the month," ad for Hearn department store, *New York Times*, December 1, 1901.

191 "to see 'Christmas,'" Schmidt, *Consumer Rites*, 150–52.

191 "The Spirit of Christmas is all over the store," Siegel Cooper ad, *New York Times*, December 1, 1901, 5.

192 "You have taken a big step," quoted in Schmidt, *Consumer Rites*, 166–67.

193 "I rejoice that it comes but once," William Mercer, quoted in Schmidt, *Consumer Rites*, 156.

193 "this silly Christmas trash," Marguerite Du Bois, quoted in Schmidt, *Consumer Rites*, 156.

194 "All traded gifts," Triangle Electronics ad, quoted by John F. Sherry, Jr., in Otnes and Beltramini, *Gift Giving*, 223–24.

195 "Isn't it funny how some," Maggie Alderson, *Shoe Money*, 1–2.

196 "Or, you say that you're '*collecting*,'" study by Sherry and McGrath, 1989, quoted by David Glen Mick, "Self-Gifts," in Otnes and Beltramini, *Gift Giving*, 101.

196 people feel guilty buying self-gifts, study by Sherry, McGrath, and Levy, 1995, quoted by Mick, "Self-Gifts," in Otnes and Beltramini, *Gift Giving*, 106–7.

196 54 college students, study by Mick and DeMoss, 1990, quoted by Mick, "Self-Gifts," in Otnes and Beltramini, *Gift Giving*, 101.

196 good price is satisfying, study by Compeau, Monroe, and Ozanne, quoted by Mick, "Self-Gifts," in Otnes and Beltramini, *Gift Giving*, 106.

## 11   Don't Miss Our Gift Shop on the Way Out

199 "I hope you will send us," Josiah Wedgwood, *Letters*, 124 (letter from Josiah Wedgwood to Thomas Bentley, June 6, 1772), quoted in Trevor Fawcett, compiler, *Voices of Eighteenth-Century Bath: An Anthology*, 32.

200–1 series of quotations from Agnes Repplier comes from "Christmas Shopping at Assuân," *The Atlantic Monthly*, May 1895.

201–2 study of the relationship between museums and merchandising, Stefan Toepler and Volker Kirchberg, *Museums, Merchandising, and Nonprofit Commercialization*, National Center on Non-Profit Enterprise, n.d.

202 Statistics Canada figures on museum gift shops, Statistics Canada, "Heritage institutions," *The Daily*, December 4, 2002, 7.

202 "We had a flurry of letters," Philippe de Montebello, *New York Times*, 2002, quoted in Toepler and Kirchberg, *Museums, Merchandising, and Nonprofit Commercialization*, National Center on Non-Profit Enterprise, 5.

203 "For some people," National Public Radio, 1998, quoted in Toepler and Kirchberg, *Museums, Merchandising, and Nonprofit Commercialization*, n.d., 5–6.

203–4 "the Museum Store," quoted in Toepler and Kirchberg, *Museums, Merchandising, and Nonprofit Commercialization*, 6.

204 The 2001 Travel Industry Association of America study was called *The Shopping Traveler*.

205 "The sales begin as private events," Suzy Gershman and Judith Thomas, *Born to Shop Los Angeles*, 142.

206 "Move over, Chelsea," Francis Lewis, "Hot Tips: Art and Antiques," *Where New York*, November 2002.

208 spending by Icelanders in Newfoundland, Economic Development St. John's, undated articles in the *St. John's Telegram*, and "Icelanders shop Newfoundland," *Tourism*, December 2002.

209 "The market can't be thought of," Daryl Adair, "Creating a shopping destination," *Tourism*, December 2002.

209 research on downtown Montreal shoppers, quoted in "Montréal a unique shopping experience," *Tourism*, December 2002.

211–12 quotes from Rosemary McCormick, telephone interview, May 2003.

212 "a '90s-style vacation," Emily Nelson, "The new '90s getaway: shopping," *Globe and Mail*, November 22, 1997 (reprinted from the *Wall Street Journal*).

212–13 "No big box stores," Southern Ontario Tourism Organization, *Shopping Getaways . . . in Southern Ontario*, promotional booklet, fall 2002.

213 "celebrity-style shopping," West Hollywood Convention and Visitors Bureau, "Two Celebrity-Magnets Announce Shopping Promotion for the Holidays," news release, October 15, 2002.

213 "VIP treatment at select stores," Hyatt International Corporation, "Shopping perks and Parisian pampering," news release, October 30, 2002.

214 "Our focus is to attract class tourists," T. Balakrishnan, quoted in Venkatachari Jagannathan, "Heavenly Destination," Domain-b.com, June 20, 2002.

215    "knickknack shops and shuffleboard," Sean Durnam, quoted in James MacPherson, "Tenakee cruisers spurned," *Juneau Empire*, August 14, 1998.

215    statistics about art auctions, Kitty Bean Yancey, "Cruise lines draw profits from selling works of art," *USA Today*, February 8, 2001.

216    statistics about spending by cruise ship passengers, Ross A. Klein, "Cruise Ships: The Industry's Dark Side," *Conscious Choice*, February 2003.

218    tourism statistics for Charlotte Amalie, Susan Thorne, "Carnival Time: Tourist sales give retailers in U.S. Virgin Islands cause to celebrate," *Shopping Centers Today*, January 1, 2000.

## 12   Extreme Retail Therapy: Shopaholics and Kleptomaniacs

Molly Harrison's *People and Shopping* provided useful information on the history of credit. Marian Fowler's *The Way She Looks Tonight* was invaluable for information on Jackie Kennedy and Empress Eugénie.

222    "In such moments," Paco Underhill, *Why We Buy*, 55–56.

226    "True kleptomania," James Bryant, *Department Store Disease*, 56.

## 13   The Politics of Shopping

232    "the poorest county," Herman P. Miller, *Rich Man, Poor Man*, 110–11.

233    "In seventeenth-century England," Thomas Hine, *I Want That! How We All Became Shoppers*, 84.

234    Canadian Health Food Association study, Neville Judd, "Lack of GMO Labeling Turns Canadians Towards Organic Foods," ENS news release, August 16, 2000.

236    "throbbing with the merits," "Ball Blasts Plan to Fill Airwaves with Ike Spots," 1952 newspaper article reproduced at <www.sit.wisc.edu/~carmona/sixthpg.htm>.

## 14   Our Conflicted Attitudes to Shopping

Details on early English commerce came from Peter Sawyer, "Early Fairs and Markets in England and Scandinavia" and Molly Harrison, *People and Shopping*. Leigh Eric Schmidt's *Consumer Rites: The Buying and Selling of American Holidays* was a rich source of information on our conflicted attitudes to shopping during Christmas and other religious holidays. Information on the legal underpinnings of Sabbath laws came from Witold Rybczynski's fascinating book, *Waiting for the Weekend*.

237–38   "As to those who hoard," Koran, 9:34–9:35.

239    "Jesus went up to Jerusalem," John 2:13-16.

239     "on those holy days," from Edith Cooperrider Rodgers' *Discussion of Holidays in the Later Middle Ages* (1940, reprinted 1967), quoted in Leigh Eric Schmidt, *Consumer Rites*, 20.

241     "The desirability of enabling parents," former Canadian chief justice Brian Dickson, quoted in Stephen Bindman, "Merchants, employees relieved by ruling," *Ottawa Citizen*, December 18, 1986.

241–42 "Stop and enjoy," Jack Dekok, "Breaking Law, and Tradition," *Ottawa Citizen*, October 29, 1986.

243     "this old-fashioned policy," "Sunday is like every day," *National Post*, April 23, 2003.

243     "Extravagance is the besetting sin," John D. McCabe, Jr., *Lights and Shadows of New York Life*, 141.

243–44 "Keen observers see every day," McCabe, *Lights and Shadows of New York Life*, 151.

244     "Don't seek to analyze her character," McCabe, *Lights and Shadows of New York Life*, 154–55.

245     "I hate the beauty business," Anita Roddick, *Body and Soul*, 9.

245     "A shopkeeper will never get," Josiah Tucker, *Four Tracts on Political and Commercial Subjects*, 1766.

246     "To found a great empire," Adam Smith, *An Inquiry into the Causes of the Wealth of Nations*, 1776, volume II, book IV, chapter 7, part 3.

246     "Let Pitt then boast," Bertrand Barère, June 11, 1794.

247     "Christmas won't be Christmas," Louisa May Alcott, *Little Women*, chapter 1.

247     "to stop Christmas from coming" and "It came without ribbons," Dr. Seuss, *How the Grinch Stole Christmas*.

247     "Very few Americans," quoted in Schmidt, *Consumer Rites*, 183.

248     "In vain our dragoman," Agnes Repplier, "Christmas Shopping at Assuân," *Atlantic Monthly*, May 1895.

250     "After Jackie was photographed," Marian Fowler, *The Way She Looks Tonight*, 292.

251     "The local man and merchant," Senator Hugo L. Black, quoted in James M. Mayo, *The American Grocery Store*, 107.

251     "sinister and anti-social," *Canadian Grocer*, 1927, quoted in Harry Bruce, *Frank Sobey*, 77.

251     "lowering the standard of Canadian citizenship," Montreal *Daily Star*, 1929, quoted in Harry Bruce, *Frank Sobey*, 77.

252     "You've got to hand it," John Greenwald, "Up Against the Wal-Mart," *Time*, August 22, 1994.

253     "Their success is measured strictly," James William Kunstler, *The Geography of Nowhere*, 182.

# Bibliography

Adair, Daryl. "Creating a shopping destination." *Tourism*, Canadian Tourism Commission, December 2002, 6.

Adburgham, Alison. *Shopping in Style: London from the Restoration to Edwardian Elegance*. London: Thames and Hudson, 1979.

Adburgham, Alison. *Shops and Shopping 1800–1914*. London: George Allen and Unwin, 1964.

Alcott, Louisa May. *Little Women*.

Alderman, Tom. Report on Robert McMath's collection of failed products. "The National." CBC Television, January 20, 2000.

Alderson, Maggie. *Shoe Money*. Ringwood, Australia: Penguin Books Australia Ltd., 1998.

Alexander, David. *Retailing in England during the Industrial Revolution*. London: The Athlone Press, University of London, 1970.

Amiel, Barbara. "The art of being precious." *National Post*, November 16, 2002.

Anon. "The Anecdotal Side of Mr. Beecher." *Ladies' Home Journal,* March 1900, 3.

Anon. "Buy on the fly: airports are discovering that travellers want more from on-site retailers than a cheap novel and a pricey cup of coffee." *Marketing Magazine*, May 11, 1998, 14.

Anon. "Counter Intelligence." *Ottawa Citizen*, May 17, 2003, E7.

Anon. "Design therapy: new trends in supermarket design can create moods that can enhance sales." *Canadian Grocer*, February 1993, 102–10.

Anon. "Grocery store puts pesky guys in their place while wives shop." *Ottawa Citizen*, February 17, 1999, B11.

Anon. "HomeRuns.com shuts down." *Boston Business Journal*, July 13, 2001.

Anon. "Icelanders shop Newfoundland." *Tourism*, December 2002, 8.

Anon. "Montréal a unique shopping experience." *Tourism*, December 2002, 8.

Anon. "New Design Throws Supermarket a Curve." *Air Conditioning Heating and Refrigeration News*, October 1, 2001, 16.

Anon. "Pots of Promise." *The Economist*, May 24, 2003, 69–71.

Anon. "Roundtable: Where We've Been, Where We're Going." *Catalog Age*, June 1, 2001.

Anon. "'Smart carts' on a roll." *Globe and Mail*, October 28, 2002.

Anon. "The spice trade: A taste of adventure." *The Economist*, December 19, 1998.

Anon. "Spring Dictionary of Style." *National Post*, March 8, 2003, FA4.

Anon. "Sunday is like every day." *National Post*, editorial, April 23, 2003, A19.

Anon. "Super markets." *Canadian Architect*, September 2001, 22–25.

Anon. "Supermarket as Theater." *Chain Store Age*, December 2000, 190.

Anon. "Supermarket design geared to big box concept." *Lighting Magazine*, February 1, 1998, 8–9.

Anon. "Tour du Metro." *Canadian Grocer*, April 1994, 16–22.

Anon. "Toying with fresh alternatives: Major shift in retailing game." *Calgary Herald*, February 15, 2003, D8.

Arizona Department of Weights and Measures. *2001 UPC Pricing Accuracy Report*. Phoenix: Arizona Department of Weights and Measures, n.d.

Asell, Vanessa. "Food & Drink: Vending machine." *Metropolis Tokyo*, n.d. <http://metropolis.japantoday.com/tokyofooddrinksarchive349/329/tokyofooddrinksinc.htm>.

Balcom, Susan. "Here comes the bridal registry: Getting married? A bridal registry is a great way to get the gifts you really want—and the good news is that they don't have to be conventional." *Vancouver Sun*, May 17, 2002, E4.

Barr, Vilma and Charles E. Brody. *Designing to Sell: A Complete Guide to Retail Store Planning and Design*. New York: McGraw-Hill Book Company, 1986.

Barreneche, Raul A. "Window Shopping." *Architecture*, March 1999.

Beer, George Louis. *The Commercial Policy of England toward the American Colonies*. New York: Smith, 1893.

Berdik, Chris. "Selling the Cure for Shopaholism." *Mother Jones*, May 23, 2000.

Bindman, Stephen. "Merchants, employees relieved by ruling." *Ottawa Citizen*, December 18, 1986, A1.

Bir, Sara. "Salesmen of the Century." *North Bay Bohemian*. April 18–24, 2002.

Bird, John. "On a Sunday shopping spree." *The United Church Observer*, March 2002.

Boroughs, Don L. "Purchasing power: QVC, television's home-shopping giant, channels big growth and products." *U.S. News and World Report*, January 31, 1994.

Bourret, Suzanne. "Super Markets: They're not just grocery stores anymore." *Hamilton Spectator*, February 26, 1997, C12.

Brand, Rachel. "DIA shop owners seek relief: nearly 100 stores ask city to extend leases 5 to 10 years." *Denver Rocky Mountain News*, February 20, 2003, 2B.

Braudel, Fernand. *The Wheels of Commerce: Civilization and Capitalism, 15th–18th Century*. Vol. 2. 1979. Translation. New York: Harper and Row, 1982.

Brooks, David. *Bobos in Paradise: The New Upper Class and How They Got There*. New York: Simon and Schuster, 2000.

Bruce, Harry. *Frank Sobey: The Man and The Empire*. Toronto: Macmillan of Canada, 1985.

Bryant, James. *Department Store Disease*. Toronto: McClelland and Stewart, 1977.

Burrows, Edwin G. and Mike Wallace. *Gotham: A History of New York City to 1898*. New York and Oxford: Oxford University Press, 1999.

Byrnes, Nanette. "Avon's New Calling." *Business Week*, September 18, 2000.

Campbell, Calvin. "Convenience, Japanese-style." *Globe and Mail*, February 22, 2003, T2.

Carlson, Les, Ann Walsh, Russell N. Laczniak, and Sanford Grossbart. "Family communication patterns and marketplace motivations, attitudes, and behaviors of children and mothers." *Journal of Consumer Affairs*, June 22, 1994.

Cassidy, Mike. "Candy-coated eBay tale was too good to be true." *The Mercury News*, June 14, 2002.

Center for Exhibition Industry Research. *Exhibition Industry Census*. Chicago: CEIR, 2002.

Coburn, Kate. "Airport retail in 9/11's wake." *Shopping Center World*, May 1, 2002.

Connelly, Mark. *Christmas: A Social History*. London: I.B. Tauris & Co. Ltd., 1999.

Dalby, Andrew. *Empire of Pleasures: Luxury and Indulgence in the Roman World*. London: Routledge, 2000.

Davis, Natalie Zemon. *The Gift in Sixteenth-Century France*. Madison WI: University of Wisconsin Press, 2000.

Defoe, Daniel. *A Tour Through the Whole Island of Great Britain*. 1724 (electronic version).

Defoe, Daniel. *The Complete English Tradesman*. Reprint. New York: Burt Franklin, 1970.

DeKok, Jack. "Breaking law, and tradition." *Ottawa Citizen*, October 29, 1986, A9.

Delap, Leanne. "Waiting a year for a purse that costs $16,000: trendy." *Globe and Mail*, July 8, 1999.

Dowd, Eric. "Sunday shopping slips in back door." *Windsor Star*, January 9, 1992, A7.

Eade, Ron, Kristin Goff and Vito Pilieci. "Shoppers mob newest big-box Loblaws superstore: West-end giant blurs distinction between food, department stores." *Ottawa Citizen*, November 28, 2002, F1.

Economic Development St. John's, *St. John's Economic Update*, January 2003, 2.

Edwards, Bob. Report on book about Ronco. "Morning Edition," National Public Radio, June 19, 2002.

Edy, Carolyn M. "Babies Mean Business." *American Demographics*, May 1, 1999.

Egan, Kelly. "Shopping areas on a human scale." *Ottawa Citizen*, December 9, 2002, C4.

——. "Shopping—maybe on Sunday?" *Ottawa Citizen*, December 14, 1985, B1.

ElBoghdady, Dina. "Airport Shops Fear War's Impact; Vendors Already Weakened by Sept. 11, Economic Slowdown." *Washington Post*, April 5, 2003, E01.

Ellie, "Wedding gift fumbles create awkward situation." *Toronto Star*, February 27, 2003.

Fairmont Hotels and Resorts, "Winter Packages at Fairmont Hotels & Resorts Offer Outdoor . . . And Indoor Adventures For All." news release, November 1, 2002.

Fawcett, Trevor, compiler. *Voices of Eighteenth-Century Bath: An Anthology*. Bath, U.K.: Ruton, 1995.

Fernandez, Kay Harwell. "Watercolors: Art auctions at sea." *Orlando Sentinel*, February 3, 2002.

Ficner, Charles. "The welcome mat is out for bad development." *Ottawa Citizen*, August 24, 2002, B7.

Fitch, Rodney and Lance Knobel. *Retail Design*. New York: Whitney Library of Design, an imprint of Watson-Guptill Publications, 1990.

Fontaine, Laurence. *History of Pedlars in Europe*. Durham, NC: Duke University Press, 1996.

Food Marketing Institute. *Food Retailing in the 21st Century—Riding a Consumer Revolution*. Washington, D.C.: Food Marketing Institute, n.d.

——. *Key Facts in the Food Retailing and Supermarket Industry*. Washington, D.C.: Food Marketing Institute, May 2003. <http://www.fmi.org/facts_figs/keyfacts/>.

——. *Industry Speaks 1992–2002*. Washington, D.C.: Food Marketing Institute, n.d.

——. *Slotting Allowances in The Supermarket Industry*. Washington, D.C.: Food Marketing Institute, n.d.

——. *Technology Review Highlights 2003*. Washington, D.C.: Food Marketing Institute, n.d.

——. *Trends in the United States: Consumer Attitudes and the Supermarket*. Washington, D.C.: Food Marketing Institute, 2003.

Foote, Denise. "Makeover madness: in the face of competition, the grocery store puts on a new face." *Canadian Grocer*, April 1999, 16–17.

Foreman, Amanda. *Georgiana: Duchess of Devonshire*. London: Harper Collins Publishers, 1998.

Fortney, Valerie. "Men make haste in malls." *Calgary Herald*, August 3, 2002, ES1.

Fowler, Marian. *The Way She Looks Tonight: Five Women of Style*. Toronto: Random House of Canada, 1996.

Frank, Thomas. *The Conquest of Cool*. Chicago: The University of Chicago Press, 1997.

Gershman, Suzy and Judith Thomas. *Born to Shop Los Angeles*. New York: Bantam Books, 1988.

Giese, Rachel. "Consuming Passion." *This Magazine*. November–December 2002, 23–25.

Gillmor, Don. "Groceryland." *Report on Business Magazine*, October 1998, 121–26.

Girouard, Mark. *Cities and People*. New Haven: Yale University Press, 1985.

Givhan, Robin. "The future of fashion is in e-commerce: And it means the death of exclusivity." *Ottawa Citizen*, December 16, 1999, E5.

Gladwell, Malcolm. "The Pitchman." *The New Yorker*, October 30, 2000.

——. *The Tipping Point: How Little Things Can Make a Big Difference*. Boston: Little, Brown and Company, 2002.

Glazenbrook, G. de T., Katharine B. Brett and Judith McErvel. *A Shopper's View of Canada's Past: Pages from Eaton's Catalogues 1886-1930*. Toronto: University of Toronto Press, 1969.

Goff, Kristin. "Westboro Loblaws mega-store gets go-ahead: Construction to begin next month." *Ottawa Citizen*, September 20, 2002, E1.

Green, William R. *The Retail Store: Design and Construction*, second edition. New York: Van Nostrand Reinhold, 1991.

Greenwald, John. "Up Against the Wal-Mart." *Time*, August 22, 1994.

Groner, Jonathan. "Tupperware: The Promise of Plastic in 1950s America" (Review). Salon.com, November 10, 1994.

Gross, Daniel. "At Your Door." *US Airways Attache Magazine*, July 2000.

Hahn, Lucinda. "Buyer's Remorse." *Chicago Magazine*, April 2002.

Hamilton, Richard. *The Social Misconstruction of Reality*. Yale University Press, 1996.

Hannigan, John. *Fantasy City: Pleasure and profit in the postmodern metropolis*. London: Routledge, 1998.

Harrison, Molly. *People and Shopping: A Social Background*. London: Ernest Benn Limited, 1975.

Heath, Joseph and Andrew Potter, "The Rebel Sell." *This Magazine*, November–December 2002, 30–34.

Hine, Thomas. *I Want That! How We All Became Shoppers*. New York: HarperCollins Publishers Inc., 2002.

Hodgson, Richard S. "It's Still the 'Catalog Age.'" *Catalog Age*, June 1, 2001.

Hoge, Sharon King. "Better shop around?" *National Review*, May 1, 1995, 54–55.

Homberger, Eric. *The Historical Atlas of New York City: A Visual Celebration of Nearly 400 Years of New York City's History*. New York: Henry Holt and Company, 1994.

Hower, Ralph M. *History of Macy's of New York 1858–1919: Chapters in the Evolution of the Department Store*. Cambridge MA: Harvard University Press, 1943.

Hughes-Hallet, Penelope, editor. *My Dear Cassandra: The Illustrated Letters of Jane Austen*. London: Collins and Brown, 1990.

Humphery, Kim. *Shelf Life: Supermarkets and the Changing Cultures of Consumption.* Cambridge, U.K.: Cambridge University Press, 1998.

Hyatt International Corporation. "Shopping perks and Parisian pampering." news release, October 30, 2002.

Jacobs, Jane. *The Death and Life of Great American Cities.* New York: Vintage Books/Random House Inc., 1961.

Jagannathan, Venkatachari. "Heavenly Destination." Domain-b.com, June 20, 2002.

Janoff, Barry. "East meets West." *Progressive Grocer,* January 2001.

Jesse, Captain W. *The Life of Beau Brummell.* 1844. Reprint. London: The Navarre Society Limited, 1927.

Johnson, Jessica. "Attention shoppers!" *Saturday Night,* November 2002, 35–36.

Judd, Neville. "Lack of GMO Labeling Turns Canadians Towards Organic Foods." ENS news release, August 16, 2000.

Katz, Helena. "Loblaws imports concept to Quebec." *Marketing,* March 2, 1998, 3.

Khouri, Rami. "So much to buy, so little to buy it with." *Globe and Mail,* April 27, 2000, A15.

Kinsella, Sophie. *Confessions of a Shopaholic.* New York: Dell Publishing, 2001.

——. *Shopaholic Ties the Knot.* New York: Bantam Dell, 2003.

Kirsner, Scott. "Express Lane." *Wired,* May 1999.

Klaffke, Pamela. "Let's get personal, shopping, that is." *Calgary Herald,* December 5, 2002, E5.

Klein, Naomi. *No Logo: Taking Aim at the Brand Bullies.* Toronto: Vintage Canada, 2000.

Klein, Ross A. "Cruise Ships: The Industry's Dark Side." *Conscious Choice,* February 2003.

Kole, William. "Anti-Santa movement backs off under fire: Austrian group urging traditional celebrations instead of the American Claus promises to lighten up." *Vancouver Sun,* December 24, 2002, A16.

Komter, Aafke E., editor. *The Gift: An Interdisciplinary Perspective.* Amsterdam: Amsterdam University Press.

Kostof, Spiro. *A History of Architecture: Settings and Rituals.* New York: Oxford University Press, 1985, 1995.

——. *The City Assembled: The Elements of Urban Form Through History.* Boston: Little, Brown and Company/Bullfinch Press, 1992.

——. *The City Shaped: Urban Patterns and Meanings Through History.* London: Thames and Hudson Limited, 1991.

Kunstler, James Howard. *The Geography of Nowhere: The Rise and Decline of America's Man-Made Landscape.* New York: Simon and Schuster/Touchstone, 1993.

LaChance, Danny. "Carleton Student Examines the Role of Avon Corporation in Brazil." *Carleton College News,* April 11, 2002.

Lancaster, Bill. *The Department Store: A Social History.* London: Leicester University Press, 1995.

Leach, William. *Land of Desire: Merchants, Power, and the Rise of a New American Culture.* New York: Pantheon Books, 1993.

Leapman, Michael, editor. *The Book of London: The Evolution of a Great City.* New York: Weidenfeld and Nicolson, 1989.

Leeming, Virginia. "Super shopper tries stores in Vancouver." *Vancouver Sun,* May 12, 1988, C5.

Le Faye, Deirdre. *Jane Austen: The World of Her Novels.* New York: Henry N. Abrams, Inc., 2002.

Lempert, Phil. *Being the Shopper: Understanding the Buyer's Choice.* New York: John Wiley and Sons, Inc., 2002.

Levy, Michael and Barton A. Weitz. *Retailing Management.* Homewood IL: Richard D. Irwin, Inc., 1992.

Lewis, Francis. "Hot Tips: Art and Antiques." *Where New York,* November 2002, 16.

Lewis, Herschell Gordon. "Catalog Copy: So It's Listed in the Catalog? So What?" *Catalog Age,* June 1, 2001.

MacDonald, Gayle. "Attention, shoppers: new products stage left." *Globe and Mail,* November 9, 2002.

MacKeith, Margaret. *The History and Conservation of Shopping Arcades.* London and New York: Mansell Publishing Limited, 1986.

MacPherson, James. "Tenakee cruisers spurned." *Juneau Empire,* August 14, 1998.

Markin, Rom J. *The Supermarket: An Analysis of Growth, Development, and Change.* Washington State University Press, 1968.

Mauss, Marcel, translated by Ian Cunnison. *The Gift: Forms and Functions of Exchange in Archaic Societies.* New York: W.W. Norton and Company, 1967.

Mayhew, Henry ("recalled for the edification of the Public by Stanley Rubinstein"), *The Street Trader's Lot—London: 1851.* London: Readers Union, by arrangement with the Sylvan Press, 1949.

Mayo, James M. *The American Grocery Store: The Business Evolution of an Architectural Space.* Westport, Connecticut: Greenwood Press, 1993.

McCabe, James D., Jr. *Lights and Shadows of New York Life, or, Sights and Sensations of The Great City.* Philadelphia: National Publishing Company, 1872. Reprint. London: André Deutsch, 1971.

McCabe-Lokos, Nick. "Grocer wants shoppers to add furniture to list." *Toronto Star,* February 16, 2003.

McMartin, Peter. "Adieu calamari, sayonara sushi." *Ottawa Citizen,* May 25, 2003.

Miller, Daniel, Peter Jackson, Nigel Thrift, Beverley Holbrook and Michael Rowlands. *Shopping, Place and Identity.* London and New York: Routledge, 1998.

Miller, Daniel. *A Theory of Shopping*. Ithaca, New York: Cornell University Press, 1998.

Miller, Herman P. *Rich Man, Poor Man*. New York: Thomas Y. Crowell Co., 1971.

Miller, Michael B. *The Bon Marché: Bourgeois Culture and the Department Store, 1869–1920*. Princeton, NJ: Princeton University Press, 1981.

Mokhiber, Russell and Robert Weissman. "Tupperware, Disney and the Selling of the Public Space." Focus on the Corporation Column, October 5, 1999.

Montgomery, L.M. *Anne's House of Dreams*. Toronto: McClelland and Stewart Limited, 1922. Reprint. Toronto: McClelland and Stewart Limited, 1972.

Moritz, Carl Philip (translated and introduced by Reginald Nettel). *Journeys of a German in England: A walking-tour of England in 1782*. Reprint. Eland Books, n.d.

National Center for Policy Analysis. *Why the Minimum Wage Law Causes Unemployment*. Dallas, Texas: National Center for Policy Analysis, 1996.

Nelson, Emily. "The new '90s getaway: shopping." *Globe and Mail*, November 22, 1997, F5 (reprinted from *Wall Street Journal*).

Ode, Kim. "Living room, salesroom: It's big bucks and strained friendships." *Minneapolis Star Tribune*, April 23, 2003, 02E.

Olijnyk, Zena. "Dot-com wonder boys." *Canadian Business*, April 14, 2003, 36.

——. "Supermarket chic." *National Post*, April 24, 2000.

Otnes, Cele and Mary Ann McGrath, "Perceptions and Realities of Male Shopping Behavior." *Journal of Retailing*, spring 2001.

Otnes, Cele and Richard F. Beltramini. *Gift Giving: A Research Anthology*. Bowling Green, Ohio: Bowling Green State University Popular Press, 1996.

Owens, Anne Marie. "Everything for the granny-to-be." *National Post*, August 12, 2002, AL1.

——. "The way we shop." *National Post*, November 9, 2002.

Painter, Sidney. *Mediaeval Society*. Ithaca: Cornell University Press, 1951.

Palmer, Susan. *The Soanes at Home: Domestic Life at Lincoln's Inn Fields*. London: Sir John Soane's Museum, 1997.

Pearsall, Kathy. "Bank accounts: aisle twenty-two: taking advantage of technology, Loblaws now leads the retail pack entering the banking industry." *Computing Canada*, March 9, 1998.

Phenix, Patricia. *Eatonians: The Story of the Family Behind the Family*. Toronto: McClelland and Stewart, 2002.

Porter, Roy. *London: A Social History*. Cambridge, Massachusetts: Harvard University Press, 1995.

Potier, Beth. "Fellow's film chronicles history of the bowl that burped." *Harvard Gazette*, April 3, 2003.

Potter, Andrew. "The marketers made me buy it." *National Post*, March 8, 2003.

Prince William County–Manassas, Virginia Convention and Visitors Bureau. "Holiday Shopping Got You Down . . . It's Time for a Shopping Holiday!" News release, November 2002.

Pritchard, Carolyn. "Brides and grooms will always take your cash." *National Post*, May 12, 2001, C7.

Publicis Dialog, "Optimists: America Needs You." News release, January 15, 2002.

Ramp, William. "If it's the thought that counts, what are you thinking about?: A sociologist confronts the myths that surround the materialistic orgy we call Christmas." *Calgary Herald*, December 22, 2002, A19.

Reginald of Durham. *Life of St. Godric*. In G. G. Coulton, editor, *Social Life in Britain from the Conquest to the Reformation* (Cambridge: Cambridge University Press, 1918), 415–420 (reproduced as part of the Internet Medieval Source Book, www.fordham.edu/halsall/source/goderic.html).

Renaud, Georges (translated by Dorothy Terry, introduction by G.D.H. Cole). *Guilds in the Middle Ages*. New York: Augustus M. Kelley, Publishers, 1968.

Repplier, Agnes. "Christmas Shopping at Assuân." *The Atlantic Monthly*, May 1895, 681–686.

Rice, Kate. "Malls of America: Not Just Shopping—Now They're Becoming Vacation Destinations." ABCNews.com, November 1, 2002.

Robinson, Jill. "Store, spa, or subculture? Go to Bloomie's." *Vogue*, August 1976.

Roddick, Anita. *Body and Soul*. London: Ebury Press, 1991.

Roseman, Ellen. "Online grocery should explain pricing policy." *Toronto Star*, May 17, 2003.

Rybczynski, Witold. *City Life: Urban Expectations in a New World*. New York: Scribner/Harper Collins Inc., 1995.

——. *Looking Around: A Journey Through Architecture*. New York: Viking Penguin, 1992.

——. *Waiting for the Weekend*. New York: Viking Penguin, 1991.

Sanati, Mercedeh. "Lisbon calling." *Report on Business Magazine*, June 2003, 99–100.

Sawyer, Peter. "Early Fairs and Markets in England and Scandinavia," in *The Market in History: Papers presented at a Symposium held 9–13 September 1984 at St George's House, Windsor Castle, under the auspices of the Liberty Fund*, edited by B.L. Anderson and A.J.H. Latham. London: Croom Helm Ltd., 1986.

Schlereth, Thomas J. *Victorian America: Transformations in Everyday Life 1876–1915*. New York: Harper Perennial, 1991.

Schmidt, Leigh Eric. *Consumer Rites: The Buying and Selling of American Holidays*. Princeton NJ: Princeton University Press, 1995.

Schmidt, Sarah. "Branded babies: Marketing turns tots into logo-conscious consumers." *Ottawa Citizen*, May 6, 2003, A1-A2.

Schor, Juliet B. and Douglas B. Holt, editors. *The Consumer Society Reader*. New York: The New Press, 2000.

Schor, Juliet B. *The Overspent American: Why We Want What We Don't Need*. New York: Harper Perennial, 1998.

Semenak, Susan. "Marrying the gift to the wedding: Picking present is no walk down aisle." *The Gazette* (Montreal), June 9, 2001, A1.

Sheikh, Fawzia. "Offering consumers more choices." *Marketing*, December 21 1998, 19.

Shelton, Jo-Ann. *As the Romans Did: A Sourcebook in Roman Social History*. New York and Oxford: Oxford University Press, 1988.

Seuss, Dr. *How the Grinch Stole Christmas*. New York: Random House, 1957.

Shop-Hound, "Tips on the shop market." *Vogue*, May 1, 1933.

Silcoff, Mireille. "Getting up our noses." *National Post*, December 7, 2002.

Silcoff, Sean. "Secrets of a Bestseller." *Canadian Business*, June 26–July 10, 1998, 90–93.

Singman, Jeffrey L. and Will McLean. *Daily Life in Chaucer's England*. Westport, Connecticut: Greenwood Press, 1995.

Smith, Liz. "Store, spa, or subculture? Trust Bloomie's." *Vogue*, August 1976.

Smith, Sarah. "Checking out the new Loblaws." *Marketing*, April 29 2002, 10–11.

——. "Loblaws has plans to pump profits." *Marketing*, May 13 2002, 3.

Southern Ontario Tourism Organization. *Shopping Getaways . . . in Southern Ontario*, promotional booklet, fall 2002.

Stanford, Jim. "Business as usual." *This Magazine*, November–December 2002, 12–15.

Staten, Vince. *Can You Trust a Tomato in January?* New York: Simon and Schuster, 1993.

Statistics Canada, "Heritage institutions." *The Daily*, December 4, 2002.

Stephenson, William. *The Store that Timothy Built*. Toronto: McClelland and Stewart, 1969.

Straub, Jeanie. "Regional shopping mall's design banks on meshing indoors, outdoors." *Boulder County Business Report*, December 17, 1999.

Summerskill, Ben and Tom Reilly. "Debt becomes the norm for middle classes." *The Observer* (London), January 19, 2003.

Summerskill, Ben. "Shopping can make you depressed." *The Observer* (London), May 6, 2001.

Symkusl, Ed. "Uncovering the Tupperware Story." Townonline.com, April 23, 2003.

Tagami, Kirsten. "Economic slump strains business at Hartsfield." *Atlanta Journal-Constitution*, March 29, 2003, A1.

Taitz, Laurice. "Retail therapy is a harmless enough way to lift a mood, but when shopping becomes compulsive it's time to get help." *Sunday Times* (South Africa), October 14, 2001.

Tedeschi, Bob. "Online Jewelry Sales Increase." *New York Times*, December 9, 2002.

Thal Larsen, Peter. "Process could trigger sale of QVC channel: Malone starts talks." *National Post*, March 4, 2003.

Thorne, Susan. "Carnival Time: Tourist sales give retailers in U.S. Virgin Islands cause to celebrate." *Shopping Centers Today*, January 1, 2000.

Toepler, Stefan, and Volker Kirchberg. "Museums, Merchandising, and Non-profit Commercialization." National Center on Non-Profit Enterprise, n.d.

Tourism Toronto, *Toronto Briefs Quarterly*, July 2002, 1.

Travel Industry Association of America, *The Shopping Traveler*. Washington, D.C.: Travel Industry Association of America, 2001.

Troy, Mike. "Kash 'N Karry store design takes a circular approach." *Discount Store News*, August 21, 2000, 2.

Turner, Chris. "The Legend of Pepsi A.M." *This Magazine*, November–December 2002, 18–22.

Twitchell, James B. *Lead Us Into Temptation: The Triumph of American Materialism*. New York: Columbia University Press, 1999.

Underhill, Paco. *Why We Buy: The Science of Shopping*. New York: Simon and Schuster, 1999.

United Nations Population Division, *World Population Prospects: The 2002 Revision*, highlights. New York: United Nations, February 26, 2003.

Vander Doelen, Chris. "It's the latest round in fight on shopping laws." *Windsor Star*, December 22, 1992, A1.

Veblen, Thorstein. *The Theory of the Leisure Class*. 1899. Reprint. New York: The Modern Library, 1934.

Vending Times. Census of the Industry 2002.

Viets, Deborah. "Why ladies go a-thieving." *Globe and Mail*, November 2, 2002, F2.

Walford, Cornelius. *Fairs Past and Present: A Chapter in the History of Commerce*. London: 1883. Reprint. New York: Burt Franklin, 1967.

Walsh, John P. *Supermarkets Transformed: Understanding Organizational and Technological Innovations*. New Brunswick NJ: Rutgers University Press, 1993.

Weiss, Paulette. "Holiday Gift Guide." *Where New York*, November 2002, 24–29.

——. "Hot Tips: Shopping." *Where New York*, November 2002, 18.

Wendt, Lloyd and Herman Kogan. *Give the Lady What She Wants! The Story of Marshall Field & Company*. South Bend, Indiana: And Books, 1952.

West Hollywood Convention and Visitors Bureau. "Two Celebrity-Magnets Announce Shopping Promotion for the Holidays." News release, October 15, 2002.

Wight, Emily. "The Easter Bride's Wardrobe." *Ladies' Home Journal*, March 1900, 29.

Yancey, Kitty Bean, "Cruise lines draw profits from selling works of art." *USA Today*, February 8, 2001.

Young, Pamela. "High Camp Roots." *Globe and Mail*, December 13, 1997, C9.

Zekas, Rita. "A shopaholic's best friend." *Toronto Star*, March 22, 2003.